Praise for Previous Editions of
The Official Ubuntu Book

"*The Official Ubuntu Book* is a great way to get you started with Ubuntu, giving you enough information to be productive without overloading you."

—John Stevenson, DZone book reviewer

"*OUB* is one of the best books I've seen for beginners."

—Bill Blinn, TechByter Worldwide

"This book is the perfect companion for users new to Linux and Ubuntu. It covers the basics in a concise and well-organized manner. General use is covered separately from troubleshooting and error-handling, making the book well-suited both for the beginner as well as the user that needs extended help."

—Thomas Petrucha, Austria Ubuntu User Group

"I have recommended this book to several users who I instruct regularly on the use of Ubuntu. All of them have been satisfied with their purchase and have even been able to use it to help them in their journey along the way."

—Chris Crisafulli, Ubuntu LoCo Council,
Florida Local Community Team

"This text demystifies a very powerful Linux operating system . . . In just a few weeks of having it, I've used it as a quick reference a half-dozen times, which saved me the time I would have spent scouring the Ubuntu forums online."

—Darren Frey, Member, Houston Local User Group

The Official Ubuntu Book

Seventh Edition

The Official Ubuntu Book

Seventh Edition

Matthew Helmke
Amber Graner

**With Kyle Rankin, Benjamin Mako Hill,
and Jono Bacon**

PRENTICE
HALL

Upper Saddle River, NJ • Boston • Indianapolis • San Francisco
New York • Toronto • Montreal • London • Munich • Paris • Madrid
Capetown • Sydney • Tokyo • Singapore • Mexico City

Many of the designations used by manufacturers and sellers to distinguish their products are claimed as trademarks. Where those designations appear in this book, and the publisher was aware of a trademark claim, the designations have been printed with initial capital letters or in all capitals.

The authors and publisher have taken care in the preparation of this book, but make no expressed or implied warranty of any kind and assume no responsibility for errors or omissions. No liability is assumed for incidental or consequential damages in connection with or arising out of the use of the information or programs contained herein.

The publisher offers excellent discounts on this book when ordered in quantity for bulk purchases or special sales, which may include electronic versions and/or custom covers and content particular to your business, training goals, marketing focus, and branding interests. For more information, please contact:

U.S. Corporate and Government Sales
(800) 382-3419
corpsales@pearsontechgroup.com

For sales outside the United States please contact:

International Sales
international@pearson.com

Visit us on the Web: informit.com/ph

Library of Congress Cataloging-in-Publication Data

Helmke, Matthew.
    The official Ubuntu book / Matthew Helmke, Amber Graner. — 7th ed.
        p. cm.
    Previous editions by Benjamin Mako Hill and others.
    Includes bibliographical references and index.
    ISBN 0-13-301760-5 (pbk. : alk. paper)
1. Ubuntu (Electronic resource) 2. Operating systems (Computers) I. Graner, Amber. II. Title.
QA76.76.774.U28H45 2013
005.4'32—dc23
                                                            2012016037

ISBN-13: 978-0-13-301760-1
ISBN-10:   0-13-301760-5
Text printed in the United States on recycled paper at RR Donnelley in Crawfordsville, Indiana.
Third Printing, November 2013

This book is dedicated to the Ubuntu community. Without your tireless hard work and commitment, none of this would be possible.

Contents at a Glance

Contents

Foreword to the Sixth Edition

THE OFFICIAL UBUNTU BOOK CAPTURES both the spirit and the precision with which Ubuntu itself is crafted. Like Ubuntu, it has evolved in a steady cadence of regular releases, and this sixth edition reflects the cumulative insight gained from prior editions, as well as some of the latest innovations driving Ubuntu forward.

2011 is a critical year of change for Ubuntu, as we move towards the new, unified interface called Unity. Our goal is to deliver what people have long wished for: the world's cleanest, most elegant desktop experience, as free software. 11.04 is the first major step in that process as we introduce Unity by default on the desktop, retaining the Classic GNOME desktop for those who cannot yet make the leap to Unity.

Our broader goal is to challenge the free software ecosystem to invest as much creativity and energy in design as it does in engineering. We know that free software can be the best in the world for performance, reliability, and security; now it's time to bring ease-of-use and stylishness into the mix too.

I hope you enjoy 11.04, and love this book. My thanks to the many folks who have made both Ubuntu and *The Official Ubuntu Book* possible. It's a great privilege to be part of this community.

—Mark Shuttleworth
Ubuntu Founder
April 2011

Foreword to the First Edition

IT'S A SMALL CELEBRATION for me to write this foreword—almost exactly two years after the first meeting of a small group of free software professionals that turned into the Ubuntu project. A celebration because two years ago none of us would have predicted that our dream would spawn several million CDs, three or four million enthusiastic users, hundreds of commitments of support from companies large and small, a minor prime time television reference, and now *The Official Ubuntu Book*.

The dream that brought us together can be simply expressed:

> To build a world-class operating system for ordinary desktop computer users, that is genuinely free and freely available, that is immediately useful, and that represents the very best that the free software world can achieve today.

In setting out to build a platform for "ordinary desktop computer users," I had no idea that I would have the privilege of meeting and working with so many *extra*ordinary desktop computer users. Some of those extraordinary individuals are the authors of this book, people who both understand the importance of the free software movement and have the talent to have been real contributors to its success. Others make up the backbone of the Ubuntu community—the small but dedicated army of a few hundred people that works to produce a new release of Ubuntu every six months. They are at the heart of a network that reaches out through the global free software community—through the world of Debian, an extraordinary project in its own right and without which Ubuntu could not exist, and on out to the thousands of projects, large and small, that produce the code and documentation that we pull together and call *Ubuntu*.

While this huge extended community can often appear to be fractured and divided along infinitesimal ideological lines, we are all broadly in agreement about four key ideas, and it is those ideas that are central to the Ubuntu promise:

- That our software should not come with a license fee. That we should be able to share our software, modify it, and then share our modifications, too.

- That this free software should be the best version available, including regular security updates, and not a tease for a better, commercial product.

- That full-scale, high-quality commercial support from local and global companies should be available for this free platform.

- That this software should be usable in as many languages as possible and usable by as many people as possible regardless of disability.

The 17 of us who met in London two years ago come from a very wide variety of countries and backgrounds, but we all agreed that the goal of producing a platform that could live up to that promise was a worthy one, one that we would devote ourselves to wholeheartedly.

For several months we worked quietly. We wanted to come to the world not only with a manifesto but also with a clear demonstration of work done toward our goals, something that people could test and comment on. We had no name (though industry insiders called us the "Super-Secret Debian Startup"), and, as a result, we hosted most of our work at www.no-name-yet.com. We were looking for a name that could express the beauty of the free software community development process—collaboration, interdependence, sharing, standing gently on the shoulders of giants, and reaching for lofty goals. The only word that comes close to that, of which I'm aware, is the African word *ubuntu*. It is found in many forms in many different African languages. And so we adopted it as the name of our project.

We knew that our first release would have blemishes—warts—and gave it the codename "The Warty Warthog." We called ourselves "the warthogs" and coordinated our work on the #warthogs IRC channel. Today, for better or worse, that's turned into a tradition of codenames such as "Breezy

Badger" and "Dapper Drake." As lighthearted as they sound, these code-names come to embody the spirit of our community as it works toward a particular release. This next one—Dapper—is exactly that: a man emerging from youth, professional, bold, confident, and energetic. This is our first release that is designed to meet the needs of large organizations as much as developers and engineers. In the same way, the Ubuntu community has moved from being something of a rebellion against the "Linux establishment" to a strong and professionally organized group.

What Makes Ubuntu So Popular?

First, this is the time for free software to come to the forefront, and Ubuntu is very much the beneficiary of the vast amount of work that has gone into building up a huge body of work in the GNU/Linux world. That work has been underway for nearly 30 years, in one form or another, but Ubuntu is one way in which it is suddenly becoming "visible" to the non-specialist computer user. We are in the middle of a great overturning of the industry status quo. The last time that happened, in the mid-1990s, was when the world suddenly found itself connected to itself—by the Internet. Every major company, especially those in the field of technology, had to examine itself and ask the question, "How do we adapt to an Internet world?" Today, every major technology company has to ask itself the question, "How do we adapt to a free software world?"

I would speculate and say that Ubuntu represents an idea whose time has come. We did not invent the free software movement—that honor goes to Richard Stallman and many others who had a vision far more profound at a time when it was hard to see how it could ever become reality. But Ubuntu has perhaps the honor of bringing that vision to a very wide audience in a form that we can all appreciate. I hope that the real visionaries—those who have led the way—will appreciate the decisions and the choices we make in bringing you this project. Some will take exception—I know Linus prefers KDE to GNOME, for example, so he's likely to be more of a fan of Kubuntu than Ubuntu. But in general, the ideas that others have had, the principles of the free software movement, are well expressed in Ubuntu.

Second, Ubuntu is a project on which you can have a real impact. It has the benefit of deep and reliable financial backing and a corporate team to give it muscle, but it is in every regard an open project, with participation at the highest levels by true volunteers. We work in a fishbowl—our meetings take place online, in a public forum. That can be tricky. Building an operating system is a fast-paced business full of compromise and tough decisions in the face of little information. There are disagreements and dirty laundry, and mistakes are made. (I should know; some of them are mine. You should hear the one about the Warty Warthog desktop artwork.) The transparency of our environment, however, means that we can count on having robust conversations about our options—all of them, even the ones the core team would never have dreamed up. It also means that mistakes are identified, discussed, and ultimately addressed faster than they would be if we lived and worked behind closed doors. You get a better platform as a result.

We work hard as a community to recognize the contributions of all sorts of individuals—advocates, artists, Web forum moderators, channel operators, community event organizers, writers, translators, people who file and triage bugs . . . whatever your particular interest or talent, we will find a way to integrate your contribution.

Perhaps most important is the way our approach to community differentiates Ubuntu from other free software projects with similar vision. We try to do all of this in a way that recognizes that disagreements are important but prevents those disagreements from creating deep divides in our community. Our code of conduct may not be perfect, but it reminds each of us to remember the meaning of the word *ubuntu*—that each of us has our best impact *through* the relationships we maintain with one another. Finding common ground and maintaining healthy communication are more important for us as a community in the long run than a particular technical decision or the specific choice of words with which to translate "File" into Spanish. Our community governance structures—our Technical Board and Community Council—exist to ensure that debates don't become personal and that decisions can be taken after all sides have been heard.

If you are a software professional or curious about Linux, this book and this platform are an excellent choice. You will learn about the world of Ubuntu and, indirectly, Debian and GNU/Linux. These are great foundations for working with the tools that I believe will come to define the "standard," the everyday computing base upon which we build our homes and offices.

I once heard a proprietary software vendor say, "Linux is more expensive because skilled Linux professionals are more costly." This is true. It means, of course, that Linux skills are more valuable! It won't be true forever because the world of Linux is expanding so rapidly that sooner or later we will have to accept a position in the mainstream, and that takes off some of the "geek points" associated with being part of the "future of technology." But right now, without a doubt, being ahead of the curve on Linux and on Ubuntu is the right place to be. If you're this far into this foreword, you are clearly going to make it. ;-)

It's difficult for me to speculate on what the future might hold for the Ubuntu project. I know that I along with many others are loving the opportunity to be at the center of such an exciting initiative and are committed to seeing where it leads us over the coming years. I believe that it will become a pervasive part of our everyday computing environment, so I would like to help make sure that we don't make too many mistakes along the way! Please, come and join us in the fishbowl to help ensure we do a very, very good job.

—Mark Shuttleworth
Ubuntu Founder
April 2006

Preface

WE HOPE YOU ENJOY *THE OFFICIAL UBUNTU BOOK*. There are many changes we made for this edition, which we believe takes an already good book to a new level.

Because Ubuntu has risen in popularity and is better known, we have expanded the intended audience from pure beginners to also include those who know a bit about Ubuntu but who want to improve their skills and become power users. These are not necessarily focused on becoming programmers or systems administrators, but regular people who want to make their day-to-day use of Ubuntu more efficient or who want to better harness Ubuntu's potential.

In 2011, Ubuntu received the first wide release of the new Unity interface. This has been refined to become more elegant, more powerful, and more useful. These changes are outlined in this book. While the first release was exciting but incomplete, we believe you will find that the 12.04 Ubuntu edition of Unity delivers a new and exciting standard for human-computer interaction.

Finally, a large part of this book has been rewritten—not because the earlier editions were bad, but because so much has happened in the last year since the previous edition was released. This book chronicles the major changes that affect typical users and will help anyone learn the foundations, the history, and how to harness the potential of the free software in Ubuntu.

As we write this, it has been several years since we penned the first edition of *The Official Ubuntu Book*. Over that time, we have seen Ubuntu continue its explosive growth. Updating this book drives this fact home in striking ways. For example, the number of users and posts in the Ubuntu Forums has nearly doubled since the last edition of this book a year ago. Again.

Once again, we feel blessed that *The Official Ubuntu Book* has been able to benefit from, and perhaps in a small way even *contribute* to, that success. Ultimately, that success paved the way for several subsequent editions, and now the seventh edition, of the book that you're reading now.

In the process, this book, like Ubuntu, continues to mature. Our job as authors, like that of the Ubuntu developers, now involves more updating and polishing than it used to. Distributed under a free license, a once-risky book on a once-risky operating system is, just a few short years later, as close to a sure thing as an author, publisher, and, if we have done our job well, a reader could hope for.

And yet with success comes responsibility to our readers and to our users with high expectations. Ubuntu's success is built in part of maturity and excellence, and it cannot sacrifice these qualities if it will succeed. We cannot either. Our job as writers is complicated because we need to accurately reflect and represent both qualities while catering to an increasing and increasingly diverse group of users.

As we've noted in the prefaces to previous editions of this book, being *Official* has carried with it a set of rights and responsibilities. Our book's title means that we must attempt to reflect and represent the whole Ubuntu community. While we, as authors, are expected to put ourselves into the book, it is understood that it can never be to the detriment of the values, principles, technologies, or structures of the Ubuntu community.

Doing this has been complicated as Ubuntu has grown. In each edition, we have added new information, because the Ubuntu community has grown to include new projects. In each revision of this book, we have needed to add to the list of related projects, tools, and community initiatives. As the Ubuntu community grows, it is impossible to give a complete accounting of what Ubuntu has to offer. Creating a summary requires some hard decisions. At the end of the day, we are constrained by page count and our own limited schedules.

Meanwhile, as with earlier editions, we needed to write this book about a new release of Ubuntu while that version was under active development and was being redesigned, rethought, and rebuilt. Every day, Ubuntu grows in different, unpredictable ways, and this growth has increased exponentially with the size of the community and the diversity of the userbase. Our book's development process had to both match and track this process as our content was crafted, rewritten, adjusted, and allowed to mature itself.

As in the previous edition, the contributors to this book go well beyond those listed on the book's cover. Invisible to most readers, dozens of members of the community left their mark on different parts of the text of this book. Although this degree of participation led to a writing process that was as hectic, and at times frustrating, as the process that builds Ubuntu, we hope we can remind readers of the level of quality that this process inspires in our book's subject. In the places where we achieve this, we have earned our book's title. With that goal in mind, we look forward to future versions of Ubuntu and editions of this book wrought through the same community-driven process.

Acknowledgments

SPECIAL THANKS TO Mark Shuttleworth, Jane Silber, and Vanessa Sammut for all their efforts to get this book out into the world for both new and veteran Ubuntu users. Thanks also to Victor Ferns, director of Canonical, Ltd., for his attention to the project. Many people at Canonical, including Gill Cole, Iain Farrell, Kat Kinnie, Julian Hubbard, Ivanka Majic, Cezzaine Haigh, James Troup, and Marcus Haslam, provided immeasurable assistance in the production of this book.

We greatly appreciate the efforts of our technical reviewers, each of whom greatly contributed to the strength of the manuscript, especially Shannon Oliver, and an anonymous group of Canonical employees and engineers for this edition. Our thanks extend back to this group of reviewers and information sources for help with the previous editions: Ashley Rose, Allen Dye, Isabelle Duchatelle, Joe Barker, Alan Pope, Jorge O. Castro, Jonathan Riddell, Oliver Grawet, Dennis Kaarsemaker, Matthew East, Quim Gil, Dinko Korunic, Abhay Kumar, Jaldhar Vyas, Richard Weideman, and Scott Ritchie.

And finally, we appreciate the efforts of the Prentice Hall team, including Debra Williams Cauley, Kim Arney, Carol Lallier, Linda Begley, Richard Evans, Kim Boedigheimer, Mark Taub, John Fuller, and Elizabeth Ryan.

About the Authors

Matthew Helmke has been an Ubuntu user since April 2005 and an Ubuntu Member since August 2006. He served from 2006 to 2011 on the Ubuntu Forum Council, providing leadership and oversight of the Ubuntu Forums, and spent two years on the Ubuntu regional membership approval board for Europe, the Middle East, and Africa. He has written articles about Ubuntu for magazines and Web sites, is the lead author of *Ubuntu Unleashed*, and has written several books and articles on other topics.

Amber Graner is an active Ubuntu community member, whose path to Ubuntu activism started as she blogged about her transition to Ubuntu in 2009. Amber contributes to the Ubuntu News Team, Ubuntu Women Project, Ubuntu North Carolina LoCo Team, and more. She assists with many of the online Ubuntu tutorial weeks and various Ubucons. Amber resides in Western North Carolina where she works as the Associate Web Editor for Linux New Media. Her writing can be found online and in print for *Linux Pro* and *Ubuntu User* magazines. Additionally Amber is often found at Linux and open source events promoting, advocating, and encouraging participation in the Ubuntu community and with the Ubuntu project.

Kyle Rankin is a senior systems administrator; the current president of the North Bay Linux Users' Group; and author of *The Official Ubuntu Server Book*, *Knoppix Hacks*, *Knoppix Pocket Reference*, *Linux Multimedia Hacks*, and *Ubuntu Hacks*. Kyle is an award-winning columnist for *Linux Journal* and has had articles featured in *PC Magazine*, *Tech Target*, and other publications.

Benjamin Mako Hill is a long time free software developer and advocate. He was part of the founding Ubuntu team whose charge at Canonical was to help grow the Ubuntu development and user community during the project's first year. Mako is currently a fellow at the MIT Center for Future Civic Media, and a researcher and Ph.D. candidate at the MIT Sloan School of Management.

Jono Bacon is the Ubuntu community manager at Canonical, author of *The Art of Community*, founder of the annual Community Leadership Summit, founder of Severed Fifth, and cocreator of the popular LugRadio podcast.

Introduction

WELCOME to *The Official Ubuntu Book, Seventh Edition*!

In recent years, the Ubuntu operating system has taken the open source and IT world by storm. From out of nowhere, the Little Operating System That Could has blossomed into a full-featured desktop and server offering that has won over the hearts of users everywhere. Aside from the strong technical platform and impressive commitment to quality, Ubuntu also enjoys success because of its sprawling community of enthusiastic users who have helped to support, document, and test every millimeter of the Ubuntu landscape.

In your hands you are holding the official, authorized guide to this impressive operating system. Each of the authors selected to work on this book has demonstrated a high level of technical competence, an unbridled commitment to Ubuntu, and the ability to share this knowledge in a simple and clear manner. These authors gathered together to create a book that offers a solid grounding to Ubuntu and explains how the many facets and features of Ubuntu work.

About This Book

At the start of every book, on every bookshelf, in every shop, is a paragraph that sums up the intentions and aims for the book. We have one very simple, down-to-earth aim: to make the Ubuntu experience even more pleasant for users. The Ubuntu developers and community have gone to great lengths to produce an easy-to-use, functional, and flexible operating system for doing, browsing, and creating all kinds of interesting things. This book augments that effort. With such an integrated and flexible operating system, this guide acts as a tour de force for the many things you can do with Ubuntu.

The Scope of the Book

With so much to cover, we had our work cut out to write a book that could cover the system in sufficient detail. However, if we were to write in depth about every possible feature in Ubuntu, you would need to buy a new bookcase to store the sheer amount of content.

Part of the challenge in creating *The Official Ubuntu Book* was selecting the topics and content that can be covered within a reasonably sized book. We have identified the most essential content and written only about it. These chosen topics not only include installation, use of the desktop, applications, multimedia, system administration, and software management, but also include a discussion of the community, online resources, and the philosophy behind Ubuntu and open source software. As a bonus, we expanded our discussion of projects related to Ubuntu that will be of interest to you. We believe this book provides an ideal one-stop shop for getting started with Ubuntu.

The Menu

Here is a short introduction to each chapter and what it covers.

- Chapter 1—The Ubuntu Story: This spirited introduction describes the Ubuntu project, its distribution, its development processes, and some of the history that made it all possible.

- Chapter 2—Installing Ubuntu: We walk through the installation process one step at a time to clearly describe how anyone interested may begin using Ubuntu on their own computer.

- Chapter 3—Getting Started with Ubuntu: This is an informative and enjoyable introductory tour of Ubuntu, and the reader's first introduction to the more practical content of the book.

- Chapter 4—Becoming an Ubuntu Power User: We explore some of the advanced ways to use Ubuntu. This is the chapter for users who want to move up from basic use, but who do not intend to become programmers or professional systems administrators.

- Chapter 5—Finding and Installing Ubuntu Applications: Here you will learn about the vast contents of the Ubuntu software repositories and how to take advantage of them. Several examples of useful software that is not installed by default are highlighted.

- Chapter 6—Customizing Ubuntu for Performance, Accessibility, and Fun: Learn how to bend Ubuntu to better fit your needs or whims.

- Chapter 7—Welcome to the Command Line: Begin to take advantage of the power and efficiency of the command line with the clear, easy-to-use examples in our brief introduction.

- Chapter 8—The Ubuntu Server: This introduction to Ubuntu Server installation and administration includes coverage of command-line package management, basic security topics, and advanced installer features like logical volume management and RAID.

- Chapter 9—Ubuntu-Related Projects and Derivatives: There are a number of Linux distributions based on Ubuntu that you will find interesting and possibly useful. We discuss some of these as well as projects that are integral to the creation of Ubuntu, such as Launchpad and Bazaar.

- Chapter 10—The Ubuntu Community: The Ubuntu community is larger and more active than many people realize. We discuss many of its facets, including what people like you do to build, promote, distribute, support, document, translate, and advocate Ubuntu—and we tell you how you can join in the fun.

The Ubuntu team offers several installation options for Ubuntu users, including CDs for desktop, alternate install, and server install. These three CD images are conveniently combined onto one DVD included in the back of this book, allowing you to install Ubuntu for different configurations from just one disk. There is also an option to test the DVD for defects as well as a memory test option to check your computer.

The first boot option on the DVD, Start or Install Ubuntu, will cover most users' needs. For more comprehensive information, check the Help feature by selecting F1 on the boot menu. You can also refer to Chapter 2, which covers the Ubuntu installation process in detail.

You can find the DVD image, the individual CD images (for those who don't have a DVD drive), and Kubuntu and Ubuntu Server on www.ubuntu.com/download.

CHAPTER 1

The Ubuntu Story

- The Vision
- Free Software, Open Source, and GNU/Linux
- How the Vision Became Ubuntu
- What Is Ubuntu?
- Ubuntu Promises and Goals
- Sustaining the Vision: Canonical and the
  Ubuntu Foundation
- Beyond the Vision: Ubuntu Subprojects,
  Derivatives, and Spin-Offs
- Summary

THIS CHAPTER brings the history of the Ubuntu Project to life and through its history and looks to its future. If you are looking to jump right in and get started with Ubuntu, you can skip this and proceed immediately to Chapter 2, Installing Ubuntu. If you are interested in first learning about where Ubuntu comes from and where it is going, this chapter provides a good introduction.

The Vision

In April 2004 Mark Shuttleworth brought together a dozen developers from the Debian, GNOME, and GNU Arch projects to brainstorm. Shuttleworth asked the developers if a better type of operating system (OS) was possible. Their answer was "Yes." He asked them what it would look like. He asked them to describe the community that would build such an OS. That group worked with Shuttleworth to come up with answers to these questions, and then they decided to try to make the answers a reality. The group named itself the Warthogs and gave itself a six-month deadline to build a proof-of-concept OS. The developers nicknamed their first release the Warty Warthog with the reasonable assumption that their first product would have its warts. Then they got down to business.

It's fulfilling, particularly for those of us who were privileged to be among those early Warthogs, to see the progress made by this project over the years. We had a strong beginning when, far from being warty, the Warty Warthog surpassed our most optimistic expectations and *everyone's* predictions. Within six months, Ubuntu was in the Number 1 spot on several popularity rankings of GNU/Linux distributions. Ubuntu has demonstrated the most explosive growth of any GNU/Linux distribution in recent memory and had one of the most impressive first years and continued growth of any free or open source software project in history.

It is staggering to think that after so few years, *millions* of individuals are using Ubuntu. As many thousands of these users give back to the Ubuntu community by developing documentation, translation, and code, Ubuntu improves every day. As many thousands of these users contribute to a thriving advocacy and support community—both online and in their local communities—Ubuntu's growth remains unchecked. Ubuntu sub-projects, a list of efforts that includes Kubuntu and Ubuntu Studio, along with other projects, are extending the reach and goals of the Ubuntu project into new realms.

Meanwhile, millions of pressed Ubuntu CDs have been shipped at no cost to universities, Internet cafés, computer shops, and community centers around the world. You can find Ubuntu almost anywhere people use computers. The authors have personally seen strangers running Ubuntu on trains in Spain, in libraries in Boston, in museums in Croatia, in high schools in Mexico, across North Africa in Morocco and Tunisia, and in many more places too numerous to list here.

Over the years, Ubuntu has continued to mature. The public took even more notice of Ubuntu beginning with the release of Ubuntu 6.06 LTS, the first polished release with long-term support for both desktops and servers, and followed by a new release every six months and a new LTS release every two years up to the current 12.04 LTS. With these releases, Ubuntu has proven it intends to stick around for the long term while also improving consistently and on a predictable schedule. Even with this maturation, the project maintains its youthful vigor, its ambitious attitude, its commitment to its principles, and its community-driven approach. As the project ages, it is proving that it can learn from its failures as well as its successes and that it can maintain growth without compromising stability.

We've come a long way—and we're still only getting started.

Free Software, Open Source, and GNU/Linux

While thousands of individuals have contributed in some form to Ubuntu, the project has succeeded only through the contributions of many thousands more who have indirectly laid the technical, social, and economic groundwork for Ubuntu's success. While introductions to free software, open source, and GNU/Linux can be found in many other places, no introduction of Ubuntu is complete without a brief discussion of these concepts and the people and history behind them. It is around these concepts and within these communities that Ubuntu was motivated and born. Ultimately, it is through these ideas that it is sustained.

Free Software and GNU

In a series of events that have almost become legend through constant repetition, Richard M. Stallman created the concept of free software in 1983. Stallman grew up with computers in the 1960s and 1970s, when computer users purchased very large and extremely expensive mainframe computers, which were then shared among large numbers of programmers. Software was, for the most part, seen as an add-on to the hardware, and every user had the ability and the right to modify or rewrite the software on his or her computer and to freely share this software. As computers became cheaper and more numerous in the late 1970s, producers of software began to see value in the software itself. Producers of computers began to argue that their software could be copyrighted and was a form of intellectual property much like a music recording, a film, or a book's text. They began to distribute their software under licenses and in forms that restricted its users' abilities to use, redistribute, or modify the code. By the early 1980s, restrictive software licenses had become the norm.

Stallman, then a programmer at MIT's Artificial Intelligence Laboratory, became increasingly concerned with what he saw as a dangerous loss of the freedoms that software users and developers had previously enjoyed. He was concerned with computer users' ability to be good neighbors and members of what he thought was an ethical and efficient computer-user community. To fight against this negative tide, Stallman articulated a vision for a community that developed liberated code—in his words, "free software." He defined free software as software that had the following four characteristics—labeled as freedoms 0 through 3 instead of 1 through 4 as a nod to computer programming tradition and a bit of an inside joke:

■ The freedom to run the program for any purpose (freedom 0)

■ The freedom to study how the program works and adapt it to your needs (freedom 1)

- The freedom to redistribute copies so you can help your neighbor (freedom 2)

- The freedom to improve the program and release your improvements to the public so that the whole community benefits (freedom 3)

Access to source code—the human-readable and modifiable blueprints of any piece of software that can be distinguished from the computer-readable version of the code that most software is distributed as—is a prerequisite to freedoms 1 and 3. In addition to releasing this definition of free software, Stallman created a project with the goal of creating a completely free OS to replace the then-popular UNIX. In 1984, Stallman announced this project and called it GNU—also in the form of common programmer humor, a recursive acronym that stands for "GNU's Not UNIX."

Linux

By the early 1990s, Stallman and a collection of other programmers working on GNU had developed a near-complete OS that could be freely shared. They were, however, missing a final essential piece in the form of a kernel—a complex system command processor that lies at the center of any OS. In 1991, Linus Torvalds wrote an early version of just such a kernel, released it under a free license, and called it Linux. Linus's kernel was paired with the GNU project's development tools and OS and with the graphical windowing system called X. With this pairing, a completely free OS was born—free both in terms of price and in Stallman's terms of freedom.

All systems referred to as Linux today are, in fact, built on the work of this collaboration. Technically, the term *Linux* refers only to the kernel. Many programmers and contributors to GNU, including Stallman, argue emphatically that the full OS should be referred to as GNU/Linux in order to give credit not only to Linux but also to the GNU project and to highlight GNU's goals of spreading software freedom—goals not necessarily shared by Linus Torvalds. Many others find this name cumbersome and prefer calling the system simply Linux. Yet others, such as those working on the Ubuntu project, attempt to avoid the controversy altogether by referring to GNU/Linux only by using their own project's name.

Open Source

Disagreements over labeling did not end with discussions about the naming of the combination of GNU and Linux. In fact, as the list of contributors to GNU and Linux grew, a vibrant world of new free software projects sprouted up, facilitated in part by growing access to the Internet. As this community grew and diversified, a number of people began to notice an unintentional side effect of Stallman's free software. Because free software was built in an open way, *anyone* could contribute to software by looking through the code, finding bugs, and fixing them. Because software ended up being examined by larger numbers of programmers, free software was higher in quality, performed better, and offered more features than similar software developed through proprietary development mechanisms. It turned out that in many situations, the development model behind free software led to software that was *inherently better* than proprietary alternatives.

As the computer and information technology industry began to move into the dot-com boom, one group of free software developers and leaders, spearheaded by two free software developers and advocates—Eric S. Raymond and Bruce Perens—saw the important business proposition offered by a model that could harness volunteer labor or interbusiness collaboration and create intrinsically better software. However, they worried that the term *free software* was problematic for at least two reasons. First, it was highly ambiguous—the English word *free* means both gratis, or at no cost (e.g., free as in free beer), and liberated in the sense of freedom (e.g., free as in free speech). Second, there was a feeling, articulated most famously by Raymond, that all this talk of freedom was scaring off the very business executives and decision makers whom the free software movement needed to impress in order to succeed.

To tackle both of these problems, this group coined a new phrase—open source—and created a new organization called the Open Source Initiative. The group set at its core a definition of open source software that overlapped completely and exclusively with both Stallman's four-part definition of free software and with other community definitions that were also based on Stallman's.

One useful way to understand the split between the free software and open source movements is to think of it as the opposite of a schism. In religious schisms, churches separate and do not work or worship together because of relatively small differences in belief, interpretation, or motivation. For example, most contemporary forms of Protestant Christianity agree on *almost* everything but have separated over some small but irreconcilable differences. However, in the case of the free software and open source movements, the two groups have fundamental disagreements about their motivation and beliefs. One group is focused on freedom, while the other is focused on pragmatics. Free software is most accurately described as a social movement, while open source is a development methodology. However, the two groups have no trouble working on projects hand in hand.

In terms of the motivations and goals, open source and free software diverge greatly. Yet in terms of the software, the projects, and the licenses they use, they are completely synonymous. While people who identify with either group see the two movements as being at odds, the Ubuntu project sees no conflict between the two ideologies. People in the Ubuntu project identify with either group and often with both. In this book, we may switch back and forth between the terms as different projects, and many people in the Ubuntu community identify more strongly with one term or the other. For the purposes of this book, though, either term should be read as implying the other unless it is stated otherwise.

How the Vision Became Ubuntu

There was a time when writing a history of Ubuntu may have seemed premature; however, that is no longer the case, as the last several years have been busy ones for Ubuntu. With its explosive growth, it is difficult even for those involved most closely with the project to track and record some of the high points. Importantly, there are some key figures whose own history must be given to fully understand Ubuntu. This brief summary provides some of the high points of Ubuntu's history to date and the necessary background knowledge to understand where Ubuntu comes from.

Mark Shuttleworth

No history of Ubuntu can call itself complete without a history of Mark Shuttleworth. Shuttleworth is, undeniably, the most visible and important person in Ubuntu. More important from the point of view of history,

Shuttleworth is also the originator and initiator of the project—he made the snowball that would eventually roll on and grow to become the Ubuntu project.

Shuttleworth was born in 1973 in Welkom, Free State, in South Africa. He attended Diocesan College and obtained a business science degree in finance and information systems at the University of Cape Town. During this period, he was an avid computer hobbyist and became involved with the free and open source software community. He was at least marginally involved in both the Apache project and the Debian project and was the first person to upload the Apache Web server, perhaps the single most important piece of server software on GNU/Linux platforms, into the Debian project's archives.

Seeing an opportunity in the early days of the Web, Shuttleworth founded a certificate authority and Internet security company called Thawte in his garage. Over the course of several years, he built Thawte into the second largest certificate authority on the Internet, trailing only the security behemoth VeriSign. Throughout this period, Thawte's products and services were built and served almost entirely from free and open source software. In December 1999, Shuttleworth sold Thawte to VeriSign for an undisclosed amount that reached into the hundreds of millions in U.S. dollars.

With his fortune made at a young age, Shuttleworth might have enjoyed a life of leisure—and probably considered it. Instead, he decided to pursue his lifelong dream of space travel. After paying approximately US$20 million to the Russian space program and devoting nearly a year to preparation, including learning Russian and spending seven months training in Star City, Russia, Shuttleworth realized his dream as a civilian cosmonaut aboard the Russian Soyuz TM-34 mission. On this mission, Shuttleworth spent two days on the Soyuz rocket and eight days on the International Space Station, where he participated in experiments related to AIDS and genome research. In early May 2002, Shuttleworth returned to Earth.

In addition to space exploration and an only slightly less impressive jaunt to Antarctica, Shuttleworth has played an active role as both a philanthropist and a venture capitalist. In 2001, Shuttleworth founded The Shuttleworth Foundation (TSF)—a nonprofit organization based in South Africa. The foundation was chartered to fund, develop, and drive social innovation in the field of education. Of course, the means by which TSF attempts to achieve these goals frequently involves free software. Through these projects, the organization has been one of the most visible proponents of free and open source software in South Africa and even the world. In the venture capital area, Shuttleworth worked to foster research, development, and entrepreneurship in South Africa with strategic injections of cash into start-ups through a new venture capital firm called HBD, an acronym for "Here Be Dragons." During this period, Shuttleworth was busy brainstorming his next big project—the project that would eventually become Ubuntu.

The Warthogs

There has been no lack of projects attempting to wrap GNU, Linux, and other pieces of free and open source software into a neat, workable, and user-friendly package. Mark Shuttleworth, like many other people, believed that the philosophical and pragmatic benefits offered by free software put it on a course for widespread success. While each had its strengths, none of the offerings were particularly impressive as a whole. Something was missing from each of them. Shuttleworth saw this as an opportunity. If someone could build *the* great free software distribution that helped push GNU/Linux into the mainstream, he would come to occupy a position of strategic importance.

Shuttleworth, like many other technically inclined people, was a huge fan of the Debian project (discussed in depth later in this chapter). However, many things about Debian did not fit with Shuttleworth's vision of an ideal OS. For a period of time, Shuttleworth considered the possibility of running for Debian project leader as a means of reforming the Debian project from within. With time, though, it became clear that the best way to bring GNU/Linux to the mainstream would not be from within the Debian project—which in many situations had very good reasons for being the way it was. Instead, Shuttleworth would create a new project that worked in symbiosis with Debian to build a new, better GNU/Linux system.

To kick off this project, Shuttleworth invited a dozen or so free and open source software developers he knew and respected to his flat in London in April 2004. It was in this meeting (alluded to in the first paragraphs of this introduction) that the groundwork for the Ubuntu project was laid. By that point, many of those involved were excited about the possibility of the project. During this meeting, the members of the team—which would in time grow into the core Ubuntu team—brainstormed a large list of the things that *they* would want to see in their ideal OS. The list is now a familiar list of features to most Ubuntu users. Many of these traits are covered in more depth later in this chapter. The group wanted

- Predictable and frequent release cycles
- A strong focus on localization and accessibility
- A strong focus on ease of use and user-friendliness on the desktop
- A strong focus on Python as the single programming language through which the entire system could be built and expanded
- A community-driven approach that worked with existing free software projects and a method by which the groups could give back as they went along—not just at the time of release
- A new set of tools designed around the process of building distributions that allowed developers to work within an ecosystem of different projects and that allowed users to give back in whatever way they could

There was consensus among the group that actions speak louder than words, so there were no public announcements or press releases. Instead, the group set a deadline for itself—six short months in the future. Shuttleworth agreed to finance the work and pay the developers full-time salaries to work on the project. After six months, they would both announce their project and reveal the first product of their work. They made a list of goals they wanted to achieve by the deadline, and the individuals present took on tasks. Collectively, they called themselves the Warthogs.

What Does *Ubuntu* Mean?

At this point, the Warthogs had a great team, a set of goals, and a decent idea of how to achieve most of them. The team did not, on the other hand, have a name for the project. Shuttleworth argued strongly that they should call the project Ubuntu.

Ubuntu is a concept and a term from several South African languages, including Zulu and Xhosa. It refers to a South African ideology or ethic that, while difficult to express in English, might roughly be translated as "humanity toward others," or "I am what I am because of who we all are." Others have described Ubuntu as "the belief in a universal bond of sharing that connects all humanity." The famous South African human rights champion Archbishop Desmond Tutu explained Ubuntu in this way:

> A person with Ubuntu is open and available to others, affirming of others, does not feel threatened that others are able and good, for he or she has a proper self-assurance that comes from knowing that he or she belongs in a greater whole and is diminished when others are humiliated or diminished, when others are tortured or oppressed.

Ubuntu played an important role as a founding principle in post-apartheid South Africa and remains a concept familiar to most South Africans today.

Shuttleworth liked *Ubuntu* as a name for the new project for several reasons. First, it is a South African concept. While the majority of the people who work on Ubuntu are not from South Africa, the roots of the project are, and Shuttleworth wanted to choose a name that represented this. Second, the project emphasizes relationships with others and provides a framework for a profound type of community and sharing—exactly the attitudes of sharing, community, and collaboration that are at the core of free software. The term represented the side of free software that the team wanted to share with the world. Third, the idea of personal relationships built on mutual respect and connections describes the fundamental ground rules for the highly functional community that the Ubuntu team wanted to build. *Ubuntu* was a term that encapsulated where the project came from, where the project was going, and how the project planned to get there. The name was perfect. It stuck.

Beyond the Vision

In order to pay developers to work on Ubuntu full time, Shuttleworth needed a company to employ them. He wanted to pick some of the best people for the jobs from within the global free and open source communities. These communities, inconveniently for Shuttleworth, know no national and geographic boundaries. Rather than move everyone to a single locale and office, Shuttleworth made the decision to employ these developers through a virtual company. While this had obvious drawbacks in the form of high-latency and low-bandwidth connections, different time zones, and much more, it also introduced some major benefits in the particular context of the project. On one hand, the distributed nature of employees meant that the new company could hire individuals without requiring them to pack up their lives and move to a new country. More important, it meant that *everyone* in the company was dependent on IRC, mailing lists, and online communication mechanisms to do their work. This unintentionally and automatically solved the water-cooler problem that plagued many other corporately funded free software projects—namely, that developers would casually speak about their work in person, and cut the community and anyone else who didn't work in the office out of the conversation completely. For the first year, the closest thing that Canonical had to an office was Shuttleworth's flat in London. While the company has grown and now has several offices around the world, it remains distributed and a large number of the engineers work from home. The group remains highly dependent on Internet collaboration.

With time, the company was named Canonical. The name was a nod to the project's optimistic goals of becoming the canonical place for services and support for free and open source software and for Ubuntu in particular. *Canonical*, of course, refers to something that is accepted as authoritative. It is a common word in the computer programmer lexicon. It's important to note that being canonical is like being standard; it is not coercive. Unlike holding a monopoly, becoming the canonical location for something implies a similar sort of success—but *never* one that cannot be undone, and *never* one that is exclusive. Other companies will support Ubuntu and build operating systems based on it, but as long as Canonical is doing a good job, its role will remain central.

What Is Ubuntu?

The Warthogs' goal and Canonical's flagship project is Ubuntu. Ubuntu is a free and open source GNU/Linux distribution and operating system. More information on what a distribution is and how other distributions have played a role in vision that is now Ubuntu can be found in Chapter 7.

What Is a Distribution?

It's clear to most people that Ubuntu is an OS. The full story is a little more complex. Ubuntu is what is called a distribution of GNU/Linux—a *distro* for short. Understanding exactly what that means requires, once again, a little bit of history. In the early days of GNU and Linux, users needed a great deal of technical knowledge. Only geeks needed to apply. There were no Linux operating systems in the sense that we usually use the term— there was no single CD or set of disks that one could use to install. Instead, the software was dozens and even hundreds of individual programs, each built differently by a different individual, and each distributed separately. Installing each of the necessary applications would be incredibly time con- suming at best. In many cases, incompatibilities and the technical trickery necessary to install software made getting a GNU/Linux system on a hard disk prohibitively difficult. A great deal of knowledge of configuration and programming was necessary just to get a system up and running. As a result, very few people who were not programmers used these early GNU/ Linux systems.

Early distributions were projects that collected all of the necessary pieces of software from all of the different places and put them together in an easier-to-install form with the most basic configuration already done. These distributions aimed to make using GNU/Linux more convenient and to bring it to larger groups of users. Today, almost nobody uses GNU/Linux without using a distribution. As a result, distribution names are well known. Ubuntu is such a project. Other popular distros include Red Hat and Fedora, Novell's SUSE, Gentoo, and of course Debian.

Most distributions contain a similar collection of software. For example, they all contain most of the core pieces of GNU and a Linux kernel. Almost all contain the X Window System and a set of applications on top of it that may include a Web browser, a desktop environment, and an office suite. While distributions started out distributing only the core pieces of the OS, they have grown to include an increasingly wide array of applications as well. A modern distribution includes all of the software that "comes with an OS," that is, several CDs or DVDs containing anything that most users might want and that the distribution is legally allowed to distribute.

Ubuntu, like other contemporary distros, offers a custom installer, a framework including software and servers to install new software once the system has been installed, a standard configuration method through which many programs can be configured, a standard method through which users can report bugs in their software, and much more. Frequently, distributions also contain large repositories of software on servers accessible through the Internet. To get a sense of scale, Ubuntu includes more than 30,000 pieces of software on its central servers—each piece of software is customized slightly and tested to work well with all of the other software on the system. That number grows daily.

What's important to realize is that the creators of distributions do not, for the most part, write or create the applications you use. The Ubuntu team did not write Linux, and it did not write GNU—although individuals on the team have contributed to both projects. Instead, the Ubuntu team takes GNU, Linux, and many thousands of other applications and then tests and integrates them to be accessible under a single installer. Ubuntu is the glue that lets you take a single CD, install hundreds of separate pieces of software, and have them work together as a single, integrated desktop system. If you were to pick up a CD of another distribution such as Debian, Red Hat, or Novell, the software installed would be nearly identical to the software in Ubuntu. The difference would be in the way the software is installed, serviced, upgraded, and presented and the way it integrates with other pieces of software on the system.

An Ecosystem of Distributions

Many hundreds of GNU/Linux distributions are in active use today. A quick look at Distrowatch's database (distrowatch.com) demonstrates the staggering number and growth of distributions. One of the first GNU/Linux distributions was called Softlanding Linux System, or SLS. For a number of reasons, a programmer named Patrick Volkerding thought he could improve on SLS. Because SLS was free software, Volkerding had the freedom to make a derivative version of SLS and distribute it. Volkerding did just this when he took SLS's code and used it as the framework or model upon which to create his own variant called Slackware. Subsequently, Slackware became the first widely successful GNU/Linux distribution and is maintained to this day.

With time, the landscape of GNU/Linux distribution has changed. However, the important role of derivation that made Slackware possible has remained fully intact and is still shaping this landscape. Today, the hundreds of GNU/Linux distributions serve a multitude of users for a myriad of purposes: There are distributions specially designed for children, for dentists, and for speakers of many of the world's languages. There are distributions for science, for business, for servers, for PDAs, for nonprofit organizations, for musicians, and for countless other groups.

Despite this diversity, the vast majority of derivatives can be traced back to one of two parent distributions: Red Hat and Debian. While it is not necessary to understand the details of how these projects differ, it's useful to know that Red Hat and Debian offer two compelling, but frequently different, platforms. Each project has strengths and weaknesses. For almost every group making a Linux-based OS, one of these projects acts as square one (with a few notable exceptions, such as the Gentoo project).

However, while the process of deriving distributions has allowed for a proliferation of OS platforms serving a vast multiplicity of needs, the derivative process has, historically, been largely a one-way process. New distributions based on Red Hat—CentOS and SUSE, for example—begin with Red Hat or a subset of Red Hat technology and then customize and diverge. Very few of these changes ever make it back into Red Hat and, with time, distributions tend to diverge to the point of irreconcilable incompatibility. While the software that each system includes remains largely consistent across all distributions, the way that it is packaged, presented, installed, and configured becomes increasingly differentiated. During this process, interdistribution sharing and collaboration grow in difficulty.

This growing divergence indicates a more general problem faced by distribution teams in getting changes upstream. Frequently, the users of GNU/Linux distributions find and report problems in their software. Frequently, distribution teams fix the bugs in question. While sometimes these bugs are in changes introduced by the distribution, they often exist in the upstream version of the software and the fix applies to *every* distribution. What is not uncommon, but is unfortunately *much* less frequent, is for these bug fixes to be pushed upstream so that all distributions and users get to use them. This lack of collaboration is rarely due to malice, incompetence, or any tactical or strategic decision made by developers or their employers. Instead, tracking and monitoring changes *across* distributions and in relation to upstream developers is complicated and difficult. It's a fact of life that sometimes changes fall on the floor. These failures are simply the product of distribution-building processes, policies, and tools that approach distributions as products in and of themselves—not processes within an ecosystem.

Like many other distributions, Ubuntu is a derivative of Debian. Unlike the creators of many derivatives, the Ubuntu community has made it one of its primary goals to explore the possibility of a better derivation process with Debian, with Debian and Ubuntu's common upstreams (e.g., projects such as Linux or GNU), and with Ubuntu's *own* derivatives. A more in-depth discussion of Debian can help explain how Ubuntu positions itself within the free software world.

The Debian Project and the Free Software Universe

Debian is a distribution backed by a volunteer project of many hundreds of official members and many more volunteers and contributors. It has expanded to encompass over 30,000 packages of free and open source applications and documentation. Debian's history and structure make it very good at certain things. For example, Debian has a well-deserved reputation for integrated package management and access to a large list of free software applications. However, as a voluntary and largely nonhierarchical organization, Debian had a challenging time providing frequent and reliable releases, corporate support and liability, and a top-down consistency.

Each new distribution exists for a reason. Creating a new distribution, even a derivative, is far from easy. In large part, Ubuntu exists to build off of the many successes of the Debian project while solving some of the problems it struggles with. The goal is to create a synthetic whole that appeals to users who had previously been unable or unwilling to use Debian.

In building off the great work of the Debian project, as well as GNU, Linux, and other projects that Debian is built on, the Ubuntu team wanted to explore a new style of derivation that focused on a tighter interproject relationship within an ecosystem of different developers. While Ubuntu tries to improve and build on Debian's success, the project is in no way trying to replace Debian. On the contrary, Ubuntu couldn't exist without the Debian project and its large volunteer and software base, as well as the high degree of quality that Debian consistently provides. This symbiotic relationship between Ubuntu and Debian is mirrored in the way that both Ubuntu and Debian depend heavily on projects such as GNU and Linux to produce great software, which they can each package and distribute. The Ubuntu project sets out explicitly to build a symbiotic relationship with both Debian and their common "upstream."

The relationship between Ubuntu and Debian has not been simple, straightforward, or painless and has involved patience and learning on both sides. While the relationship has yet to be perfected, with time it has improved consistently, and both groups have found ways to work together that seem to offer major benefits over the traditional derive-and-forget model. It is through a complex series of technological, social, and even political processes—many of which are described in the rest of this chapter—that Ubuntu tries to create a better way to build a free software distribution.

The Ubuntu Community

Ubuntu would not be what it is today without the Ubuntu community. Even the definition of *ubuntu* is one that revolves around people interacting in a community. The Ubuntu community and how it is organized as well as how those who choose can get involved will be discussed in detail in Chapter 10.

Ubuntu Promises and Goals

So far, this book has been about the prehistory, history, and context of the Ubuntu project. After this chapter, the book focuses on the distribution itself. Before proceeding, it's important to understand the goals that motivated the project.

Philosophical Goals

The most important goals of the Ubuntu project are philosophical in nature. The Ubuntu project lays out its philosophy in a series of documents on its Web site. In the most central of these documents, the team summarizes the charter and the major philosophical goals and underpinnings.

▪ **Our philosophy**

Our work is driven by a philosophy of software freedom that aims to spread and bring the benefits of software to all parts of the world. At the core of the Ubuntu Philosophy are these core ideals:

1. Every computer user should have the freedom to download, run, copy, distribute, study, share, change and improve their software for any purpose, without paying licensing fees.

2. Every computer user should be able to use their software in the language of their choice.

3. Every computer user should be given every opportunity to use software, even if they work under a disability.

Our philosophy is reflected in the software we produce and included in our distribution. As a result, the licensing terms of the software we distribute are measured against our philosophy, using the Ubuntu License Policy.

When you install Ubuntu, almost all of the software installed already meets these ideals, and we are working to ensure that every single piece of software you need is available under a license that gives you those freedoms.

Currently, we make a specific exception for some "drivers" that are available only in binary form, without which many computers will not complete the Ubuntu installation. We place these in a restricted section of your system, which makes them easy to remove if you do not need them.

▪ **Free software**

For Ubuntu, the "free" in free software is used primarily in reference to freedom and not to price—although we are committed to not charging for Ubuntu. The most important thing about Ubuntu is that it confers rights of software freedom on the people who install and use it. These freedoms enable the Ubuntu community to grow and to continue to share its collective experience and expertise to improve Ubuntu and make it suitable for use in new countries and new industries.

Quoting the Free Software Foundation's "What Is Free Software?" the freedoms at the core of free software are defined as

▪ The freedom to run the program for any purpose

▪ The freedom to study how the program works and adapt it to your needs

  - The freedom to redistribute copies so you can help others

  - The freedom to improve the program and release your improvements to the public so that everyone benefits

- **Open source**

  Open source is a term coined in 1998 to remove the ambiguity in the English word *free*. The Open Source Initiative described open source software in the Open Source Definition. Open source continues to enjoy growing success and wide recognition.

  Ubuntu is happy to call itself open source. While some refer to free and open source as competing movements with different ends, we do not see free and open source software as either distinct or incompatible. Ubuntu proudly includes members who identify with both movements.

Here, the Ubuntu project makes explicit its goals that every user of software should have the freedoms required by free software. This is important for a number of reasons. First, it offers users all of the practical benefits of software that runs better, faster, and more flexibly. More important, it gives every user the capability to transcend his or her role as a user and a consumer of software. Ubuntu wants software to be empowering and to work in the ways that users want it to work. Ubuntu wants all users to have the ability to make sure it works for them. To do this, software *must* be free, so Ubuntu makes this a requirement and a philosophical promise.

Of course, the core goals of Ubuntu do not end with the free software definition. Instead, the project articulates two new but equally important goals. The first of these, that all computer users should be able to use their computers in their chosen languages, is a nod to the fact that the majority of the world's population does not speak English, while the vast majority of software interacts only in that language. To be useful, source code comments, programming languages, documentation, and the texts and menus in computer programs must be written in *some* language. Arguably, the world's most international language is a reasonably good choice. However, there is no language that everyone speaks, and English is not useful to the majority of the world's population that does not speak it. A computer can be a great tool for empowerment and education, but *only* if the user can understand the words in the computer's interface. As a result, Ubuntu believes that it is the project's—and community's—responsibility to ensure that *every* user can easily use Ubuntu to read and write in the language with which he or she is most comfortable.

The ability to make modifications—a requirement of free software and of Ubuntu's first philosophical point—makes this type of translation possible. This book is a case in point. While it helps explain Ubuntu only to the relatively small subset of the world that already speaks English, the choice to write this book in English was made to enable it to have the widest impact. More important, it is distributed under a Creative Commons license that allows for translation, modification, and redistribution. The authors of this book cannot write this book in all of the world's languages—or even more than one of them. Instead, we have attempted to eliminate unnecessary legal restrictions and other barriers that might keep the community from taking on the translation work. As a result, the complete text of the several editions have been translated into other languages like German, Japanese, Polish, and Spanish.

Finally, just as no person should be blocked from using a computer simply because he or she does not know a particular language, no user should be blocked from using a computer because of a disability. Ubuntu must be accessible to users with motor disabilities, vision disabilities, and hearing disabilities. It should provide input and output in a variety of forms to account for each of these situations and for others. A significant percentage of the world's most intelligent and creative individuals also have disabilities. Ubuntu's usefulness should not be limited when it can be inclusive. More important, Ubuntu wants to welcome and to be able to harness the ability of these individuals as community members to build a better and more effective community.

Conduct Goals and Code of Conduct

If Ubuntu's philosophical commitments describe the *why* of the Ubuntu project, the Code of Conduct (CoC) describes Ubuntu's *how*. Ubuntu's CoC is, arguably, the most important document in the day-to-day operation of the Ubuntu community and sets the ground rules for work and cooperation within the project. Explicit agreement to the document is the only criterion for becoming an officially recognized Ubuntu activist—an Ubuntero—and is an essential step toward membership in the project.

Signing the Ubuntu Code of Conduct and becoming an Ubuntu member is described in more depth in Chapter 10.

The CoC covers "behavior as a member of the Ubuntu community, in any forum, mailing list, wiki, Web site, IRC channel, install-fest, public meeting, or private correspondence." The CoC goes into some degree of depth on a series of points that fall under the following headings.

- Be considerate.
- Be respectful.
- Be collaborative.
- When you disagree, consult others.
- When you are unsure, ask for help.
- Step down considerately.

Many of these headings seem like common sense or common courtesy to many, and that is by design. Nothing in the CoC is controversial or radical, and it was never designed to be.

More difficult is that nothing is easy to enforce or decide because acting considerately, respectfully, and collaboratively is often very subjective. There is room for honest disagreements and occasional hurt feelings. These are accepted shortcomings. The CoC was not designed to be a law with explicit prohibitions on phrases, language, or actions. Instead, it aims to provide a constitution and a reminder that considerate and respectful discussion is *essential* to the health and vitality of the project. In situations where there is a serious disagreement on whether a community member has violated or is violating the code, the Community Council—a body that is discussed in depth in Chapter 10—is available to arbitrate disputes and decide what action, if any, is appropriate.

Nobody involved in the Ubuntu project, including Mark Shuttleworth and the other members of the Community Council, is above the CoC. The CoC is *never* optional and *never* waived. In fact, the Ubuntu community has also created a Leadership Code of Conduct (LCoC), which extends and expands on the CoC and describes additional requirements and expectations for those in leadership positions in the community. Of course, in no way was either code designed to eliminate conflict or disagreement. Arguments are at least as common in Ubuntu as they are in other projects and online communities. However, there is a common understanding within the project that arguments should happen in an environment of collaboration and mutual respect. This allows for *better* arguments with *better* results—and with less hurt feelings and fewer bruised egos.

While they have been sometimes incorrectly used as such, the CoC and LCoC are not sticks to be wielded against an opponent in an argument. Instead, they are useful points of reference upon which we can assume consensus within the Ubuntu community. Much more frequently, if a group in the community feels a member is acting in a way that is out of line with the code, the group will gently remind the community member, often privately, that the CoC is in effect. In almost all situations, this is enough to avoid any further action or conflict. Very few CoC violations are ever brought before the Community Council.

Technical Goals

While a respectful community and adherence to a set of philosophical goals provide an important frame in which the Ubuntu project works, Ubuntu is, at the end of the day, a technical project. As a result, it only makes sense that in addition to philosophical goals and a project constitution, Ubuntu also has a set of technical goals.

The first technical goal of the project, and perhaps the most important one, is the coordination of regular and predictable releases. In April 2004, at the Warthogs meeting, the project set a goal for its initial proof-of-concept release six months out. In part due to the resounding success of that project, and in larger part due to the GNOME release schedule, the team has stuck to a regular and predictable six-month release cycle and has only once chosen to extend the release schedule—by six weeks for the first LTS release to ensure it was done right—and only then after obtaining community consensus on the decision. The team then doubled its efforts and made the next release in a mere four and a half months, putting its release schedule back on track. Frequent releases are important because users can then use the latest and greatest free software available—something that is essential in a development environment as vibrant and rapidly changing and improving as the free software community. Predictable releases are important, especially to businesses, because it means that they can organize their business plans around Ubuntu. Through consistent releases, Ubuntu can provide a platform that businesses and derivative distributions can rely upon to grow and build.

While releasing frequently and reliably is important, the released software must then be supported. Ubuntu, like all distributions, must deal with the fact that all software has bugs. Most bugs are minor, but fixing them may introduce even worse issues. Therefore, fixing bugs after a release must be done carefully or not at all. The Ubuntu project engages in major changes, including bug fixes, between releases only when the changes can be extensively tested. However, some bugs risk the loss of users' information or pose a serious security vulnerability. These bugs are fixed immediately and made available as updates for the released distribution. The Ubuntu community works hard to find and minimize all types of bugs before releases and is largely successful in squashing the worst. However, because there is always the possibility that more of these bugs will be found, Ubuntu commits to supporting every release for 18 months after it is released. In the case of LTS releases such as the original LTS, Ubuntu 6.06 LTS, released in 2006, the project went well beyond even this and committed to support the release for three full years on desktop computers and for five years in a server configuration. This proved so popular with businesses, institutions, and the users of Ubuntu servers that in 2008 and 2010, Ubuntu 8.04 LTS and 10.04 LTS were released with similar three- and five-year desktop and server extended support commitments. The most recent release, Ubuntu 12.04 LTS, continues the pattern.

This bipartite approach to servers and desktops implies the third major technical commitment of the Ubuntu project: support for both servers and desktop computers in separate but equally emphasized modes. While Ubuntu continues to be more well known, and perhaps more popular, in desktop configurations, there exist teams of Ubuntu developers focused both on server and desktop users. The Ubuntu project believes that both desktops and servers are essential and provides installation methods on every CD for both types of systems. Ubuntu provides tested and supported software appropriate to the most common actions in both environments and documentation for each. This book contains information on running Ubuntu both on the desktop and on a server. The release of 6.06 LTS with long-term support successfully helped pave the way for reliable long-term server support for Ubuntu and helped grow the now-vibrant Ubuntu server community. The 8.04 LTS release repeated this success with a more up-to-date platform, then 10.04 LTS, and now 12.04 LTS.

Finally, the Ubuntu project is committed to making it as easy as possible for users to transcend their role as consumers and users of software and to take advantage of each of the freedoms central to our philosophy. As a result, Ubuntu has tried to focus its development around the use and promotion of a single programming language, Python. The project has worked to ensure that Python is widely used throughout the system. By ensuring that desktop applications, text-based or console applications, and many of the "guts" of the system are written in or extensible in Python, Ubuntu is working to ensure that users need learn only one language in order to take advantage of, automate, and tweak many parts of their computer systems.

Bug #1

Of course, Ubuntu's goals are not only to build an OS that lives up to our philosophy or technical goals and to do it on our terms—although we probably would be happy if we achieved only that. Our *ultimate goal*, the one that supersedes and influences all others, is to spread our great software, our frequent releases, and the freedoms enshrined in our philosophy to as many computer users in as many countries as possible. Ubuntu's ultimate goal is not to become the most used *GNU/Linux distribution* in the world; it is to become the most widely used *OS* in the world.

The first bug recorded for Ubuntu illustrates this fact. The bug, filed by Shuttleworth and marked as severity critical, remains open today and can be viewed online at https://launchpad.net/distros/ubuntu/+bug/1. The text of the bug reads as follows.

> Microsoft has a majority market share | Non-free software is holding back innovation in the IT industry, restricting access to IT to a small part of the world's population and limiting the ability of software developers to reach their full potential, globally. This bug is widely evident in the PC industry.

Steps to repeat:

1. Visit a local PC store.

What happens:

2. Observe that a majority of PCs for sale have non-free software preinstalled.
3. Observe very few PCs with Ubuntu and free software preinstalled.

What should happen:

1. A majority of the PCs for sale should include only free software such as Ubuntu.
2. Ubuntu should be marketed in a way such that its amazing features and benefits would be apparent and known by all.
3. The system shall become more and more user friendly as time passes.

Many have described Ubuntu's success in the last several years as amazing. For a new GNU/Linux distribution, the level and speed of success have been unprecedented. During this period, Ubuntu has lived up to both its philosophical and technical commitments, achieved many of its goals, and built a vibrant community of users and contributors who have accomplished monumental amounts while collaborating in a culture of respect and understanding fully in line with the Ubuntu Code of Conduct. However, Bug #1 demonstrates that the Ubuntu project will be declared a complete success only when Ubuntu's standards of freedom, technical excellence, and conduct are the norm *everywhere* in the software world.

Sustaining the Vision: Canonical and the Ubuntu Foundation

While Ubuntu is driven by a community, several groups play an important role in its structure and organization. Foremost among these are Canonical, Ltd., a for-profit company introduced as part of the Ubuntu history description, and the Ubuntu Foundation, which is introduced later in this section.

Canonical, Ltd.

Canonical, Ltd. is a company founded by Mark Shuttleworth with the primary goal of developing and supporting the Ubuntu distribution. Many of the core developers on Ubuntu—although no longer a majority of them—work full time or part time as employees of Canonical, Ltd. This funding by Canonical allows Ubuntu to make the type of support commitments that it does. Ubuntu can claim that it will release in six months because releasing, in one form or another, is something that the paid workers at Canonical can ensure. As an all-volunteer organization, Debian suffered from an inability to set and meet deadlines—volunteers become busy or have other deadlines in their paying jobs that take precedence. By offering paying jobs to a subset of developers, Canonical can set support and release deadlines and ensure that they are met.

In this way, Canonical ensures that Ubuntu's bottom-line commitments are kept. Of course, Canonical does not fund all Ubuntu work, nor could it. Canonical can release *a distribution* every six months, but that distribution will be made *much* better and more usable through contributions from the community of users. Most features, most new pieces of software, almost all translations, almost all documentation, and much more are created outside of Canonical. Instead, Canonical ensures that deadlines are met and that the essential work, regardless of whether it's fun, gets done.

Canonical, Ltd. was incorporated on the Isle of Man—a tiny island nation between Wales and Ireland that is mostly well known as a haven for international businesses. Since Canonical's staff is sprinkled across the globe and no proper office is necessary, the Isle of Man seemed like as good a place as any for the company to hang its sign.

In early 2010, Mark Shuttleworth, Canonical's first CEO, stepped down, and longtime Chief Operating Officer, Jane Silber, became the new CEO. Shuttleworth retains his position as the head of the Ubuntu Community Council and Ubuntu Technical boards. He focuses his energy on product design and working with enterprise customers and partners, and leaves the day-to-day running of Canonical to Silber. Silber has been with Canonical since before the first release, and the company is expected to continue expanding and operating on its current path.

Canonical's Service and Support

While it is surprising to many users, fewer than half of Canonical's employees work on the Ubuntu project. The rest of the employees fall into several categories: business development, support and administration, and development of other projects such as Bazaar and Launchpad, which are discussed a bit later in this chapter.

Individuals involved in business development help create strategic deals and certification programs with other companies—primarily around Ubuntu. In large part, these are things that the community is either ill suited for or uninterested in as a whole. One example of business development work is the process of working with companies to ensure that their software (usually proprietary) is built and certified to run on Ubuntu. For example, Canonical worked with IBM to ensure that its popular DB2 database would run on Ubuntu and, when this was achieved, worked to have Ubuntu certified as a platform that would run DB2. Similarly, Canonical worked with Dell to ensure that Ubuntu could be installed and supported on Dell laptops and desktops as an option for its customers. A third example is the production of this book, which, published by Pearson Education's Prentice Hall imprint, was a product of work with Canonical.

Canonical also plays an important support role in the Ubuntu project in three ways. First, Canonical supports the development of the Ubuntu project. For example, Canonical system administrators keep servers up that support development and distribution of Ubuntu. Second, Canonical helps Ubuntu users and businesses directly by offering phone and e-mail support. Additionally, Canonical has helped build a large commercial Ubuntu support operation by arranging for support contracts with larger companies and organizations. This support is over and above the free (i.e., gratis) support offered by the community—this commercial support is offered at a fee and is either part of a longer-term flat-fee support contract or is pay-per-instance. By offering commercial support for Ubuntu in a variety of ways, Canonical has made a business for itself and helps make Ubuntu a more palatable option for the businesses, large and small, that are looking for an enterprise or enterprise-class GNU/Linux product with support contracts like those offered by other commercial GNU/Linux distributions.

Finally, Ubuntu supports other support organizations. Canonical does not seek or try to enforce a monopoly on Ubuntu support; it proudly lists *hundreds* of other organizations offering support for Ubuntu on the Ubuntu Web pages. Instead, Canonical offers what is called second-tier support to these organizations. Because Canonical employs many of the core Ubuntu developers, the company is very well suited to taking action on many of the tougher problems that these support organizations may run into. With its concentrated expertise, Canonical can offer this type of backup, or secondary support, to these organizations.

Bazaar and Launchpad

In addition to support and development on Ubuntu, Canonical, Ltd. funds the development of Bazaar, a distributed version control tool, and the Launchpad project. Bazaar is a tool for developing software that is used heavily in Ubuntu and plays an important role in the technical processes through which Ubuntu is forged. However, the software, which is similar in functionality to other version control systems such as CVS, Subversion, or BitKeeper, is useful in a variety of other projects as well. More important, Bazaar acts as the workhorse behind Launchpad.

More than half of Canonical's technical employees work on the Launchpad project. Launchpad is an ambitious Web-based superstructure application that consists of several highly integrated tools. The software plays a central role in Ubuntu development but is also used for the development of other distributions—especially those based on Ubuntu. Launchpad consists of the following major pieces.

■ **Rosetta:**
  A Web-based system for easily translating almost any piece of free software from English into almost any language. Rosetta is named after the Rosetta Stone, which helped linguists finally crack the code of Egyptian hieroglyphics.

■ **Malone:**
  The bug-tracking system that Ubuntu uses to manage and track bugs. It both tracks bugs across different versions of Ubuntu and allows the Ubuntu community to see the status of that bug in other places, including other distributions and potentially upstream. Malone is a reference to the gangster movie musical *Bugsy Malone*.

■ **Blueprint:**
  The specification writing and tracking software that Ubuntu and a small number of other projects use to track desired features and their status and to help manage and report on release processes.

- **Answers:**
  A simple support tracker built into Launchpad that provides one venue where users can make support requests and the community can help answer them in ways that are documented and connected to the other related functionality in Launchpad.

- **Soyuz:**
  The distribution management part of Launchpad that now controls the processes by which Ubuntu packages are built, tested, and migrated between different parts of the distribution. Soyuz is a reference to the type of Russian rocket that took Mark Shuttleworth to space. The word *soyuz*, in Russian, means "union."

- **Code:**
  Code allows Launchpad users to publish Bazaar branches of their code and should they choose, can associate them with projects. Code also allows users to mirror or watch Bazaar branches that are hosted elsewhere and even import Subversion and CVS repositories into Bazaar branches.

Launchpad and its components are discussed in more depth in Chapter 9. The importance of Launchpad in the Ubuntu project cannot be overstated. In addition to handling bugs, translations, and distribution building, Launchpad also handles Web site authentication and codifies team membership in the Ubuntu project. It is the place where all work in Ubuntu is tracked and recorded. Any member of the Ubuntu community and any person who contributes to Ubuntu in almost any way will, in due course, create an account in Launchpad.

The Ubuntu Foundation

Finally, in addition to Canonical and the full Ubuntu community, the Ubuntu project is supported by the Ubuntu Foundation, which was announced by Shuttleworth with an initial funding commitment of $10 million. The foundation, like Canonical, is based on the Isle of Man. The organization is advised by the Ubuntu Community Council.

Unlike Canonical, the Foundation does not play an active role in the day-to-day life of Ubuntu. At the moment, the Foundation is little more than a pile of money that exists to endow and ensure Ubuntu's future. Because Canonical is a young company, some companies and individuals found it difficult early on to trust that Canonical would be able to provide support for Ubuntu for the time frames (e.g., three to five years) that it claims it can. The Ubuntu Foundation exists to allay those fears. Time and consistency has also contributed greatly to the confidence of companies and individuals in Ubuntu, and the foundation will remain to ensure that consistency in the future.

If something unexpected were to happen to Shuttleworth or to Canonical that caused either to be unable to support Ubuntu development and maintain the distribution, the Ubuntu Foundation exists to carry on many of Canonical's core activities well into the future. Through the existence of the Foundation, the Ubuntu project can make the types of long-term commitments and promises it does.

The one activity that the Foundation can and does engage in is receiving donations on behalf of the Ubuntu project. These donations, and only these donations, are then put into action on behalf of Ubuntu in accordance with the wishes of the development team and the Technical Board. For the most part, these contributions are spent on "bounties" given to community members who have achieved important feature goals for the Ubuntu project.

Beyond the Vision: Ubuntu Subprojects, Derivatives, and Spin-Offs

No introduction to Ubuntu is complete without an introduction to a growing list of Ubuntu subprojects and derivatives. While Ubuntu was derived from Debian, the project has also developed a number of derivatives of its own.

First among these is Kubuntu—a version of Ubuntu that uses KDE instead of GNOME as the default desktop environment. The relationship between Kubuntu and Ubuntu is different from the relationship between Ubuntu and Debian. From a technical perspective, Kubuntu is *fully* within the Ubuntu distribution. Organizationally, the Kubuntu team works fully within Ubuntu as well.

A similar organization exists with the Edubuntu project, which aims to help develop Ubuntu so that a configuration of the distribution can be easily and effectively put into use in schools. Although the project has undergone a few changes in recent years, it remains focused on both educational and school-related software and on a Linux Terminal Server Project (LTSP) setup that allows schools to run many students' computers using one or more powerful servers and many "dumb" terminals that connect to the server and run software off it. This relatively simple technical trick translates into huge cost savings in educational settings.

The Xubuntu project is based on the lightweight window manager Xfce. Xubuntu is designed to be appropriate on older or less powerful computers with less memory or slower processors—or just for people who prefer a more responsive environment and a slimmer set of features. While started as an unofficial project, Xubuntu has enjoyed great popularity and has become integrated as an official part of the core distribution.

These and other derivatives are discussed in Chapter 9.

In a way, it is through these derivatives that the work and goals of the Ubuntu project come together and are crystallized. It is only through the free and open source software movements' commitment to freely accessible source code that Ubuntu could be built at all. Similarly, it is only through Ubuntu's continued commitment to these ideals that derivatives can spring from Ubuntu. As a derivative with a view of distributions within an ecosystem, Ubuntu does not see the process of derivation as an insult or criticism. Far from it—Ubuntu thinks derivation is the highest form of compliment.

Outside of Ubuntu, Canonical's work is largely based around software projects such as Launchpad and Bazaar that are designed to facilitate precisely this sort of derivative process. This process, when practiced right, is one that describes an ecosystem of development in which *everyone* benefits—the derivative, Ubuntu, and Ubuntu's upstreams. Only through this derivative process does everyone get what they want.

Derivation, done correctly, allows groups to diverge where necessary while working together where possible. Ultimately, it leads to more work done, more happy users, and more overall collaboration. Through this enhanced collaboration, Ubuntu's philosophical and technical goals will be achieved. Through this profound community involvement, Bug #1 will be closed. Through this type of meaningful cooperation, internal and external to the project itself, the incredible growth of Ubuntu in its first four years will be sustained into the next four and the next forty.

Summary

This chapter looks at how the vision of a better distribution and OS became the phenomenon that is Ubuntu. It moves through the relationship Ubuntu has with Canonical, Ltd. and the Ubuntu Foundation and finishes with some discussion of the various Ubuntu subprojects, derivatives, and spin-offs that go beyond its original vision.

CHAPTER 2

Installing Ubuntu

- Choosing Your Ubuntu Version
- Getting Ubuntu
- Booting and Installing
- Installing from the Alternate Install CD
- Installing from within Windows
- Summary

IF YOU ARE READING THIS, it is probably safe to assume that you have decided to give Ubuntu a try. You will find that Ubuntu is flexible and powerful not only as an operating system but also in how you evaluate and install it.

Trying Ubuntu is simple. The Ubuntu desktop CD is a special "live" CD. You can use this disk to run Ubuntu from the CD itself without Ubuntu removing or even interacting with your hard disk. This is ideal if you are already using another operating system like Windows or Mac OS X; you can try Ubuntu by running it from the CD, and you don't have to worry about it overwriting the data on your hard drive or changing any part of your current operating system unless you intentionally choose to do so.

Choosing Your Ubuntu Version

The developers behind Ubuntu have worked to make the software as easy and flexible to install as possible. They understand that people will be installing Ubuntu on computers with varying purposes (desktops, servers, laptops, and so on) and using different types of computers (PCs and Macs, 32-bit and 64-bit computers, and so on). To cater to as many people as possible, there are two Ubuntu CDs that can be used. The DVD with this book is equivalent to the downloadable desktop CD but with additional packages included for your convenience.

- **Desktop:** The desktop CD is the one recommended for *desktops* and *laptops*. With this CD, you can boot Ubuntu from the CD and, if you like it, you have the option to install it to your hard drive. Note that running from the disk without installing directly to the hard drive is the default option to help prevent accidental data loss.

- **Alternate install:** The alternate install CD is recommended for use in any scenario where the desktop version is unusable (e.g., not enough RAM) or for those with more advanced needs (e.g., automated deployments or special partitioning requirements). With this CD, you boot into an installer and then run Ubuntu when the installation is complete.

Ubuntu 12.04 officially supports three main computer types, or architectures, and a couple of additional variations:

- **i386:** This supports all Intel or compatible processors except those that require AMD64. This includes current Apple hardware. If you are not certain which you need, use this one. It will work on either 32-bit or 64-bit systems, so it is the default choice.

- **AMD64:** If you know you are using a processor based on the AMD64 or EM64T architecture (e.g., Athlon64, Opteron, EM64T Xeon, or Core2), you should choose this version because it will be a bit more efficient on your hardware.

- **ARM:** ARM is a low-powered chip commonly found in cell phones and similar mobile devices. ARM Inc., the makers of ARM, and Canonical have an agreement to build the entire Ubuntu archive on ARM, which makes Ubuntu the first major distribution to support ARM as a standard rather than custom device–specific distribution, such as OpenWRT is for routers. For a list of the current ARM chip version being supported and other information, please see wiki.ubuntu.com/ARM.

TIP **Where to Download**
If you lose the installation disk that accompanies this book, or if you want to use some of the other options available, such as installation from a USB drive (discussed later in the chapter), you will find what you need at help.ubuntu.com/community/GettingUbuntu.

TIP **What about PowerPC and Others?**
PowerPC and a few other architectures are not officially supported, but do have unofficial builds available. See help.ubuntu.com/12.04/installation-guide/index.html for current details.

Other Ubuntu Distributions

In addition to the official Ubuntu release, some distributions are based on Ubuntu but are slightly different. Here are some examples:

- **Kubuntu:** Kubuntu is Ubuntu, but instead of using the default interface, Kubuntu uses the KDE desktop. See http://kubuntu.org or Chapter 9 for more information.

- **Ubuntu Server Edition:** Ubuntu Server Edition makes Ubuntu easy to install and use on servers. It initially focused on making certain that the highest quality server applications were available for easy installation and configuration, including MySQL, Apache, and others. The most recent work has improved the cloud computing capabilities of Ubuntu Server via the Ubuntu Enterprise Cloud. See Chapter 8 for more information.

- **Xubuntu:** The Xubuntu distribution replaces the default interface with the Xfce 4 environment. Xubuntu is particularly useful for those of you who want to run Ubuntu on older hardware as it has lighter system requirements. See http://xubuntu.org or Chapter 9 for more information.

- **Edubuntu:** Edubuntu is a derivative of Ubuntu aimed at educational use and schools. To install it, you should first install the default desktop version of Ubuntu. Then use either the downloadable add-on Edubuntu CD or the Ubuntu Software Center in your Applications menu on the desktop to install the Edubuntu environment and applications. See Chapter 9 for more information.

TIP   **Downloading Edubuntu**
You may download the Edubuntu add-on CD and learn more about Edubuntu at www.edubuntu.org.

With a range of different distributions and options available, Ubuntu is flexible enough to be used in virtually all situations.

Is It Still Ubuntu?

Some of you may be reading about Kubuntu, Ubuntu Server Edition, and Xubuntu and wondering how different they are from the regular Ubuntu release. These distributions differ mainly in which applications and user interface are included. As such, they may differ quite a bit, especially in the user interface look and feel, but the underlying OS and software install system is the same.

Getting Ubuntu

Ubuntu is an entirely free OS. When you have a copy of it, you can give it to as many people as you like. This free characteristic of Ubuntu means that it is simple to get a copy. If you have a high-speed Internet connection, go to www.ubuntu.com/download, and follow the instructions. You can select a desktop or alternate install CD image and download it.

TIP   See the upcoming Burning a CD section for details on how to create your Ubuntu CD from the file you just downloaded. You can also create a bootable USB stick, as described in the Creating a Bootable USB Stick section, just below Burning a CD.

If you are willing to wait, you can buy authorized Ubuntu CDs at www. ubuntu.com/download/ubuntu/cds.

Burning a CD

When you download an Ubuntu CD, you download a special .iso file, which is the same size as a CD (around 650MB). This file is an "image" of the installation CD. When you burn the .iso file to the CD-ROM, you have a complete installation CD all ready to go.

TIP   **Which Image?**
When you are reading about .iso files, you will often see them referred to as CD images. The term *image* here does not refer to a visual image such as a photo or picture but to an exact digital copy of the contents of a CD.

You need to use a CD-burning application to burn your .iso file to the CD correctly. Inside the application should be a menu option called Burn from Disk Image or something similar. The wording and details will vary according to the program you use to burn the image. You should select the .iso file, insert a blank CD, and after a few minutes, out will pop a fresh Ubuntu installation CD.

To give you a head start, the following subsections present instructions for burning a CD in some popular tools.

In Windows 7   To burn your image using Windows 7, follow these steps.

1. Right-click on the icon for your downloaded .iso image and select Open with > Windows Disc Image Burner.

2. Select a writable CD/CVD drive from the drop-down box.

3. Click Burn.

In Older Versions of Windows with ISO Recorder   To burn your .iso file with the freely available ISO Recorder, first go to http://isorecorder.alexfeinman.com, and then download and install ISO Recorder. To burn your image, follow these steps.

1. Insert a blank CD into your CD writer.

2. Locate the .iso file you downloaded, right-click it, and select Copy Image to CD.

3. Click Next, and the recording process begins.

4. When the image has been written, click Finish to exit ISO Recorder.

In Mac OS X   To burn your image using Mac OS X, follow these steps.

1. Load the Disk Utility application (found in your Utilities folder).

2. Insert a blank CD, and then choose Images > Burn and select the .iso file.

In Ubuntu   To burn your image using Ubuntu, follow these steps. To burn your image using Mac OS X, follow these steps.

1. Insert a blank CD into your CD writer.

2. In the File Browser, right-click on the file you just downloaded, and choose Write to Disk. The Write to Disk dialog box opens.

3. In the dialog box, choose your CD writer and speed, and then click on Write. The Writing Files to Disk Progress dialog box opens, and File Browser begins writing the disk.

TIP   **Use the Right Option**

Be sure to use the Burn from Disk Image or similar option rather than just copy the .iso image onto the CD to be burned. If you just burn the file directly, you will have a CD containing the single .iso file. This won't work.

The Burn from Disk Image function takes the .iso file and restores all the original files from the installation CD onto the disk. This ensures you have a proper installation CD.

Creating a Bootable USB Stick

To create a bootable USB stick, follow these directions for your current operating system.

TIP **Use the Right Size USB Stick**
Use a USB stick with at least 2 GB of free space.

In Windows To create your bootable USB stick using Windows, follow these steps.

1. Download the USB installer provided by pendrivelinux.com at www.pendrivelinux.com/universal-usb-installer-easy-as-1-2-3/ and follow the installation instructions.

2. Insert your USB stick into the computer and run the USB installer from pendrivelinux.com.

3. Select Ubuntu Desktop Edition from the drop-down menu.

4. Click Browse and select the Ubuntu .iso image you downloaded.

5. Select the USB drive for installation and click Create.

In Mac OS X The Ubuntu download page recommends that Mac users install using a CD because the workarounds required to create a bootable USB stick on OS X are complex.

In Ubuntu To create your bootable USB stick using Ubuntu, follow these steps.

1. Insert your USB stick into the computer.

2. Open the Dash (see Chapter 3 if you don't yet know what the Dash is) and search for Startup Disk Creator. Click the icon for Startup Disk Creator to run the program.

3. Select your downloaded Ubuntu .iso image. If your downloaded .iso image does not automatically appear in the list in Startup Disk Creator, click Other to select it.

4. Select the USB stick in the bottom box.

5. Click Make Startup Disk.

NOTE   You will need to have administrative privileges on your computer to use the USB Startup Disk Creator.

Booting and Installing

This section begins with instructions for running Ubuntu from the desktop CD that you burned earlier, from the DVD that came with this book, or from a bootable USB stick. You can explore and test Ubuntu without making any changes to your hard drive. If you don't like it, reboot and remove the CD/DVD/USB stick to return to what you already have.

TIP   **Try before You Buy**
Take some time to test before you make the permanent decision to erase your hard drive and current operating system and install Ubuntu. Once you do so, you cannot recover old files or return to how things were. This is why you are given the opportunity to test from the CD/DVD or USB stick. Take advantage of the opportunity and make sure you like what you see.

Place your CD or DVD into your CD/DVD drive or your bootable USB stick into a USB port, and reboot your computer. If your computer does not boot from the CD/DVD, you should enter your computer's BIOS and change the boot order to ensure that the boot medium you are using is first in the boot order. Save your BIOS changes, and then restart again.

TIP   **BIOS Problems**
If you have problems configuring your BIOS to boot from the CD, you should consult the manual. If you don't have the manual, visit the manufacturer's Web site, and see if you can download the manual.

After a few seconds, the Ubuntu logo and boot screen appear and then you are presented with a list of languages on the left of the screen and two options on the right. Use your mouse to select your language. Then decide whether you want to Try Ubuntu 12.04, which allows you to try out Ubuntu without making any changes to your computer and install it later if you decide you want to, or whether you want to install Ubuntu 12.04, which will jump straight into the installer. Select the first option, and Ubuntu will begin to boot. After a minute or so, the Ubuntu desktop will appear, and you can use the system right away. Under this scenario, the system is running from the CD and will not touch your hard disk. Do bear in mind that because Ubuntu is running from the CD, it will run slower than if it were installed to your hard disk.

NOTE   **CD/DVD/USB Stick**

It takes a lot of space to write to a CD/DVD/USB stick every time. For simplicity and easier reading, unless explicitly stated, assume we mean any of the three throughout the remainder of this chapter when we refer to the live or install CD.

If you decide you want to install the system permanently on your computer's hard disk, there are two ways you can do so:

1. Double-click the Install icon located on the left side of the desktop.

2. Reboot and select Install Ubuntu from the initial menu.

TIP   If you choose to install from the live CD while running Ubuntu, you can continue to use the computer while the install is happening. If you choose to reboot, the process will go a bit faster.

Using either option, an installer application will walk you through the steps to permanently install your Ubuntu system. The remainder of this chapter describes each part of the process.

Migration

Ubuntu provides a migration assistant, which aims to ease your transition to your new OS. If a supported OS is found during installation, you are presented with a list of accounts and the features that can be migrated. If you choose to migrate anything, you must provide details for the new user to whom the features will be migrated.

TIP It is recommended that you back up any important files before you perform the installation. Although Ubuntu installations can safely resize Windows partitions, this is not guaranteed, and installations can result in data loss, so it is wise to be careful.

Language

The first screen you are presented with when you boot the computer introduces you to the installation program and asks you to select your language, as shown in Figure 2-1, and whether you want to Try Ubuntu (run the operating system from the CD without changing anything on your hard drive, which we suggest for first time users before committing to an installation) or whether you want to Install Ubuntu.

Ubuntu supports a huge range of different languages. Select your language from the list, and then click Install Ubuntu to continue with the installation.

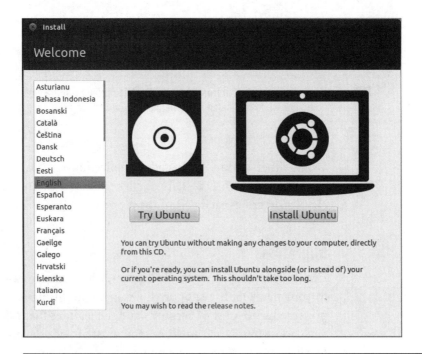

Figure 2-1 Pick your language.

Preparing to Install Ubuntu

You will be informed of the install requirements, as in Figure 2-2. We strongly suggest selecting the option to Download Updates While Installing because this option will end your installation with an up-to-the-minute current system that includes any existing security updates or bug fixes. A nice feature is that these updates will be downloaded while installation is in process, in parallel to other operations, so it happens with great efficiency.

You may also choose to install third-party software to enable your computer to play certain media files immediately after installation. This will also save you time later, although some users may not want to install closed-source software and will choose not to enable this option. Click Continue after making your selection(s).

Allocate Drive Space

To prepare your hard disk to store the Ubuntu system and your files, hard disks are divided into partitions. Each partition reserves a specific portion

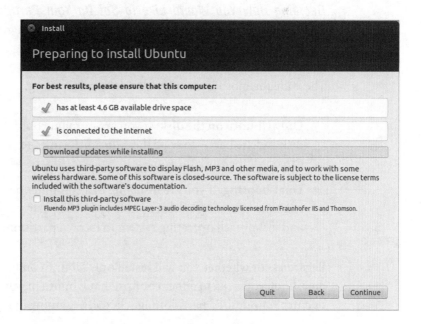

Figure 2-2 Preparing to install Ubuntu

of the hard disk for use by a particular operating system. As an example, you may use the entire hard disk for your new Ubuntu system, or you may share the disk so that both Windows and Ubuntu are installed. This shared scenario is known as *dual-booting*. In a dual-booting situation, your hard disk typically has Windows partitions as well as Linux partitions, and when it boots it gives you a menu so you can select whether to boot Windows or Linux.

In this part of the installer you create the partitions for your new system. This can be the trickiest part of the installation and can also be the most dangerous. If you have existing partitions (such as a Windows installation) on the disk, it is highly recommended that you back up your important files.

TIP   **Seriously, We Mean It**
Really, really, really do back up any important files. If you make a mistake in this part of the installation, you could lose your files and stop your system from booting.

Deciding How You Would Like to Set Up Your Partitions Before You Create Them   If you have a clear idea of how your hard disk should be partitioned, it is easier to get everything up and running quickly.

These are the most common methods of partitioning.

- **Only Ubuntu on the disk:** If you are installing only Ubuntu on the disk and are happy to wipe the *entire disk*, your life is simple. Ubuntu can do all the work for you.
- **Dual-booting:** If you are installing to a computer that will have multiple operating system options, you will partition your hard drive and install each operating system to its own partition.

Regardless of whether you will install only Ubuntu on the disk or you will dual-boot, you need to either confirm that Ubuntu may use the entire disk or enter your desired partitioning scheme, beginning in Figure 2-3.

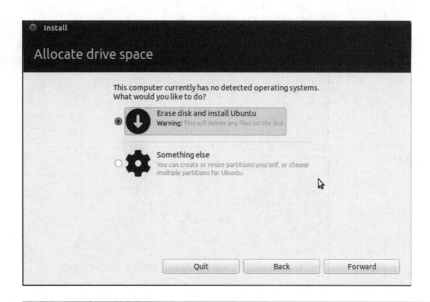

Figure 2-3 Allocate all drive space to Ubuntu

Ubuntu Only   If you are happy to erase your entire hard disk, select Erase Disk and Install Ubuntu. If you choose this option, skip ahead to the next section of the book, Installation Begins.

Manual Partitioning   If you will install only Ubuntu or will dual-boot with an existing operating system but want more control over the process, you must set the partitions manually. To do this, select Something Else and click Forward to continue. You will see the screens shown in Figures 2-4, 2-5, and 2-6.

The main part of this screen displays available drives and configured partitions. Clicking on a drive or partition changes the actions available to you below the list. Select the relevant disk to add partitions to. The disks are listed by device name in the order they are connected within your computer.

QUICK TIP   The name of the device indicates how it is connected to your computer. For example, hda is the first IDE drive, and sdb is the second SCSI or SATA drive.

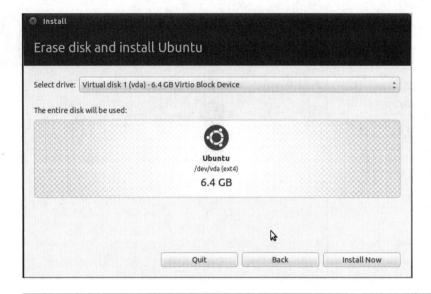

Figure 2-4 Erase disk and install Ubuntu

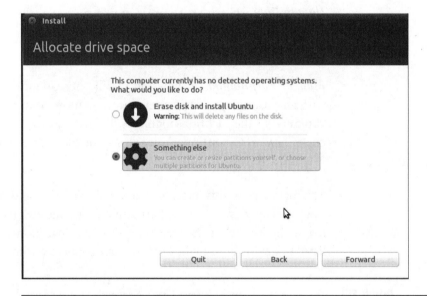

Figure 2-5 Allocate drive space another way

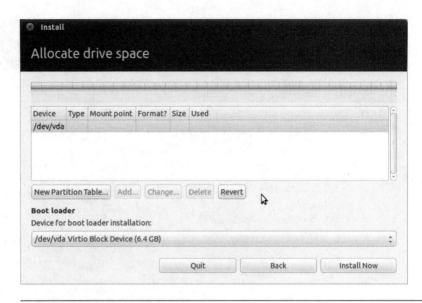

Figure 2-6 Create partitions manually

Before you begin, you should prepare the disk for your partitions. If you want to completely wipe a disk, right-click on the name of the device (/dev/sda in Figure 2-6), then click New Partition Table. You'll be asked if you're sure, so click Continue. The disk is now filled with unallocated data. Now you can add your Ubuntu partitions.

To add a partition, click a free space entry in the list and then click the New button. A new window appears like that shown in Figure 2-7.

Set the values according to your requirements. The Type combo box lets you select which one of the many filesystem types you want the partition to use. The default filesystem included with Ubuntu is ext4, and it is recommended that you use ext4 for any Ubuntu partitions. Although ext4 is a good choice for Ubuntu, you cannot read an ext4 partition in Windows. If you need to create a partition that is shared between Windows and Ubuntu, you should use either the FAT32 filesystem or NTFS.

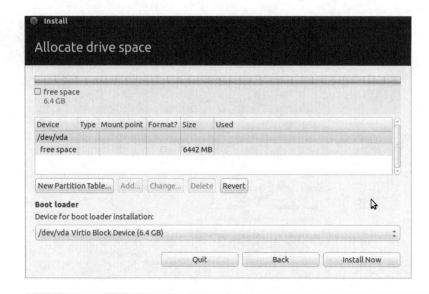

Figure 2-7 Configuring a partition

Use the Mount Point combo box to select one of the different mount points, which tells Ubuntu where the partition should be used. You need to have a root partition, which has a mount point of /. Click OK to finish configuring this partition.

Once you've completed configuring all your partitions, click Forward to proceed with the installation. Please note that if you have read all of these comments on partitioning and feel a bit overwhelmed or confused, you don't need to worry. You may simply use the default settings given by the installer and all will work well.

Installation Begins

At this point, the installation begins. While it progresses, you are asked some questions to customize your installation appropriately. Doing this concurrently saves time.

Tell the installer where in the world you live (Figure 2-8).

Figure 2-8 Click the map to select a location.

You can select your location in one of several ways. First, you can hover your mouse over the time zone on your part of the world map to select your location. When you are happy with the time zone selection, click it, and select the city nearest to you. Alternatively, use the Selected City drop down to find the city nearest to you.

When you are done, click Continue.

Configuring Your Keyboard

The next screen (shown in Figure 2-9) configures your keyboard.

The installer will suggest a keyboard option for you based on your location choice, but you may choose a different one if you desire. You can also use the box at the bottom of the window to test whether your keyboard layout works. Try typing some of the symbols on your keyboard (such as ", /, |) to make sure they work. If you press a symbol and a different one appears, you have selected the wrong keyboard layout.

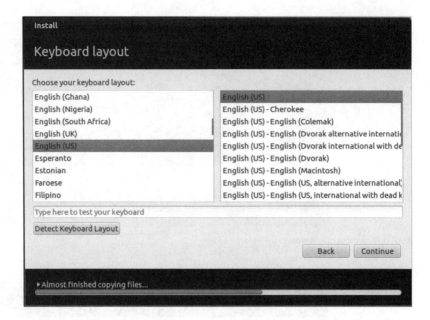

Figure 2-9 Select the correct keyboard to ensure the symbols on the keys work correctly.

Identification

The next step is to enter some details about you that can be used to create a user account on the computer (Figure 2-10).

In the first box, enter your full name. The information from this box is used in different parts of the system to indicate who the user is behind the account.

Enter a computer name in the last box. Also called a "hostname," this is a single word that identifies your current machine. This is used on a local network so that you can identify which machine is which.

Hostnames can be great fun. Many people pick themes for their hostnames, such as superheroes, and name each computer on their network after a superhero (Superman, Batman, Spiderman, and so on). Think of a fun hostname theme you can use. For many people, this ends up being the hardest part of the install!

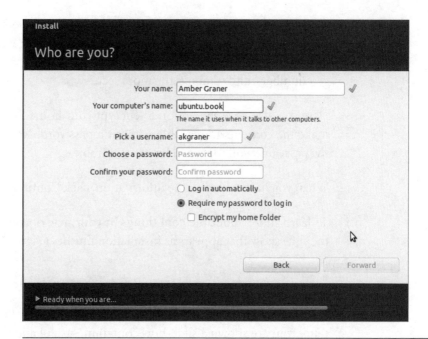

Figure 2-10 Enter your personal details to create your user account.

In the next box, set a username for yourself (the installer will provide a suggestion based on your full name). Your username should be something easy to remember. Many people either use their first name or add an initial to their first or last name (such as jbacon or jonob). Each username on your computer must be unique—you cannot have two accounts with the same username. Usernames must begin with a lowercase letter—only lowercase letters and numbers are permitted after that.

In the next two boxes, add a password and then confirm it. This password is used when you log in to your computer with the username you just created. When choosing a password, follow these simple guidelines.

- Make sure you can remember your password. If you need to write it down, keep it somewhere secure. Don't make the mistake of putting the password somewhere easily accessible and known to others.

- Avoid using dictionary words ("real words") such as "chicken" or "beard" when choosing a password, and try to input numbers and punctuation.

- Your password should ideally be longer than six letters and contain a combination of letters, symbols, and numbers. The longer the password and the more it mixes upper and lowercase letters, numbers, and symbols, the more secure it is.

Here you also have the option to encrypt your home folder. Select this to make the contents unreadable without a password. Note that if you lose the password, your data will be unrecoverable.

When you have added all the information, click Continue.

To learn more about the cool things in your new operating system, view the slide show that appears as installation finishes (Figure 2-11).

Finishing Up

From here, as the Ubuntu software continues to be installed on your computer, you are shown a slideshow containing useful and interesting infor-

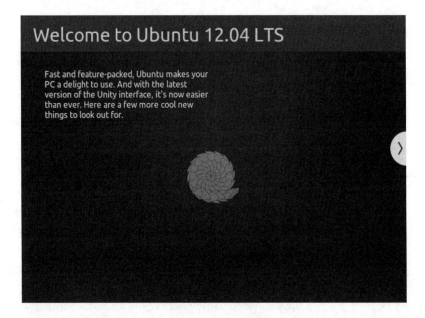

Figure 2-11 Slide show users can watch as installation finishes to find out more about Ubuntu.

mation about the operating system. At the end of this process, you are asked to restart your computer. You are now finished and can skip ahead to Chapter 3 to get started with using Ubuntu.

TIP   **Better Use of Your Valuable, Valuable Time**
One of the great benefits of the desktop live CD installer is that while the files are being copied from the disk, you can still use the system. Instead of sitting at your computer staring at the progress bar, you can play a few games to while away the time.

Installing from the Alternate Install CD

Although the desktop CD is ideal for installing Ubuntu, you may want to use the traditional installer method to install the system. This method involves booting the alternate install CD, running through the installer, and then starting the system. This kind of installer is ideal for installation on older hardware.

To get started, put the CD in the drive, and restart your computer.

Select the Install Ubuntu option with the arrow keys, and press Enter. After a few moments, the installation process begins by asking you to choose a language. Select from the different languages by using the up and down arrow keys, and then use the Tab key to jump to the red buttons to continue through the setup.

TIP   **Installing a Server**
You can obtain a third version of Ubuntu that is especially tailored for server environments. For more information about this version, see www.ubuntu.com/server, or read Chapter 8 for more details about running Ubuntu as a server.

Choosing Your Spot in the World

Next you are asked to specify your location. First you need to choose your language.

Then you need to pick which country you are in, again pressing Enter to accept your choice.

Now you need to select your keyboard layout. Keyboard layouts vary across the world to take into account the many and varied symbols and letters used in different countries. Even if you are using the typical Latin character set (as used in most European countries, America, Africa, and Australia), there are variations and additions (e.g., German umlauts). You can let Ubuntu detect your layout for you, or you can choose from a list of options. If you want your layout detected, you will be asked a series of questions until a guess can be made. If the guess is wrong, you can repeat the process. Otherwise, choose your keyboard layout from the options available.

Hardware

Next, the system will attempt to load the rest of the installer and to detect hardware. In most situations, this happens without prompting you for anything, although sometimes you might need to provide input such as choosing a primary network device. Once this is set up, your computer will also configure itself with your local network—if possible. If it cannot configure itself with a local network, it will tell you this and you'll have the option of configuring it manually or choosing to not configure it at that time. You can always come back and change things later once the installation is done.

Setting the Hostname and Time Zone

You are next asked for a hostname for the computer.

Use the text box to add your own hostname, or use the default Ubuntu hostname if required. Feel free to let your imagination go wild, and create a theme for your hostnames (such as superheroes).

After choosing a hostname, you will be asked to select your time zone. Choosing this should be a fairly straightforward operation.

Creating Partitions

The system will then read your disks to find out the current partition information. You will be asked to create or select partitions for Ubuntu to install on to. Creating partitions is the most challenging part of the installation routine. Before you partition your disk, think about how your partitions should be organized.

You are given a number of partition options:

- Guided—Use Entire Disk
- Guided—Use Entire Disk and Set Up LVM
- Guided—Use Entire Disk and Set Up Encrypted LVM
- Manual

In most cases, you probably want to use the Guided—Use Entire Disk option. This will erase everything on the hard drive in your computer and set everything up for you. The second option, Guided—Use Entire Disk and Set Up LVM, allows you to use the Logical Volume Manager (LVM). The third is identical to the second option but also employs disk encryption, which will make your data safer and more secure in some circumstances. Finally, if you want to set up specific partitions, use the Manual option.

Let's look at each of these options in turn and how they are used.

Guided—Use Entire Disk   When you select this option, your entire disk is partitioned automatically. The installer tells you that a primary and logical partition will be created, and then it asks if you want to go ahead and create the partitions. Click Yes, and you are done.

Guided—Use Entire Disk and Set Up LVM   Configuring LVM is covered in Chapter 8.

Guided—Use Entire Disk and Set Up Encrypted LVM   Configuring LVM is identical to the previous option except that it also uses a secure encryption layer to provide additional security and protection for your data. If you choose to do this, during the process you will be asked to provide a passphrase. Be very careful to choose one that is impossible to guess and that you will also remember. You will need to use this passphrase to access your data every time you boot the computer, and if you lose or forget the passphrase, all your data will be permanently inaccessible. There is no way to recover a lost or forgotten encryption passphrase.

TIP   **Disk Encryption**
You may also decide to encrypt specific partitions manually. Simply choose "Use Physical Volume for Encryption" in the "Use As:" option. Note: You never want to encrypt the boot partition.

Manual   Select this option if you want to create your own partitions manually. Here you can create a number of different types of partitions, set their sizes, and configure their properties. Creating these partitions is not done in the same graphical way as the live CD installer, so it is a little more complex. However, doing so is still largely a process of selecting something and pressing Enter.

Depending on your configuration (and the options you selected), you are given a number of options from which to choose:

- Configure Software RAID
- Configure the Logical Volume Manager
- Guided Partitioning

QUICK TIP   Discussion of software RAID and the Logical Volume Manager is covered in Chapter 8.

Your disk is listed below these options, and it may display a few existing partitions. If you want to delete the existing partitions, select each one, press Enter, and select Delete the Partition. When you have deleted some partitions, you should see a FREE SPACE line. The FREE SPACE line is used to create new partitions. If the disk was empty already and you don't see a FREE SPACE line, select the hard disk, and press Enter. When it asks if you want to create an empty partition table, click Yes. You should now see the FREE SPACE line.

To create a new partition, select the FREE SPACE line, and press Enter. In the next screen, click Create a New Partition, and press Enter. Now enter the size the partition should be. You can use gigabytes (GB) and megabytes

(M) to indicate size. For example, 4.2 GB is 4.2 gigabytes, and 100 M is 100 megabytes. You can also use a percentage or just add max to use the entire disk. Add the size, and then press the Tab key to select Continue. Press Enter. You are next asked whether the partition should be primary or logical. It is likely that you will want a primary partition. Make your choice and continue.

If this is the first partition, you are asked if the partition should be at the beginning or end of the disk. It is recommended that when creating the root partition (known as /) on older computers, it should be placed at the beginning of the disk. This gets around some potential BIOS problems on older hardware. On newer computers, this is no longer a problem, and you can put the partition where you like on the disk.

On the next screen to display, you can configure some settings for the partition.

Table 2-1 describes the settings.

When the partition is configured, choose the Done Setting Up the Partition option.

You can now select FREE SPACE again (if there is free space left, of course) to create another partition. When you have finished partitioning, click the Finish Partitioning and Write Changes to Disk option.

The system will now install the Ubuntu core to your newly partitioned disk. Depending on the speed of your computer and your CD drive, this installation could take some time.

Configuring a User

The next part of the installation routine configures a user for the computer. This user role is important because it not only can be used as a normal user but also has the ability to use sudo to perform system administrator tasks.

You are first asked to enter a full name for the user (such as Matthew Helmke). Next you are asked for a username, or one will be picked for you

Table 2-1 Partition Settings

Setting	Description	Example
Use as	This is the type of filesystem. For a normal Ubuntu system, ext4 is recommended.	ext4
Format the partition	This setting appears when editing an existing partition.	yes
Mount point	This specifies which part of the filesystem will live on the partition. See earlier in this chapter for details about the kind of partitions you should set up.	/
Mount options	A number of options can be passed to the mount point, although the default setting should be fine.	defaults
Label	A text label describes the partition. Usually it is set to the same value as the mount point.	/
Reserved blocks	This is the percentage of the filesystem reserved for the super-user; 5% is a good default.	5.00%
Typical usage	This option can be used to optimize how the filesystem is organized, although the standard setting is typically used.	standard
Bootable flag	Does this partition contain the kernel and bootloader? If this is the root partition (known as /), set this to *on*.	on

from your full name (such as matthew). If you want another username, enter it there. Finally, you are asked to enter a password for the user and asked to repeat the password for verification.

QUICK TIP   A good password will have at least eight characters, will use both uppercase and lowercase letters, will use at least one number, will use at least one nonletter character like & or @, will not spell a word that can be found in a dictionary, and will also be easy for you to remember while being difficult for others to guess. A modified phrase can work well, something like Gimm1e@x3ss could work well, although that one may still be a bit too obvious ("give me access" is not much better than "password").

Finishing Up

At this point, the installation routine will install the full system for you. After this, the computer will reboot, and the installation will be complete.

Installing from within Windows

Another way to install Ubuntu is to use Ubuntu Windows Installer, or Wubi. This is perhaps the easiest of all methods. Go to www.ubuntu.com/getubuntu/download-wubi and download the program and run it within Windows. Then answer the questions that come up and wait. The process can take a long time because it will download the entire installation .iso, but once finished, a dialog box will appear telling you that you need to reboot. When you do, you will find that you will boot to a menu giving you the option to boot into either Windows or Ubuntu. More detailed information is available at the link above.

Summary

In this chapter we outlined several methods for installing Ubuntu. Once this task is complete, you are ready to move on to more interesting topics. The next chapter will help you get started.

Getting Started with Ubuntu

DUE DATE: 06--11-2015

BARCODE: 33390003210875
LOCATION: syanf
TITLE: Candlestick charting for dummies
DUE DATE: 06--11-2015

BARCODE: 30641005064089
LOCATION: lwanf
TITLE: The Zurich axioms / Max Gunther.
DUE DATE: 06--11-2015

BARCODE: 30641003339202
LOCATION: lwadf
TITLE: Polish. 1, A [sound recording CD]
DUE DATE: 06--11-2015

BARCODE: 30641005009654
LOCATION: lwanf
TITLE: The official Ubuntu book / Matthe
DUE DATE: 06--12-2015

BARCODE: 30620004506365
LOCATION: cwagm
TITLE: Saga. Volume 2 / Brian K. Vaughan
DUE DATE: 06--12-2015

BARCODE: 30641005044537
LOCATION: lwanf
TITLE: The 10 essentials of Forex tradin
DUE DATE: 06--12-2015

BARCODE: 061291000897165
LOCATION: bbagn
TITLE: The shattered eye / Bill Granger.
DUE DATE: 06--18-2015

WITH UBUNTU INSTALLED and ready to go, it's time to get started using your new operating system. Unlike other operating systems, such as Microsoft Windows or Mac OS X, Ubuntu includes everything you need to get started: an office suite, media tools, a Web browser, an e-mail client, and more. Now that the installation is complete, you are up and running without having to install any additional software.

Different people use their computers in different ways, and every user has her own personal preference for look and feel. Recognizing this desire, Linux has the capability to use any one of a number of different graphical interfaces. This flexibility, combined with the ballooning popularity of Linux and open source, has resulted in literally hundreds of different graphical environments springing up, each covering these different types of users and ways of working.

Even though there is a huge range of different environments available, there are two clear leaders in KDE and GNOME. Each environment provides a good-looking, comprehensive, and easy-to-use desktop, but they differ in how that desktop is used as well as in how further personalization can take place.

The KDE system aims for complete control and configurability of the desktop. Any desktop configuration options that exist are available to the user, who has easy access and can change the behavior and look of almost everything.

The competing GNOME desktop takes inspiration from both Windows and Mac OS X and sets a priority on simplicity and ease of use. GNOME is also easy to customize, but the less common options are either eliminated or well hidden to prevent user overload.

Ubuntu users are blessed with the choice of either desktop, along with several others. Many of these are mentioned in Chapter 9.

TIP   **The Ubuntu Desktop Is Unity**
When reading about Ubuntu, you may see terms like Unity and Ubuntu desktop used interchangeably. The Ubuntu community, with sponsorship from Canonical, has created the Unity desktop as the next stage in graphical interface evolution. Time will tell if other Linux distributions follow suit or if they choose to use one of the other existing options.

In this chapter, we help you get started with Unity, the default desktop for Ubuntu, and show how you can use it to do the normal things you face every day with your computer and a few not-so-normal things. This includes opening and running applications, managing your files, adjusting the look and feel, using applications, managing your media, and more.

Getting Acquainted with Unity

When you start your Ubuntu system, you are presented with a list of users. Once you select your username from the list, you are asked for a password to log in with. In the last chapter, you specified a user account when installing the system, so use that account to log in. First select your username and press Enter, then your password and press Enter. Your password will appear as a series of *s. This is a security feature.

After a few seconds you will see the Ubuntu desktop appear. Your desktop will look like Figure 3-1.

Figure 3-1 Ubuntu Unity

You may have noticed that, unlike other operating systems, there are no icons on the Unity desktop. The reason for this is that desktop icons typically get covered by applications, and, as such, you can't get at them.

TIP   **Device Icons**
Although there are no application icons on the desktop, when you plug in USB devices such as portable music players, keyring drives, or digital cameras, a device icon will appear on the desktop.

Finding and Running Applications with the Launcher

To find or run an application, you use the Launcher. The Launcher sits on the left of the screen. This icon bar shows icon links for applications and indicates with a small arrow which applications are currently open. The Launcher also has a few other handy features.

To find an application in Unity, click the Ubuntu logo at the top of the Launcher at the left side of the desktop (Figure 3-2).

This opens the Dash, which is the main method for finding programs, folders, and files on your computer. At the bottom of the Dash is a row of icons. These are Lenses. Each Lens helps you focus your search in a different way. Any time the Dash is open, you can begin to type the name of a program, folder, or file and it will search for matches as you type (Figure 3-3). You don't even have to know the exact name because the search also looks for near matches, similar names, and even does some semantic matching by searching program descriptions and some file contents.

Some of the Dash Lenses include predefined filters to further narrow your search (Figure 3-4). Click Filter Results at the upper right of the Dash Lens to view available Filters.

Figure 3-2 The Unity Launcher with the Ubuntu logo at the top

Other Lenses are available beyond those installed by default. Later in this chapter, you will learn how to

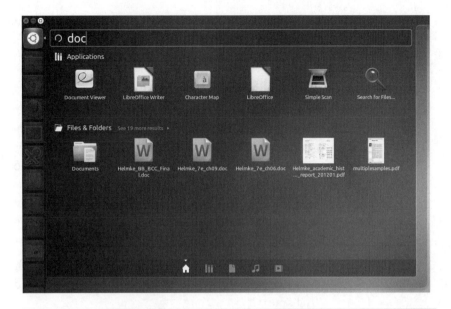

Figure 3-3 The Dash with sorted results from a partial search

Figure 3-4 The Dash Applications Lens with Filter Results shown

use the Ubuntu Software Center. You can find additional Lenses there by searching with the terms *unity lens*.

Other Icons in the Launcher

In addition to the Ubuntu logo icon described earlier, the Launcher includes several useful entries by default. Most are obvious in their intent and use. Even so, these deserve a quick mention, listed in the order they appear in the Launcher from top to bottom, skipping some more obvious entries.

▪ **Home Folder:** This icon opens your home folder using the file manager, which is described next. Your home folder is where all of your personal files and folders should be placed.

▪ **Ubuntu Software Center:** This icon opens your primary software management system for Ubuntu, which is described later in the chapter.

▪ **Workplace Switcher:** This tool allows you to have four different screens for your desktop, with different programs active in each, and switch between them. This is great if you tend to have many things open at once and run out of space on your screen. Click it to show all of your desktop workspaces (it also shows you what is open in each, which is convenient). As an example, you may be using your Web browser and e-mail client while talking to your friends in a chat client on the first desktop and working on a document on the second desktop. You can just click each virtual desktop to switch to it to access your different applications. Click the desktop you want to use. Essentially, this expands the screen real estate you have available and creates an easy way to keep many programs open without their blocking one another.

▪ **Trash:** This is where files you throw away go until you empty the Trash to remove them permanently. Files dragged onto this icon or right-clicked and moved to trash are destined to be deleted. To fully delete these files, right-click the Trash and select Empty Trash.

QUICK TIP   You can switch between multiple applications in Ubuntu just like in Windows by pressing Alt-Tab. When you press this key combination, a small window appears that can be used to switch between active applications on the current workspace.

Using Applications

When applications are loaded, the window border has three buttons on the top on the left-hand side:

- **Red button with a black X:** This button closes the application.

- **White button with a gray –:** This button minimizes the application, taking it off of your screen, and puts it in the Launcher for easy access when you need it again.

- **White button with a gray square:** This button is used to maximize the window to take up the full desktop area. Not all application windows use this button, so don't be surprised if you don't see it for an application that has a small window.

Every application that is currently in use has an entry in the Launcher on the left of the desktop. You can click these entries to minimize or restore the application, and you can right-click to see some other options, such as one to keep the program icon listed in the Launcher at all times. This is available so that you only need to click the icon to start the program rather than search for it in the Dash, which makes it convenient for frequently used programs.

Any menus with options that exist for a program currently in use in the foreground will appear in the top panel of the desktop. When you switch programs, the contents of the top panel will change accordingly. Hover over the name of the program at the top of a screen for a list of menus to appear. Click any one for a drop down list of options.

NOTE   Because this is a new interface, not all applications have been modified to take advantage of the idea; some applications may retain a menu within the application's window.

Managing Files and Folders

When using your computer, you often need to open and save files and folders, move them around, and perform other tasks. Click the Home Folder icon from the Launcher to open the file manager. Here are some of the main folders you will find contained in your home folder by default (Figure 3-5):

- **Desktop:** This folder contains files that visually appear on your desktop as icons. If you drag a file onto your desktop, it appears in the Desktop folder. Similarly, moving a file out of this folder or deleting it removes it from your desktop.

- **Documents:** This folder is intended to contain word processing files and other documents you create.

- **Downloads:** This folder is intended to contain items you download from the Internet.

- **Music:** This folder is intended to contain music files.

- **Pictures:** This folder is intended to contain image files.

- **Public:** This is a folder into which you can place files you want other users on your system or network to be able to access. The permissions on this folder are set differently, as by default all the other folders and their contents may only be accessed and opened by you.

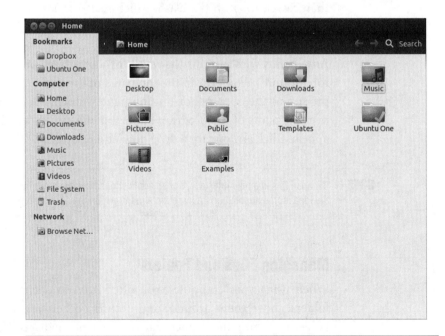

Figure 3-5 The main file manager window, open to the home folder

- **Templates:** This folder is intended to contain templates for applications like your word processor.

- **Videos:** This folder is intended to contain visual media files.

To the left of the file manager is a menu with several options. Most are repeats of commonly used folders listed previously. These deserve further mention:

- **Browse Network:** This option accesses all networked and shared devices, such as file servers or printers, that are available on your local network. This is the equivalent of the Network Neighborhood or Network Places in various versions of Windows.

- **File System:** This option allows you to browse the other files and folders on your system that are not contained in your home folder and that you have permission to view.

- **Trash:** This is where files you throw away go, until you empty the Trash to remove them permanently.

Connect to Server is an option available in the file manager from the File menu that is accessed by hovering over the words Home Folder at the top of the screen when the application is open. Click Connect to Server to run a wizard to create a connection to a network server; you will need to know the name of the server you want to connect to, and some details about it like the port being used. Use this feature to add an icon to the desktop that, when clicked, provides a list of remote files in the desktop file manager. You can then treat this window like any other file manager window and drag files back and forth. This is really useful for copying files to and from other computers.

TIP   **Usability and the Ubuntu Desktop**

Throughout the development of the Ubuntu desktop, great care and attention have gone into usability. As an example, the corners of the screen are established as areas that are simple to access—you don't need to carefully mouse over the area and can instead just throw your mouse to the appropriate corner. This is why important features are in corners. It makes accessing each feature a little bit easier.

Ubuntu is filled with tiny usability improvements such as this that help make using it as intuitive and powerful as possible. Canonical has created a collective project called Ayatana to spearhead this development. More on Ayatana can be found at https://wiki.ubuntu.com/Ayatana.

Adding Additional Users

Many computers these days are used by more than one person. Rather than forcing everyone to use the same desktop settings or making the computer less secure by allowing everyone who uses it to have access to administrative functions, it is easy and recommended to create an account for every person who will use the computer. This allows each user to customize how the computer works and looks without interfering with anyone else's preferences, and it allows you to grant administrator privileges to only select users to prevent others from accessing functions that may affect everyone or even damage the installation if used incorrectly.

Click your name at the upper right of the top panel and select User Accounts from the menu that appears to add a new user. In the dialog box that appears, there is a list of current users. Click Unlock at the top right corner of the window to make changes. Next click the "+" symbol at the bottom of the user list or Add to create a new account, as in Figure 3-6.

TIP   A password is required to make changes to users and groups, and only those users with administrative access are able to do so. Click the Lock/Unlock button to enter your password and make changes.

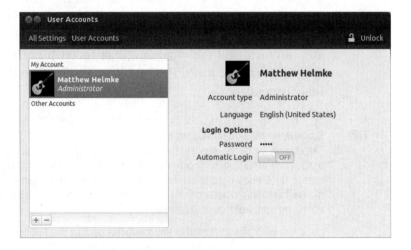

Figure 3-6 The User Settings dialog

You must now provide a full name for the new user and a short username that will be used by that user to log in. Click OK, and in the next dialog box, enter a password for that user, confirm the password by entering it a second time, and click OK again.

Once your user account is created, you may customize your login options and click the Password field to set a password, allow the user to log in without a password, or to enable the account without setting a password. Allowing a user to login without a password or automatically is not generally a good idea but can be useful. For example, if the users are small children who are not expected to perform administrative tasks, the children could have an account that automatically logs in at boot time, and the administrator would have an additional account, accessed by a password, to perform changes and updates when necessary.

Finally, now that the account is created, we may customize its settings. Highlight the username in the list, and click the field at the right next to Account Type.

If you prefer to do this from the terminal, use the `adduser` command while logged in to an account with administrative privileges:

```
matt@laptop:~$ sudo adduser corey
```

After you enter your password, this will add a new user named `corey`. You will be asked several questions in the process. Answer them, and at the end, the account will be created.

To delete a user from the command line, use the `deluser` command in place of `adduser` in the preceding example. You can learn more about dealing with users from the command line in Chapter 7.

The Notification Area

On the right-hand side of the top of the desktop is the notification area and the clock. The notification area is similar to the Windows system tray in that it provides a series of small icons that indicate something specific. A good example of this is Network Manager, which looks after your network connections—both wired and wireless—for you.

You can adjust the notification area items by right-clicking them to view a context menu. Some icons (such as the volume control) allow you to left-click on them to view them. As an example, try clicking the little speaker icon and adjusting the slider.

QUICK TIP Left-click the volume icon and select Sound Settings to access a large number of sound settings. These settings configure the speakers, microphone, line-in, any other sound card inputs or outputs, and more.

Network Manager Network Manager is a network interface created to help you manage your network devices and connections and is accessed using the network manager applet. The goal is to make networking "just work" easily and without requiring users to know how to hand-configure the settings (although that is still available for those who want to do so). A left-click of the mouse on the applet shows you the dialog box and enables quick changes between network types. It even provides an easy way to set up access through a virtual private network (VPN), such as many of us are required to use to securely access files from work or school. A right-click lets you enable or disable both wired and wireless networking, see information about your current connection, and edit connections quickly and easily (Figure 3-7).

The Clock Next to the notification area is the clock. Click on the clock to view a calendar. Later, when you use Evolution, items that are added to your calendar appear in the clock applet too. Instead of opening up Evolution to find out when your dentist appointment is, just click on the clock to see it immediately. More information about Evolution is contained later in this chapter.

QUICK TIP Customize your clock by clicking it and selecting Time & Date Settings.

User Account Menu Here you can switch which user account you use, without logging out of your current user. You can initiate a Guest Session, which is a limited account with permissions that allow simple things like

Figure 3-7 The Network Manager applet, right-clicked to show connections menu

internet access and is perfect for when a friend stops by and asks to check their e-mail. Click User Accounts at the bottom of this menu to adjust users and settings.

The Gear Menu   Click the Gear at the top right of the screen to access these options (Figure 3-8).

- **System Settings:** This option opens a window from which you may adjust your computer according to your needs or preferences. Options include Keyboard Layouts, Screen and Display settings, Printers, Power, Sound, and much more.

- **Displays:** This shortcut is useful to adjust the settings for your current display or add others, such as when you connect to a projector or add an additional monitor.

- **Startup Applications:** Here you can configure or add specific programs to be run when you log in.

- **Updates Available:** Here you are informed about software updates.

- **Attached Devices:** Under this heading are entries for things like a Webcam. Each entry links to a settings window.

Figure 3-8 Ahh, the possibilities. . . .

- **Printers:** Here you will find a link to the settings for each installed printer.

- **Lock Screen:** This option locks the screen, which is useful when you need to use the bathroom or grab some lunch. It locks the computer and asks for your password to reenable the desktop.

- **Log Out:** This option lets you log out of the current session and go back to the main login screen.

- **Suspend:** If your computer supports it, this option will be included in the list, and you can click it to save the current state of your system in RAM. The next time your computer is turned on, the desktop will be resumed. This option continues to use power, but only a minimal amount.

- **Shut Down:** Click this to shut down your computer.

Using Applications

Now that you have become familiar with the desktop, let's explore some of the many applications included on your new system. By default, Ubuntu comes with a wide range of popular and established applications to listen to music, watch videos, create documents, browse the Web, manage your appointments, read your e-mail, create images, and much more. These applications have been vetted by the developers to ensure they are the best-of-breed Linux applications available.

Although Ubuntu includes a range of software applications, it is likely you will want to install extra applications and explore other available software. Fortunately, the Ubuntu system is built on a powerful foundation that makes software installation as simple as pointing and clicking in the Ubuntu Software Center, covered later in this chapter.

TIP **Another Way to Run Applications**
Although you will most typically start your applications by selecting them from the Applications menu, you can also press Alt-F2 (on Mac hardware, use Fn-Alt-F2) to bring up the Run a command box where you can type in the name of an application and run it.

Browsing the Web with Firefox

Firefox is the default Ubuntu Web browser and provides you with a simple, safe, and powerful browsing experience. Firefox is developed by Mozilla and has become one of the most successful open source projects in the world and continues to garner huge popularity. With hundreds of millions of downloads and rapidly increasing browser share, Firefox has been an unparalleled success.

QUICK TIP You can learn more about Mozilla and Firefox, as well as their other software products, at www.mozilla.org.

Click the Firefox icon in the Launcher or open the Dash and search for *Firefox* to begin. This will open the main Firefox window (Figure 3-9).

Firefox looks similar to most Web browsers and includes the usual back, forward, reload, and stop buttons, an address bar, and some menus. These familiar-looking elements help you become acquainted with Firefox, and if you have used Internet Explorer, Opera, Chrome, or Safari before, you will have no problems.

Navigating your way around the Internet is no different in Firefox than in any other browser—just type the Web address into the address bar and press Enter. Firefox also has a few nice features that make it easy to access your favorite sites. As an example, if you want to visit the Ubuntu Web site, you can just enter www.ubuntu.com (you can leave off http://).

Figure 3-9 The Firefox interface is sleek but extensible.

Alternatively, you can just type in *Ubuntu*, and Firefox will do the equivalent of going off to Google, entering *Ubuntu* as the search term, and taking you to the first result for the search. This feature is incredibly handy for popular sites that are likely to be at the top of the search results page.

TIP   The search box next to the address bar can be used to do searches. By default, these searches are on Google. To do a Google search, just type in your search term and press Enter. You can also click the down arrow next to the Google box next to the address bar and select from a variety of other sites to search, including sites like Amazon.com and Wikipedia.

This search box can be used to search just about anything. To add more search engines, click the small icon and then select Manage Search Engines.

Bookmarking Your Favorite Sites   To bookmark the page you are viewing, hover over Firefox Web Browser to display the menu. Click Bookmarks > Bookmark This Page or click Ctrl-D. In the drop down box that pops up, use the combo box to select the folder to store the bookmark in. You also have the option to add "tags" to your bookmark, which are like keywords that can be used to sort and search for your bookmarks in the future. When you have finished naming and tagging your bookmark, click Done to save the bookmark.

Save Time with Live Bookmarks Firefox also includes a special feature called live bookmarks that automatically grabs content from a Web site without your needing to visit it. As an example, go to http://fridge.ubuntu.com (a popular Ubuntu news site), and you will see a small orange icon—which indicates that this site has a feed available—on the right side of the address bar. Click this orange square, and you will be taken to a new page that previews the feed and gives you the option of what you would like to use to subscribe to it. Use the default option (Live Bookmarks), and click Subscribe Now. A dialog box will pop up. Use the default values provided and click OK. A new toolbar button is added, and when you click on it, a list of the items from the Web site are displayed. Each time you start Firefox, it will quietly go away and update this list so that you don't need to visit the site yourself. The "Latest Headlines" toolbar entry is an example of this.

TIP **If You Liked the Fridge**
You may also like Planet Ubuntu at http://planet.ubuntu.com. This site collects the personal blogs of a number of different Ubuntu developers and other community members. Planet Ubuntu gives a unique insight into what the developers are working on and/or interested in.

Bolt It On, Make It Cool Although Firefox is already a powerful and flexible Web browser, it can be extended even further using special plug-in extensions. These extensions cover not only typical browsing needs but also other more specialized extras that extend the browser itself.

If you visit a site that requires a normal Web plug-in, a yellow bar will appear at the top of the page, indicating that you are missing a plug-in necessary to fully take advantage of the page you are visiting. Click the Install Missing Plug-ins button to grab the required plug-in. For example, Ubuntu does not come with the Adobe Flash plug-in because it does not live up to Ubuntu software freedom requirements. As a result, you will have the option to install either Adobe Flash or the free software version Gnash if you want to use Flash.

To extend the browser itself with additional features, go to https://addons.mozilla.org and browse for an extension that you are interested in. When you find something you would like to install, select Add to Firefox, then click the Install Now button. A dialog box will pop up asking you to confirm the installation. Click Install Now. Your new extension will now download and install automatically. Typically, this requires a restart of Firefox, and then your extension is available.

TIP   **Be Careful Where You Download**
It is recommended that you download extensions only from http://addons.mozilla.org. If you do need to install an extension from another site, make sure it is a site you trust. Otherwise, the extension may contain unsafe software, viruses, or spyware.

Creating Documents with LibreOffice

Included with Ubuntu is a full office suite called LibreOffice. This comprehensive collection contains applications for creating word processing documents, spreadsheets, and presentations installed by default with the ability to easily manipulate and create databases, drawings, and mathematical equations—all just a click away. The suite provides an extensive range of functionality, including reading and writing Microsoft Office file formats, and can also export documents as Web pages, PDF files, and even animations.

TIP   **History of LibreOffice**
Years ago, a company called Sun Microsystems acquired an office suite called StarOffice when it bought the company that developed it, StarDivision. Sun Microsystems continued to develop StarOffice as a proprietary office suite, but a few years later released an open source version called OpenOffice.org. OpenOffice.org had slightly fewer features, but was still very mature and gathered a large following. When Sun Microsystems was bought by Oracle, some developers were unhappy with the direction the new company was leading development and, since the code was open source, these developers created what is called a fork, a project based on the same open source code up to that point, but which would then diverge for all future development. This new office suite is called LibreOffice.

Let's give LibreOffice a whirl by creating a letter with it. Start LibreOffice word processor by clicking Dash Home in the Launcher and then searching for LibreOffice. When it has loaded, you will be presented with the interface shown in Figure 3-10.

If you have used a word processing program before, many of the common interface elements, such as the buttons for setting font type and

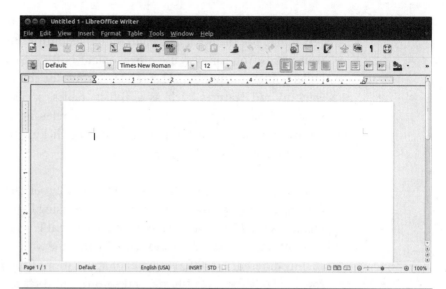

Figure 3-10 LibreOffice looks similar to Microsoft Office and is therefore quite simple to adjust to the interface.

size, bold, italic, underline, and alignment, look and behave the same. The LibreOffice developers have designed the suite to be easy to migrate to if you have used a program like Microsoft Office before. After a few minutes playing with LibreOffice, you will be confident that you can find the functions you need.

Start your letter by first choosing a nice font. In the font combo box, you should see Liberation Serif (which is a free-as-in-liberty font similar to Times) selected as the default. You can click the box and choose another if you prefer, such as the lovely DejaVu Sans or the Ubuntu font. Change the font size by clicking the combo box to the right of the font box and selecting 10 as the size. With the cursor on the left side of the page, add your home address to the letter.

Now press Enter to leave a blank line under the address, and click the Align Right toolbar button (the icon looks like some lines aligned to the right). If you are unsure of what a button does, hover your mouse over it to pop up a tool tip. Now add to your letter the address of the recipient.

Press Enter again to leave a blank line, and type the main body of the letter. Feel free to use the bold, italic, and underline buttons to add emphasis to your words. You can also use other toolbar buttons to add items such as bullet points and numbered lists and to change the color of the font. If you want to add features such as graphics, tables, special characters, and frames, click the Insert menu and select the relevant item. You can customize each item added to the page by right-clicking the item and using the options shown in the context menu.

When your letter is complete, you can save it by selecting File > Save, by clicking the floppy disk toolbar icon, or by pressing Ctrl-S. The default file format used by LibreOffice is the OpenDocument Format. This file format is an official open standard and is used across the world. The file format is slightly different for different types of applications (.odt for word processor files, .ods for spreadsheets, and so on), but each format provides an open standard free from vendor lock-in. You can also save in a variety of other formats, including the default formats for Microsoft Office.

TIP   **Vendor Lock-In?**
In the proprietary software world, it is common for each application to have its own closed file format that only the vendor knows how to implement. When a person uses the software to create documents, the closed format means that only that specific tool can read and write the format. As long as you want to access your documents, you need that tool. This is known as vendor lock-in.

To combat this problem, the LibreOffice suite (and the vast majority of other open source applications) uses an open file format that is publicly documented. In fact, the format is a published standard under ISO/IEC 26300:3006. This means that other applications can implement the OpenDocument file format, and you can be safe in the knowledge that your documents will always be available and you are not locked in to any specific tool.

Another useful feature wedged into LibreOffice is the capability to save your documents in the Adobe PDF format. PDF files have been increasingly used in the last few years and are useful for sending people documents that they should not change (such as invoices). PDF files provide a high-quality copy of the document and are well supported across all operating systems. This makes PDFs ideal for creating catalogs, leaflets, and flyers. To save a document as a PDF file, click the PDF button on the main toolbar (next to the printer icon). Click the button, enter a filename, and you are done. Simple.

Connecting with Empathy and Gwibber and the Indicator Applet

Empathy is a chat program that can interact with Google Talk, AIM, Windows Live, and many other chat programs. It has audio and video capability as well. Left-click the indicator applet (it is a small icon that looks like an envelope) on the top panel and choose Chat to begin. You will then be given an opportunity to enter your account information for various services and to begin communicating.

Gwibber, listed in this menu as Broadcast, is accessible from the same location and can be set up to allow you to integrate online services like Flickr, Twitter, identi.ca, and Facebook into your desktop for even easier access to what is happening in your social networks. Open it, enter your account information as directed, and you can begin to interact with all your circles from one location on your desktop.

This location also gives you a convenient place to mark yourself available for chat or away, update your information for social accounts that use either Empathy or Gwibber, and use your Ubuntu One services.

Ubuntu One

Ubuntu One is an online cloud storage application that is free for any Ubuntu user. This enables any user to create an Ubuntu One account and store up to 2GB on remote servers (more space is available for a fee) that may be accessed from anywhere. The service is built in to the Ubuntu desktop and, once activated, integrates smoothly. You can get started configuring your account by searching for Ubuntu One in Dash Home. More information is available in Chapter 4 and at one.ubuntu.com.

Managing Your E-Mail with Thunderbird

Thunderbird is a traditional desktop e-mail client created by Mozilla, the same people responsible for the Firefox Web browser. It is the default choice in Ubuntu and works the same as the Thunderbird versions for other operating systems. Here is how you set it up.

Open the Dash and search for *Thunderbird* to get started. When it opens for the first time, you are presented with a opportunity to create a new e-mail address using specific services. If you already have an e-mail account you want to use, select Skip this. A wizard will appear to help you configure Thunderbird (Figure 3-11).

Enter your name, e-mail address, and password to begin. Thunderbird performs a search of a Mozilla database of Internet service providers (ISPs) and attempts to set up the technical aspects for you (Figure 3-12). Click Create Account.

Figure 3-11 Thunderbird startup wizard

Figure 3-12 Thunderbird found the details for my domain.

If all goes well, you won't need to do anything else. If it does not find your ISP, you will need to know your mail server information, available from your service provider, so that you can configure Thunderbird manually.

From here on, Thunderbird works as e-mail clients have worked for the last 15 years or more. You can download your e-mail, reply to messages or send new messages, sort messages into folders, configure multiple accounts, and so on, all using a clear, standard interface (Figure 3-13).

Figure 3-13 Thunderbird's interface is easy to use.

Using Ubuntu in Your Language

When you installed Ubuntu, you were asked which language the system should use. Although this sets the initial language for the system, you may want to change the language at a later date. To do this, search the Dash for System Settings and find Language Support.

Ubuntu supports a huge range of different languages, and many applications include a Translate This Application menu option in the Help menu so that all Ubuntu users can contribute translations in their language(s). If you would like to help with this effort, it is a fantastic contribution to the Ubuntu project.

When the language selector first loads, it may ask you to update your language packs. Just click Yes to continue. Inside the dialog box a number of languages are listed, each of which has a Support checkbox listed next to it. For each language that you want available on the system, check the relevant boxes.

When you have selected the boxes, click the Apply button, and the appropriate language packs are downloaded and installed. Now use the Default Language combo box to choose the new language. You need to log out and log back in for the changes to take effect.

TIP   Choosing a New Language
When you see the login screen, you can use the Language button to choose a language for that specific login session. When you select the language, you are asked if you want to make it the default language or use it just for that specific session.

Configuring a Printer

In the Linux world, configuring a printer has traditionally been a challenge. For years, newcomers to Linux have been repeatedly challenged and even bludgeoned with scary terms, commands, and phrases that sound like a language from another planet. Users often had to edit fairly complex text files by hand and spend a good deal of time learning how to insert arcane instructions just to get a printer to work. However, things have changed with Ubuntu.

Most of the time, it is possible to add or configure a printer easily and quickly. The one caveat is that not all printer manufacturers provide Linux drivers for their devices. While the Linux community works very hard to write drivers, many times the newest printer models do not have adequate software to interact with Linux. Most printer models that are older than 6 or 9 months seem to work quite well, though.

TIP You can check before buying a printer to see what other people have experienced by looking at the list of models and the state of their drivers at www.openprinting.org/printers. The Linux Foundation maintains that list, which is a pretty good gauge for determining how well your model should work out of the box with Ubuntu, making this an excellent resource when shopping for new hardware as well as useful for troubleshooting when problems are encountered.

To get started installing your printer, click the Gear icon in the upper right of the top panel, and select Printers from the menu. This option brings up the Printers window, as shown in Figure 3-14.

The Printer configuration window lets you add printers and modify their settings. In the upcoming example, you will add a new printer and then view its settings.

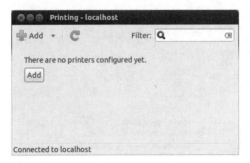

Figure 3-14 The Printers window

Gathering Information

The most important thing to remember when configuring a printer is to not get ahead of yourself. Before you start clicking on icons and running anything, make sure you have completed the following steps.

1. Note the make and model of the printer. This information is usually printed clearly on the hardware itself. In our example, we add a Brother MFC-7820N.

2. Plug the printer in to your computer or to the network, and turn it on.

Launching the Wizard

Once you have properly prepared to install your printer, click Add to bring up the the New Printer window. The system automatically searches for any new connected printers and launches a New Printer wizard, shown in Figure 3-15.

In most cases, the wizards can detect an attached printer automatically and will include it in a list of devices on the left. If your printer is plugged

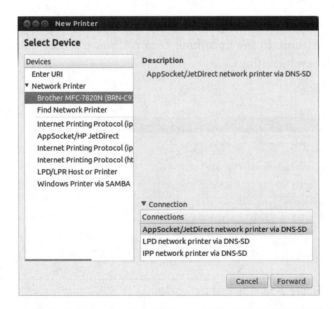

Figure 3-15 Selecting a printer

directly into a router, it is possible for the printer Wizard to find it by selecting Find Network Printer.

Select the device with your printer's name, and then hit Forward.

At this point, you must choose a printer manufacturer. If your printer has been automatically detected, the wizard will choose a manufacturer. Click Forward.

In the next screen, you are asked to choose both a model and a driver. For autodetected printers, both should be automatically selected, and the default driver should work. You can always change it later. If no driver is selected, scroll through the list of options by manufacturer.

Sometimes you may not find the exact model or driver for your specific printer. Generally, if the driver does not exist for your exact model, choose the closest one, and then test it. If that doesn't work, you can try other drivers intended for printers from the same manufacturer.

Click Forward to proceed with the installation. If you need to install a custom driver, click the Install Driver button.

Finally, you can enter a description and location for your printer, as shown in Figure 3-16. Click Apply to complete the process and set up your printer.

Mission Accomplished!

After you click Apply, you will see your printer's name under the Local Printers heading. You can click on it and then print out a test page. Do so, and make sure the page prints correctly. If you find that the page prints well, you are finished. You can now print from the applications you have installed, such as LibreOffice.

Remote Printing

You can also configure your Ubuntu system to send print jobs to a remote print server. If, for example, you have a Windows system with a printer attached on your network, simply choose the Network Printer radio button

Figure 3-16 Entering printer location and description

during configuration and specify the host name or IP address of the Windows system. You will then have to specify a connection protocol.

If your Windows system is sharing a printer, you will have to specify Samba, which is the standard way to get Linux and Windows systems to communicate with each other. You will still have to specify a print driver, as described earlier.

Keeping Your Computer Updated

While Ubuntu already includes the things most people need, sometimes you want or need something extra, such as a desktop publishing application for school or a game to pass the time. The easiest way to add these is with Ubuntu Software Center, which is extremely simple to use but has a few limitations. This section also highlights a couple of other options. Work done using one tool to add or remove software is recognized by the related tools, so it is okay to mix and match which ones you use.

Using Ubuntu Software Center

Like other tools discussed later in this chapter, Ubuntu Software Center installs software from the online Ubuntu software repositories.

To launch Ubuntu Software Center, click the Ubuntu Software Center icon in the Launcher. When it is run for the first time, and occasionally afterward, it will take a few moments to initialize itself and the list of available and installed applications. Once this is complete, you will see the main screen, shown in Figure 3-17.

Figure 3-17 Ubuntu Software Center main screen

Click a category to help you refine the listing of available software for specific applications, or use the search box at the upper right to find programs using keywords or program names.

The icons at the top of the window give you access to other features or information. You can sort software by source by changing All Software to one of the other options, such as For Purchase. Click Installed to list all installed software. History shows you what you have installed, updated, or uninstalled and when.

You can change your software sources further using the menu in the top panel and selecting Edit > Software Sources.

By default, Ubuntu Software Center shows all applications that are supported by Ubuntu, including those supported by community volunteers called MOTUs, for Masters of the Universe (more on them in Chapter 10). Although using Ubuntu Software Center to install new applications from both the officially supported Ubuntu-provided repositories as well as the community repositories is perfect for most users, there are times when a more conservative approach to software choices may be appropriate. In this case, you may limit the number of applications shown from the View menu by selecting Canonical-Maintained Applications to see only those pieces of software that are actively watched over and updated by Canonical, the company behind Ubuntu. This is sometimes preferred in corporate environments that desire or require a stronger guarantee of support.

For many people, this is all you need to know to install or uninstall software. Chapter 4 goes into a bit more detail for those who are interested in the technological aspects.

Adding and Removing Programs and Packages

No operating system or piece of software is perfect. In addition, new features may be added that users want or need. Because of this, Ubuntu developers periodically release security and other updates to software. These updates are placed into the Ubuntu repositories and are easy to install.

Most of the updates to your machine will be security related. This means that the developers have found a weakness in a particular program in Ubuntu and have released a fix for it. There will also be a small number of updates to fix some critical bugs. For a home user, there is generally no reason not to install these updates right away, as not installing them might leave your computer open to security breaches.

TIP   Although Ubuntu is significantly more secure from the main concerns of some operating systems, such as fears involving viruses and spyware, no computer is perfectly secure because no software is perfect.

When problems are discovered that could lead to security issues, like buffer overflows or remote exploits, they are fixed and released as quickly as possible, even though the danger is usually remote. Ubuntu developers also have a very strict policy about not putting new release versions of programs with significant and untested function changes or new features into stable versions of Ubuntu. This practice keeps your system more stable by not introducing new problems.

Installing Updates

Ubuntu checks the Ubuntu repositories once a day to see if there are any new versions of software you have installed, and it tells you when you need to update your machine. If security updates exist, a pop-up window will appear. If other updates are found, they will also be made available. You can check to see if updates are available in the Gear menu at the upper right of the top panel. An entry either will say Software Up to Date or will inform you of available updates. Click either message at any time to open the program.

Ubuntu 12.04 handles package updates by launching update manager. Users are notified of security updates on a daily basis and are also notified when new Ubuntu versions are released. Because 12.04 is a Long Term Support (LTS) release, by default it will only notify of new LTS releases, meaning that it would likely be silent until April 2014. This behavior may be changed by clicking Settings at the bottom left of the Update Manager window.

NOTE   LTS stands for Long Term Support and is used to designate specific Ubuntu releases that are intended for extreme stability and complete support for a longer amount of time than regular biannual releases. More information about Ubuntu releases is coming later in this chapter.

Learning about What Was Updated

The update window, shown in Figure 3-18, shows you what is going to be changed. In the details pane, it shows you what got fixed and how. It might also list a Common Vulnerabilities and Exposures (CVE) number. The CVE number is a unique identifier for a security vulnerability. You can look it up on http://cve.mitre.org to see what the exact flaw was. However, most people don't need to worry (and really don't care) about these details.

Installing an Application That Is Not in the Repositories

Although the repositories contain a huge selection of packages, sometimes the package you need is not included. The first thing you should check is that you have enabled the additional repositories such as universe and mul-

Figure 3-18 The update window

tiverse. You can do this from Update Manager by clicking the Gear icon at the top right of the desktop and selecting Updates Available. Hover over Ubuntu Software Center to view its menu. Under Edit, select Software Sources to ensure that the boxes are checked for main, universe, restricted, and multiverse. (See help.ubuntu.com/community/Repositories/Ubuntu for more details.)

TIP   **The Repository Rundown**

The *universe* repository contains the thousands of packages that are part of the Debian distribution upon which Ubuntu is based. All of these packages are entirely free and supported by a community of Ubuntu contributors.

The *multiverse* repository contains a number of packages that are freely available to download but are not fully open source. If you want to run only open source software, you may not want to use this repository.

If you have enabled these extra repositories and your package is still not there, have a quick hunt around with a search engine to see if you can find a repository (known as a Debian or APT repository) for your package. If you find one, use the Repositories dialog box you have just played with to add the new repository, and then use Synaptic to install the package.

One common type of extra repository you may encounter is called a PPA, or personal package archive. There is good information available for using PPAs at https://help.launchpad.net/Packaging/PPA/InstallingSoftware.

If no repository is available, look for a Debian package (.deb) for the application, most likely available from the software company's Web site, such as Adobe does with its Reader software or Skype with its VOIP software. If you find one, download it, and double-click it to install.

Finally, if all else fails, you may need to download the source code and compile it using instructions found at https://help.ubuntu.com/community/CompilingSoftware.

Upgrading to the Next Ubuntu Release

One of the original goals for Ubuntu was to have frequent releases, and with only one notable exception (the 6.06 LTS release, which was delayed by two months), there have been six months between each release since 4.10.

This book has been revised for the latest version—12.04—but another release will be along soon. Release 12.04, like the earlier 10.04, 8.04, and 6.06, is a Long Term Support (LTS) version of Ubuntu, supported for three years on the desktop and five on the server.

All other versions, such as 11.10, are supported for eighteen months and at the same time are superseded by a new version every six months. Essentially, if you are running the LTS version, you might not be too interested in moving to the latest and greatest until the next LTS version comes out, but if you are running a regular release version, you might be the sort of person who is more interested in the latest and greatest software updates. In either case, this is how you perform the upgrade.

TIP   All Ubuntu releases are intended to be stable. The LTS releases are intended to be extra stable, as they represent the culmination of two years of planning and feature changes. The intermediate releases will include incremental changes that are stable but that may not be feature-complete. For example, the Unity desktop was first released in 10.10, the first release after 10.04 LTS, but its features became more complete and development more mature for 12.04 LTS.

Doing the Actual Upgrade

A graphical tool called Update Manager tells you when a new version of Ubuntu is available and walks you through the upgrade process. Note that if you already know or want to learn the manual method, that is fine too. Both means will achieve the same result.

When a new release is available, Update Manager alerts you, as in Figure 3-19. All you need to do is click on the Upgrade button to start the process. You are first shown the release notes, which mention new features or any outstanding bugs. After you click on the Upgrade button on this screen, the necessary changes to your software repositories are made, and then the program downloads and installs the new distribution. You may be prompted if you have changed any configuration files. After the actual installation is complete, you are told which, if any, packages are no longer officially supported by Ubuntu (have moved to the universe repository). Last, all you need to do is restart your computer when prompted, and you will begin enjoying the new release.

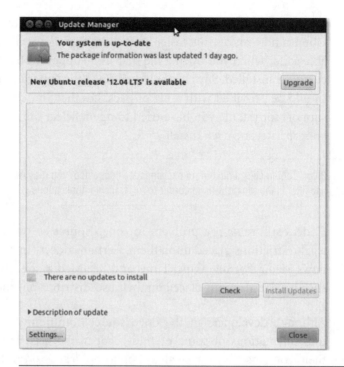

Figure 3-19 Upgrading from Ubuntu 11.10 using Update Manager and an Internet connection

Ubuntu and Multimedia

In recent years, multimedia has become an essential part of computing. Watching DVDs and Web videos and listening to music have become an integral part of modern computer use. These multimedia capabilities have been further bolstered by the huge popularity of legal music downloading. With a range of online stores for a variety of different types of music, it is not uncommon to listen to most of your music without ever seeing a little shiny silver disk.

Installing Codecs

Multimedia files and disks come in a variety of different types, and each type uses a special codec, or coder/decoder software, to compress the content to a smaller size while retaining a particular level of quality. To play this media, you need to ensure that you have the relevant codecs installed. Ubuntu now makes this easier by suggesting packages that provide a suitable codec when you open a file that isn't supported by the ones that are currently installed. Simply double-click the file you want to open, and you should be provided with a list of packages that you can install to enable support for the file you have tried to open. Select the packages that seem appropriate, and click Install.

QUICK TIP   If you double-click a file but no packages are suggested, you may need to change the package filter in the top right-hand corner to All Available Applications.

Codecs still remain a problem for open source software because of the legal restrictions placed upon them. Certain codecs (including MP3, Windows Media Format, QuickTime, and RealMedia) are proprietary and as such have restrictions placed on their use, distribution, and licensing.

Although developers in the open source community have created free implementations of some of these codecs, the licensing that surrounds them conflicts with the legal and philosophical position that Ubuntu has set. These codecs are excluded not only because they are legally dubious but also because they disagree with Ubuntu's ethic of creating a distribution that consists entirely of free software in the most free sense of the word.

QUICK TIP   If you want to find out more about installing these codecs, see https://help.ubuntu.com/community/RestrictedFormats.

To work toward resolving these problems, a number of developers are working on free codecs such as Ogg Vorbis and Ogg Theora that provide high-quality results and open licensing. The Ogg Vorbis codec is used on audio and can provide better results than MP3 at a smaller file size. The Ogg Theora codec is used for video and competes with the MPEG-4 codec. Ubuntu includes the Ogg Vorbis and Ogg Theora codecs by default, and you can encode and play back any media that uses those codecs out of the box.

Although the world would be a better place if all codecs were free, the reality is different, and many Ubuntu users still want to play media compressed with proprietary codecs. Table 3-1 shows the most typical codecs used to encode and play back media and lists their support in Ubuntu.

Table 3-1 Codec Support

Codec	File Type	Included	Supported
MP3	.mp3	No	Yes
Ogg	.ogg	Yes	N/A
Flac	.flac	Yes	N/A
Windows Media Audio	.wma	No	Yes*
Wave	.wav	Yes	N/A
MPEG-1	.mpg	No	Yes
MPEG-2	.mpg	No	Yes
Raw DV	.dv	Yes	N/A
Quicktime	.mov	No	Yes*
Windows Media Video	.wmv	No	Yes*
AAC Audio	.m4a	No	Yes*

* These codecs involve the installation of nonfree software that may or may not be legal in your country.

Listening to Audio Files

Ubuntu includes a powerful music player called Rhythmbox Music Player to organize and play your music file collection. By default, Ubuntu will look for music in the Music directory accessible in the Places menu.

Using Rhythmbox   Load Rhythmbox (Figure 3-20) by searching the Dash to find Rhythmbox Music Player. You can also access Rhythmbox quickly using the Sound icon in the Notification area at the right of the top panel. Click the icon for quick access to open or minimize the Rhythmbox window, to volume controls, playlists, and the Sound Settings menu.

The Rhythmbox window is split into a number of different panes, each displaying different details about your music collection. The left pane (Source) lets you select the source of the music, such as your media library, podcasts, and Internet radio. Each of these options has a browser pane available to display the source of the content.

Figure 3-20 Rhythmbox is a great place to look after your music collection.

Listening to Podcasts   Podcasts are audio shows that you can subscribe to, and they are increasingly becoming the new way to listen to audio and music. When you subscribe to a podcast, each new release is automatically downloaded for you. This makes it extremely convenient to regularly listen to audio shows.

Rhythmbox has good support for Podcast feeds, and subscribing to a feed is simple. In the sidebar, right-click the Podcasts entry and click New Podcast Feed. Paste in the feed by right-clicking the box and selecting Paste. The files are automatically downloaded, and you can listen to them by double-clicking on them. Each time you start Rhythmbox, a check is made to see if any new episodes exist, and if so, they are downloaded.

NOTE   **Rhythmbox and iPods and Other Media Players**
Rhythmbox can also read songs from your iPod—just plug it in and it will display in Rhythmbox. Rhythmbox can read from the iPod but may not be able to write to all iPods. Support is quite good for most other media players, including the author's Android-based phone.

Playing and Ripping CDs

Insert a music CD into your computer and Ubuntu will respond with a pop-up box giving you the option to rip (copy) the music to your hard drive or play the CD. If you rip the CD, you can adjust the metadata during the process, such as the song titles or artist names.

Buying Music

Canonical has added options within Rhythmbox. You may now buy music through the Ubuntu One Music Store alongside Jamendo, Magnatune, and the Amazon MP3 Store. While Jamendo and Magnatune are great sources for creative commons and other open-licensed music, for the first time, major and minor label artists will have their music available directly from within Ubuntu. These are the songs you would typically find in your local record shop or on a radio station. Music in the Ubuntu One Music Store will be encoded at a minimum of 256 kbps in MP3 format without any digital rights management (DRM). An Ubuntu One account (described in Chapter 4) is required to purchase music.

NOTE   You can learn more about the Ubuntu One Music Store at https://wiki.ubuntu.com/ UbuntuOne/MusicStore.

Interacting with Photos

Shotwell is a photo management program that you may use to import your pictures, organize them, and perform basic touch-ups like removing red eye, cropping, or simple color adjustment. When Shotwell imports photos, it reads the metadata embedded in the image file and then sorts the images by date. Once done, it creates a timeline that allows you to view photos easily as a group, individually, and even as a full-screen slideshow. You can export your photos individually or in groups directly from Shotwell to well-known Web services like Flickr or Google's Picasa, to a folder, or even to a CD you could give to a friend or family member.

Watching Videos

To watch videos in Ubuntu, you need to ensure that you have the correct codecs installed. As discussed earlier, some of these codecs are available separately due to the legal implications of including them with the Ubuntu system. Although the new process for suggesting and installing codecs should cover most popular types of files, you should still refer to the Ubuntu wiki at http://wiki.ubuntu.com for details of how to install ones that are not recognized.

Using Movie Player   To watch videos in Ubuntu, you use the Movie Player (Figure 3-21). Load it by clicking Dash Home from the Launcher and searching for Movie Player.

To watch a video on your hard disk, click Movie > Open, and select the file from the disk.

TIP   **Another Way to Load Files into Movie Player**
You can also load multimedia files into Movie Player by double-clicking them on your desktop or in the file manager.

Movie Player also supports video streams. To watch a stream, click Movie > Open Location, and enter the Internet address for the stream. The video feed is then loaded and displayed.

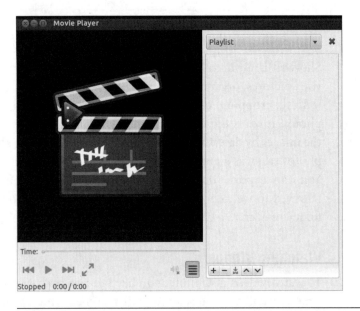

Figure 3-21 Movie Player is a simple and flexible media player.

Getting DVDs to Work Ubuntu comes with DVD support for unencrypted DVDs. With the DVD industry being what it is, the majority of DVDs come encrypted, and if you want to watch them, you need to ensure that a software library that can decrypt these DVDs is installed. Unfortunately, this software library needs to be installed separately and is not included with Ubuntu. Refer to the Ubuntu restricted formats page at https://help.ubuntu.com/community/RestrictedFormats for details.

With the library installed, insert a disk into your computer, and Ubuntu will automatically start Movie Player to view the disk. Alternatively, fire up Movie Player, and click Movie > Play Disk to play the DVD. Movie Player doesn't support DVD menus but you can still use it to play a DVD.

If you are settling down to watch a movie, you may want to configure a few other settings. First click View > Aspect Ratio to select the correct aspect ratio for your screen, and then select View > Fullscreen to switch to full-screen mode. To exit full-screen mode, just move your mouse, and some on-screen controls will appear.

TIP   **Control Movie Player with a Remote Control**
Movie Player supports the Linux Infrared Control (LIRC) library so you can use a remote control while watching your media.

If you want to use a remote control with your Ubuntu computer, you need to install the Linux Infrared Control (LIRC) package. LIRC is the library, and it supports a wide range of remote control units.

The first step is to determine which LIRC driver is required for your particular remote control. Take a look at the list of remotes on the LIRC site at www.lirc.org, or use your favorite search engine if your remote is not listed on the site.

LIRC includes a number of built-in drivers. You can see which ones are included by running the following command:

```
lircd –driver=help
```

When you know which driver is required and you know your installed LIRC supports your hardware, you can edit the hardware.conf file in the /etc/lirc file to configure which one is used. Simply set the DRIVER line to the driver you selected. Then restart LIRC:

```
sudo /etc/init.d/lirc restart
```

When you press the buttons on your remote control, a code should appear. This code can be mapped to a button on your remote by editing the lircd.cònf file in /etc/lirc. For more information, see http://help.ubuntu.com/community/LIRC.

Backing Up

Everyone who has used a computer for any length of time has heard the advice, "Back up, back up often, test the backups, repeat." Few people actually do it. Ignoring this advice is dangerous and can cause the loss of important documents, files, pictures, and more.

To prevent this loss, prudent computer users, regardless of operating system, pick a method of copying their files to a safe location for storage and use that method on a regular basis. To help you devise a strategy that best suits you, we have come up with a few options to consider. This topic is a big one, and how you deal with it is a very personal decision. Rather than give step-by-step instructions, we mention a few options to consider and leave it to you to research them further and decide on one that looks appropriate and inviting.

Some users find that the easiest thing for them to do is buy an external hard drive and copy all of their files to it every week or two. Others look at this and think to themselves, "There has to be a better way." Perhaps they noticed that these methods require every single file to be copied every time, even if the file has not changed in ages. In these cases, an incremental backup is ideal, where the computer is told to compare the files in the original location with stored files in a backup location (like an external hard drive) and copy only new or changed files.

Several GUI programs for backing up are available from the Ubuntu repositories. Each comes with a basic and useful graphic interface that is easy to figure out and use, and each is configurable to allow you to do full or incremental backups. A backup program is installed by default and can be found by searching for *backup* in the Dash. The program lets you configure automatic or manual backups, specify the location for those backups, specify what will be backed up, set scheduling for automatic backups, restore files from the backup, and more (Figure 3-22).

For users who are a little more advanced (or a little braver) and who love the raw power available from learning a command-line program, the best two programs for backups are rar and rsync, which are both available from the Ubuntu repositories. Once they are installed, you can read the manual pages and learn how to use them by typing man rar or man rsync from a terminal. They are complicated but are also fast and amazingly effective both at making the backups and restoring them.

Unfortunately, this quick mention in a small section of a very diverse chapter can only get you thinking about the need for good backups and help guide you in your search for the perfect method for you. However you decide to back up your data, we strongly encourage you not to ignore the need but to find a way to do it. If you have any questions about this or

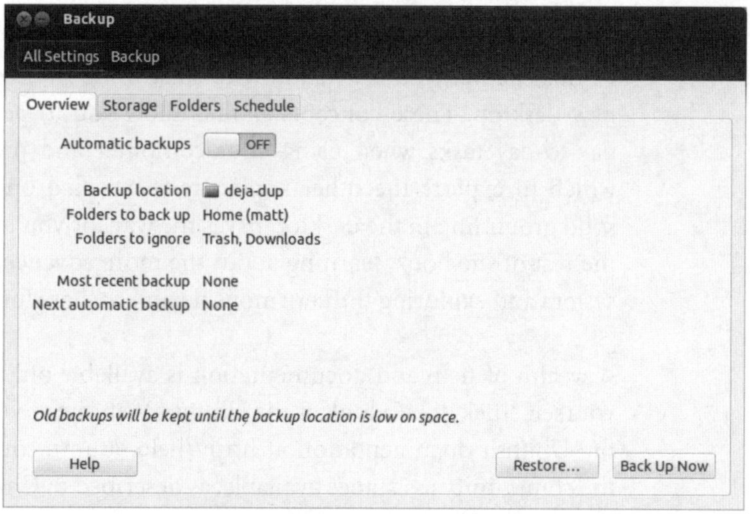

Figure 3-22 The main Backup settings window

other topics, the Ubuntu community has a large number of very helpful people you can ask for help, and we recommend you start by searching or asking questions in the Ubuntu Forums at http://ubuntuforums.org.

Customizing Ubuntu's Look and Feel

Click the Gear icon at the right of the top panel and select System Settings to configure and customize your system. You can find other settings in the Dash using the Applications Lens and the System filter. Feel free to customize anything you like, but pay attention to what you are doing so you know how to change it back if you don't like the result. Chapter 6 has more information on customizing Ubuntu.

TIP   **Feel the Power**

When you installed Ubuntu, you were asked for a username and password for the system. That first user account (and its password) has access to not just your normal user account but also to the all-powerful administration features. Therefore, when you access the menu options while using this account and are asked for a password, just enter this user account's password to use those features.

This feature applies only to the user account created during installation. If you add other users, you need to explicitly allow them access to administration options.

Summary

In this chapter, you learned how to start using the core features of your new desktop. These concepts should allow you to perform most of the day-to-day tasks when using your computer and provide a base from which to explore the other applications installed on your system. This solid grounding in the desktop paves the way for you to meander through the rest of the book, learning about the more advanced uses of your new system and exploring the enormous flexibility that Ubuntu provides.

A wealth of help and documentation is available online. If you ever find yourself stuck, take a look at the Ubuntu Web site at www.ubuntu.com or the Ubuntu documentation at http://help.ubuntu.com and make use of the community assistance available, as described in Chapter 10.

CHAPTER 4

Becoming an Ubuntu Power User

- Administering System and User Settings
- Understanding How Linux Stores and Organizes Files
- Learning Unity Keyboard Shortcuts
- Using the Terminal
- Working with Windows Programs
- Installing Software from PPAs
- Compiling Software from Source
- Summary

UBUNTU IS RELATIVELY STRAIGHTFORWARD to set up and use for the common day-to-day tasks. With time, though, most users want to learn how to be more efficient performing their tasks on that computer. It is this efficiency, this elegance in the way tasks are performed, that forms the basis of the separation between beginners and power users. Those who are content to learn just enough to get a task done need not read this chapter. Those who want to perform these tasks more easily, more quickly, or more smoothly and with a deeper understanding of what they are doing and why are the target audience here. This chapter is not about customization; for that see Chapter 6. This chapter is about understanding and learning how to use what you already have to its fullest potential.

Administering System and User Settings

To begin, search for Settings in the Dash and open System Settings (Figure 4-1).

From here you can adjust many aspects of your system, as shown in Figure 4-2.

Click an item to select it and modify its settings. When you are done, you may close the window or click All Settings in the upper left to return to the menu. Some settings require you to unlock them by clicking the Unlock button at the upper right and entering a password before you can modify their settings (Figure 4-3). You must have administrative privileges to do this.

Figure 4-1 Click System Settings to begin.

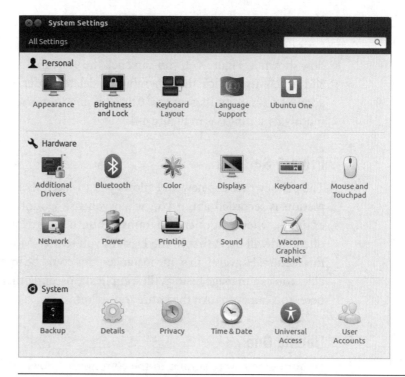

Figure 4-2 Choose from among many options in the System Settings window.

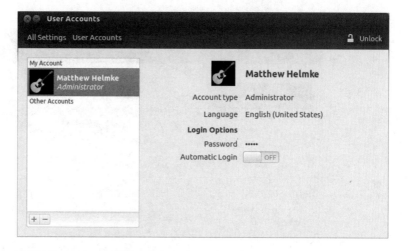

Figure 4-3 Click All Settings to return to the main menu or Unlock to continue.

User Settings

Let's begin with a look at available user settings. Once you unlock the window shown in Figure 4-3, you can click the + symbol at the bottom left to add a new user, click the – symbol to delete a user, or click on a user account to modify its settings. Click on any item shown at the right to modify its settings, as in Figure 4-4.

Privacy Settings

The privacy menu is new and allows you to carefully manage what information is recorded about you when you use Ubuntu (Figure 4-5). For example, when you open programs, Ubuntu records what you use most often and will list it first in the Dash as you search. Most users appreciate this feature. However, in some instances, this could be insecure or undesirable. You can manage history, files, applications, and other privacy features here. You can even turn the entire feature off.

Ubuntu One

Ubuntu One is very similar to the commonly known and used Dropbox, which allows you to store data in the cloud for use on multiple computers. This feature is built in to Ubuntu and does not require any additional software to be installed, but you do need to register so that your information can be kept secure (Figure 4-6).

Figure 4-4 Items have either menus or their own pop-up windows.

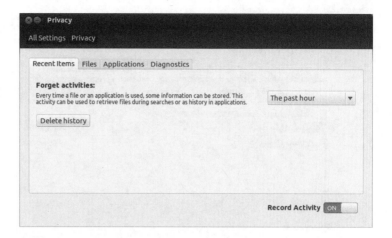

Figure 4-5 Want to delete information recorded only in the last hour? Easy.

Figure 4-6 You need to log in or create an account to use Ubuntu One.

Once you have logged in, you can use Ubuntu One to store data, settings, and other information, as in Figure 4-7. It can automatically sync these settings across multiple computers, if all of them are running Ubuntu, and you can control or revoke access by any of these devices using this menu.

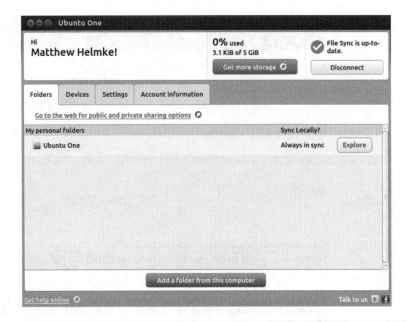

Figure 4-7 Ubuntu One has many menus to make setup and use easy.

In addition, any music you purchase from the Ubuntu Music Store using the music player will also be stored in Ubuntu One and accessible from a Web interface through your username and password using any computer and Web browser as well as by any device you permit to access, including Windows computers and Android phones. Access for more operating systems is in process and may be available by the time you read this. See https://one.ubuntu.com for more details.

Default Settings

Default settings generally make sense for most users. However, what if you want a different program to open when you try to play a certain media file? Click the Details icon in the System Settings menu to change from the default settings, as in Figure 4-8. Select different items from the menu at the left for other options.

TIP   There are lots of settings available. Feel free to change any of them to suit your needs or preferences. You may want to take note of the current settings before you make changes, just in case you change your mind and want to go back to what you had.

Figure 4-8 Changing your default applications is easy: just make sure you install what you want to use before you try to tell Ubuntu to use it.

Understanding How Linux Stores and Organizes Files

If you have not used Linux before, the way that Linux stores and organizes files is likely to be new to you because the layout is quite different from Windows and Mac OS X.

TIP   **Folders and Directories**
When reading about file management, don't get confused by the terms *folders* and *directories—both* words describe the same thing.

In the Windows world, each disk drive is labeled with an identifying letter such as C: for your hard disk and D: for the CD/DVD drive. In the Linux world, however, everything is part of the same filesystem organization. As such, if you have two or three hard disks, a CD drive, and a USB stick all plugged in, they will all be part of the same folder structure.

The diagram shown in Figure 4-9 should give you an idea of how everything hangs together.

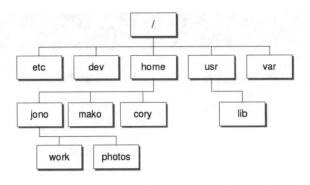

Figure 4-9 Linux filesystem organization

Right at the top of the tree is the root folder, referred to as /. Inside this folder are a number of special system folders, each with a specific use. As an example, the /home folder contains a number of home directories for each user on the system. As such, the user account has the home folder set to /home/matthew.

Which Folder Does What?   The folder structure in a modern Linux distribution such as Ubuntu was largely inspired by the original UNIX foundations that were created by men with large beards. Although you don't really need to know what these folders do, since Ubuntu looks after the housekeeping for you, some of you may be interested in the more important folders. To help, we present the Linux folder hit list in Table 4-1.

Configuration Files   In Table 4-1, /etc is described as storing systemwide configuration files for your computer. Aside from these files that affect everyone, there are also configuration files for each specific user. Earlier, when you customized Ubuntu's look and feel, the settings were applied only to your current user account. So where are those settings stored?

Inside your home directory are a number of folders that begin with a dot (.), such as .config and .libreoffice. These folders contain the configuration settings for user-specific applications. By default, these dot folders are hidden in the graphical file viewer because you rarely need to access them. You can view these hidden files and folders when you are viewing your home folder by clicking View > Show Hidden Files in the menu or by pressing Ctrl-H.

Table 4-1 Linux Folders

Folder	Use
/boot	This folder contains important files to boot the computer, including the bootloader configuration and the kernel.
/dev	Each device on your system (such as sound cards, Webcams, etc.) has an entry in this folder. Each application accesses the device by using the relevant items inside /dev.
/etc	Systemwide configuration files for the software installed on your system are stored here.
/home	Each user account on the system has a home directory that is stored here.
/lib	Important system software libraries are stored here. You should never need to delve into this world of the unknown.
/media	Media devices such as CD drives and USB sticks are referenced here when they are plugged in. More on this later.
/mnt	Other devices can be mounted too. Again, more on this later.
/opt	Optional software can be installed here. This folder is usually used when you want to build your own software. If you don't build your own software, you ignore this folder.
/proc/sys	Information about the current running status of the system is stored here.
/root	This is the home directory for the main superuser.
/bin	Software that is vital for the system to be able to boot is stored here.
/sbin	Software that should be run only by the superuser is stored here.
/usr	General software is installed here.
/var	This folder contains log files about the software on your computer.

Using Windows Files on Another Partition

For those of you who spend a considerable amount of your life on Windows partitions, you may want to be able to access these partitions from Ubuntu. This is no problem, although you will need to edit a special configuration file to do this. Luckily, you need to edit this file only once, and then everything will be set up.

Ubuntu should automatically recognize any Windows partitions you have on your computer and set them up for you; however, you may need to modify them or add your own. Search for Disk Utility in the Dash and write down the partition numbers and filesystem for your Windows partitions. The partition number will look something like /dev/hdb1 or /dev/sdb1, and the filesystem will be either FAT, VFAT, or NTFS.

The next step is to create some mount points. When your Windows partitions are enabled, they are accessed via a particular folder in Ubuntu. This is called a mount point. As an example, if you have a mount point as /media/win1 and on your Windows partition you want to access your Work folder, you would access it from Ubuntu as /media/win1/work.

Mount points usually live in the /media folder. Create a different mount point for each Windows partition. As an example, if you have three Windows partitions, run the following commands:

```
foo@bar:~$ sudo mkdir /media/win1
foo@bar:~$ sudo mkdir /media/win2
foo@bar:~$ sudo mkdir /media/win3
```

Now open up the following configuration file:

```
foo@bar:~$ sudo gedit /etc/fstab
```

The /etc/fstab file maps partition numbers to mount points. At the bottom of the file, add a line like this for each mount point:

```
/dev/hdb1 media/win1 vfat users,rw,owner,umask=000 0 0
```

You will need to change the partition number (the first column), mount point (second column), and filesystem (third column) for your relevant partitions.

Now reload /etc/fstab to enable the partitions:

```
foo@bar:~$ sudo mount -a
```

Some hard disk icons for the new partitions now appear.

TIP   You can find more about fstab at https://help.ubuntu.com/community/Fstab.

Learning Unity Keyboard Shortcuts

Using a mouse is intuitive because of the direct interaction between your hand, your eyes, and the cursor, but for repeated actions, keyboard shortcuts enable you to work (and play) faster. No need to take the time to pick up your hand, move it to a different spot on the desk, use the mouse, click something, move your hand back to the keyboard to type a few letters, go back to the mouse to click something else, and so on. The more you can do from one place, the more efficient your actions will be. Here is a list of things you can do with Unity without moving your hands away from the keyboard. Of course, you don't have to do things this way, but power users love to save time and energy, even if it means spending a little more time up front learning how; in the long term, the savings add up.

TIP   These keyboard shortcuts are new. Some are very different from what you may have used with previous operating systems or even earlier desktops with Ubuntu. Also, they are actively being developed and tested with end users for maximum usability and memorability. This means some may change from the time this was written, although we hope not.

The Super key is used for several of the shortcuts. It is sometimes known as the Windows key. In the following tables, it is simply called Super.

Table 4-2 lists keyboard shortcuts related to using the Launcher.

Dash

Table 4-3 lists keyboard shortcuts related to using the Dash.

Table 4-2 Launcher Shortcuts

Key Combination	Action
Super (long press)	Open Launcher, display shortcuts
Super-Tab	Switch applications via the Launcher
Super-# (1–9)	Same as clicking on a Launcher icon
Super-Shift-# (1–9)	Open a new window for the same application
Super-T	Open Trash

Table 4-3 Dash Shortcuts

Key Combination	Action
Super (quick tap)	Open the Dash home
Super-A	Open the Dash App Lens
Super-F	Open the Dash Files Lens
Super-M	Open the Dash Music Lens
Ctrl-Tab	Switch between Lenses
Cursor keys	Move the focus
Enter & Return	Open the item that currently has focus

Switching

Table 4-4 lists keyboard shortcuts related to switching between applications.

Windows

Table 4-5 lists keyboard shortcuts related to windows and managing them.

Workspaces

Table 4-6 lists keyboard shortcuts related to using workspaces.

Other

Table 4-7 lists keyboard shortcuts that don't fit in any of the previous categories.

Table 4-4 Switching Shortcuts

Key Combination	Action
Alt-Tab	Switch between applications
Alt-`	Hold Alt and press ` to switch between windows of current application
Cursor left or right	Move the focus within lists or images of applications when switching or in a menu

Table 4-5 Windows Management Shortcuts

Key Combination	Action
Super-W	Spread all windows in the current workspace
Super-D	Minimize all windows
Super-Cursor up	Maximize the current window
Super-Cursor down	Restore or minimize current window
Super-Cursor left or right	Semi-maximize current window
Alt-F4	Close current window
Alt-Space	Open window accessibility menu
Ctrl-Alt-Num	Place window in corresponding positions on the screen
Alt-Left mouse drag	Move window
Alt-Middle mouse drag	Resize window
Ctrl-Alt-Numpad 7	Place window in top left corner of screen; pressing a second time does nothing
Ctrl-Alt-Numpad 8	Place window in top half of screen; pressing a second time does nothing
Ctrl-Alt-Numpad 9	Place window in top right corner of screen; pressing a second time does nothing
Ctrl-Alt-Numpad 4	Place window on the left side of the screen in semi-maximized state (it is important that the window is actually semi-maximized, not just the same size and position as a semi-maximized window); pressing a second time does nothing
Ctrl-Alt-Numpad 5	Maximize window; if window is already maximized, pressing this key combo restores the window to the same size, shape, and position as before it was maximized
Ctrl-Alt-Numpad 6	Place window on the right side of the screen (it is important that the window is actually semi-maximized, not just the same size and position as a semi-maximized window); pressing a second time does nothing
Ctrl-Alt-Numpad 1	Place window in the bottom left corner of the screen; pressing a second time does nothing
Ctrl-Alt-Numpad 2	Place window in the bottom half of the screen; pressing a second time does nothing
Ctrl-Alt-Numpad 3	Place window in the bottom right corner of the screen; pressing a second time does nothing
Ctrl-Alt-Numpad 0	Minimize window; if window is already minimized, pressing this key combo restores the window to the same size, shape, and position as before it was minimized

Table 4-6 Workspace Shortcuts

Key Combination	Action
Super-S	Spread workspaces
Super-Ctrl-Cursor Keys	Switch workspaces
Super-Alt-Cursor Keys	Move focused window to different workspace

Table 4-7 Other Shortcuts

Key Combination	Action
Super-L	Lock screen
Ctrl-Super	Display an overlay image of the main keyboard shortcuts for Unity

Using the Terminal

Although Ubuntu is a desktop-driven OS, the system is running on a powerful and incredibly flexible command-line core. Inspired by more than 30 years of UNIX heritage, the command-line environment present on Linux systems enables you to perform some incredibly powerful tasks by stringing together different commands in different ways.

The philosophy behind UNIX is to create a large number of small tools, each of which is designed to do one task but do it incredibly well. As a quick example to whet your appetite, there is a command called ls that does nothing more than list files in a folder. Although listing files is its singular function in life, it has every option imaginable for listing files.

Now, ls is limited by itself, but it can be combined with other commands that have equal levels of flexibility to create impressively powerful combinations. To do this, a *pipeline* is created using the | symbol to connect these different commands. Pipelines can be constructed in any number of different ways, and once the user has even a basic knowledge of what a few different commands do, stringing together a pipeline of commands can solve virtually any task you can imagine in quick and powerful ways.

It should be made 100 percent clear that using the command line is *not* an essential skill required to use Ubuntu, but it is a skill that can increase the flexibility of your computer for more advanced, customized tasks. Rather than cover the use of the terminal here, we have included an excellent introduction in Chapter 7 and we strongly recommend that all who seek to become power users read it.

Working with Windows Programs

Although Linux offers an increasingly compelling platform for the desktop, some situations arise when there is just no alternative other than an application written for Windows. This is generally the case with specific business applications, some educational tools, and many games. Luckily, there is a way you can run many of these applications on your Ubuntu desktop.

For more than fifteen years, the Wine project team members have been working to create a free way to run Windows applications on Linux. While not every application works perfectly, and some don't work at all, the number of programs that do work in Wine has dramatically increased and continues to do so. However, it is recommended that you thoroughly test the applications you want to run in Wine before you use them for important work, and if you run into trouble, try consulting help resources, use virtualization to run Windows on top of Ubuntu, or search for a different application to use.

TIP   You can find some useful help resources for Wine at www.winehq.org/help/, and you can learn more about alternatives to Wine at www.winehq.org/docs/wineusr-guide/alternatives.

Install the Wine package from the Ubuntu Software Center or simply double-click an .exe file, and you will be prompted to install the package. You can configure Wine by searching for Wine Applications in the Applications Dash after clicking the Applications icon in the Launcher. Your C:\ drive will appear in your Places menu for easy access, and you will be able to uninstall Wine from the Ubuntu Software Center.

Running Applications

To run an application, simply double-click on the install .exe file. Once installed, the program should appear in your menu under Applications > Wine.

TIP   You can find even more about Wine from the Ubuntu perspective at https://help.ubuntu.com/community/Wine.

Installing Software from PPAs

Sometimes software is not available in the Ubuntu repositories; perhaps it is too new, perhaps there is a new version available, or perhaps it is software that no one has had the opportunity to build and get approved for inclusion in the Ubuntu repositories. You can often find this software in a Personal Package Archive, or PPA. The main Launchpad page for PPAs says, "Personal Package Archives (PPA) allow you to upload Ubuntu source packages to be built and published as an apt repository by Launchpad" (see https://launchpad.net/ubuntu/+ppas).

In short, a PPA is a small repository that contains software that is not found in the main Ubuntu repositories, perhaps for one of the reasons listed earlier or for other reasons. If a software package or version you want to install is not available from the main Ubuntu repositories, use your Web browser to search the main Launchpad site for the software and see if a PPA exists.

TIP   **Be Careful!**
Some PPAs are created for development or for beta or even alpha testing. They are not guaranteed to include stable or well-tested software. Use at your own risk.

For our example, we install a bleeding-edge testing version of LibreOffice. Unless you absolutely need something offered from a PPA, we suggest you stick with packages from the Ubuntu repositories.

To add the PPA to your system, make a note of its location from the specific PPA's Web page in Launchpad. In this case, the PPA is at ppa:libreoffice/ppa, as seen in Figure 4-10.

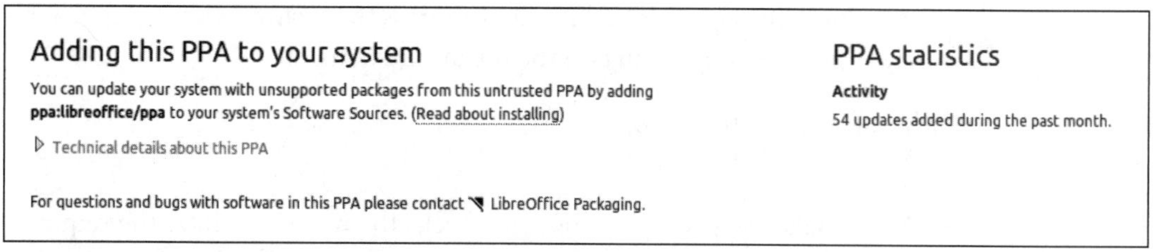

Adding this PPA to your system

You can update your system with unsupported packages from this untrusted PPA by adding **ppa:libreoffice/ppa** to your system's Software Sources. (Read about installing)

▷ Technical details about this PPA

For questions and bugs with software in this PPA please contact ✎ LibreOffice Packaging.

PPA statistics

Activity

54 updates added during the past month.

Figure 4-10 You can find technical details and installation instructions on all PPA pages.

The easiest way to add the PPA is to use the Terminal. Enter the following at the command line to add the LibreOffice PPA and to update your package manager's listing.

```
$ sudo add-apt-repository ppa:libreoffice/ppa
$ sudo apt-get update
```

Then, you can access the contents of the PPA from your preferred package manager: Ubuntu Software Center, Synaptic, the command line, and so on.

Compiling Software from Source

Some software cannot be found in any repository. The traditional way of installing software on Linux works just as well on Ubuntu. Download your software and put it in an otherwise empty directory. Sometimes, it will include installation instructions. If so, follow them. Most instructions will be the same as those listed here.

Before you can install a source code package, it must be compiled into a binary that your computer can run. For that, you need to install some packages that are not included by default. All you should need is included as a dependency of one package. Install it, and you should be all set.

```
$ sudo apt-get install build-essential
```

Next, browse to the directory where you placed the downloaded source code. It was most likely provided as a compressed archive, with a filename extension like tar.gz or tar.bz2. Decompress the archive with the appropriate command, depending on the filename extension:

```
$ tar -xvf file.tar.gz
$ tar -xvf file.tar.bz2
```

Next, make the package. This step checks to ensure you have the required dependencies installed and will tell you if you don't—if not, you need to install them separately, hopefully using Synaptic or via the command line with apt. It will also build the package from source code into something installable.

```
$ make
```

Next, install the package. The traditional way is to use:

```
$ sudo make install
```

And although this works, there is a better method. Using make install will install the package, but it will not use your package manager. If you ever want to remove the package from your system, it can be quite a chore to figure out how. Instead, install the following:

```
$ sudo apt-get install checkinstall
```

and use it to install the software, which, like any software installed from an official repository, cannot be removed using your package manager.

```
$ sudo checkinstall
```

Summary

In this chapter we looked at a variety of advanced subjects related to running and managing your Ubuntu system. Installation, removal, and upgrade of software using the Ubuntu Software Center and other options were discussed. We also looked at the installation and use of several different types of hardware devices. We perused some of the methods of accessing remote files and mentioned the powerful Ubuntu terminal and the need for learning how to back up your data regularly. Finally, we looked at a possibility of running certain programs written for Microsoft Windows under Ubuntu and even compiling software from source code.

CHAPTER 5

Finding and Installing Ubuntu Applications

- Using Ubuntu Software Center
- Learning Terminology and Foundations
- Using Synaptic
- Useful Software Packages to Explore
- Playing to Learn with Educational Programs
- Summary

IN ADDITION TO THOSE INSTALLED BY DEFAULT, Ubuntu offers a wealth of other applications to help you make the most of your computer. Different people use their computers in different ways, and it is for that reason that we wanted to help you discover how to enable your Ubuntu computer to do even more.

Chapter 3 includes a brief introduction to the Ubuntu Software Center as one way to install or remove software. Here we cover this and other methods as well. Work done using one tool to add or remove software is recognized by the related tools, so it is okay to mix and match which ones you use.

Additionally, we show you just a few of the thousands of additional applications that you can install on your Ubuntu system. Each section showcases one application, starting with the name of the package you need to install and what Windows/OS X equivalents might exist.

Using Ubuntu Software Center

Like other tools discussed later in this chapter, Ubuntu Software Center installs software from the online Ubuntu software repositories.

To launch Ubuntu Software Center, click the Dash Home icon in the launcher at the left of the desktop. In the search box at the top of the menu that appears, type *Ubuntu* and the search will begin automatically. Click the Ubuntu Software Center icon that appears in the box. When it is run for the first time, and occasionally afterward, it will take a few moments to initialize itself and the list of available and installed applications. Once this is complete, you will see the main screen shown in Figure 5-1.

We introduced the basics of the Ubuntu Software Center earlier in Chapter 3. Let's look at some of the other aspects now.

Ubuntu Software Center Account

Some features require an Ubuntu Software Center account, mainly those that require money or allow tracking (which will automatically reinstall

Figure 5-1 Ubuntu Software Center main screen

previous purchases). When required, it is noted in the section. This account is the same as the Ubuntu Single Sign-On account that is required for using Ubuntu One and other Ubuntu services that are available online like the Launchpad bug tracker described in Chapter 9. If a feature requires an account, a window will pop up to make signing up simple, as in Figure 5-2.

Recommendations

Click Turn On Recommendations at the bottom of the Ubuntu Software Center window (Figure 5-1) to allow the program to send nonidentifying information about the software you have already installed. This information is used to generate suggestions for you based on statistical trends. The

Figure 5-2 Create an Ubuntu Software Center account or sign in.

software you have installed is compared to the software other people have installed on their machines as recorded in an anonymous database, and suggestions are given to you. This works kind of like Amazon's "people who like *the book you are looking at now* also like . . ." feature and is quite convenient. Although the database used for this feature is anonymous, people who care deeply about their privacy and don't want to take chances are not forced to use it; this is why you must choose to turn it on rather than it being enabled by default.

You need to create an Ubuntu Software Center account to use this feature.

Sorting

Click a category name at the left of the Ubuntu Software Center window to sort the listed software by category. Some categories are further broken down into smaller subcategories, such as the Games listing shown in Figure 5-3. Note that books and magazines are now available instantly in their digital format via the center.

You can also sort packages from the top of the window using the buttons, as in Figure 5-4. Click the arrow next to All Software or Installed to limit

Figure 5-3 Many sorts of games are available.

Figure 5-4 More about software sources coming up

what is displayed by whether it is provided by the Ubuntu community, by Canonical partners, or available only for purchase. Click the All Software or Installed buttons to alternately show all available packages or only those currently on your machine. Click History to list all changes, installations, updates, and removals of software that have occurred on your machine.

Searching

Type search terms in the search box at the upper right to find related software. The search is a live search, meaning that the results are updated as you type; you do not have to hit Enter first, and you can change the terms and get new results instantly, as in Figure 5-5.

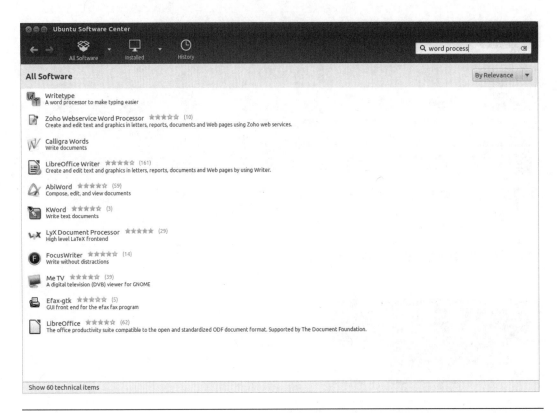

Figure 5-5 It was not necessary to finish typing "word processing" to get results.

Learning More about a Package and Installing It

Click on a title to learn more about it (Figure 5-6). Notice the line that says Free at the left (more on that in the next section) and has an Install button on the right. Click Install to install the software.

At the bottom of the information section is a link titled Developer Web Site, which opens the software developer's Web site, giving you easy access to more information to assist your decision. Further information about a package—the specific version of the package, its size and license, and more—is included below this and just above the Reviews section.

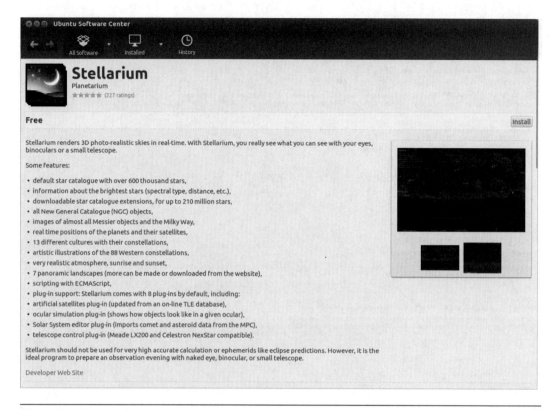

Figure 5-6 Most package listings include screenshots and valuable information.

Scroll down to read reviews and ratings, if any have been posted for the package (Figure 5-7). You can sort the reviews using the drop down boxes just above the first review.

No-Cost Software

Most of the software available from the Ubuntu Software Center is free, as in it will not cost you anything to download and install it (and is also free in the licensing sense as well). These are marked Free, like Stellarium is in Figure 5-6. You pay nothing for this software and it is completely legal for you to copy it, use it, share it, and so on.

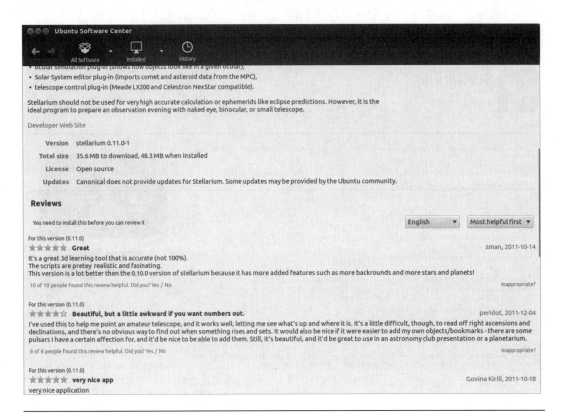

Figure 5-7 Users tend to be honest in their software reviews.

Software for Purchase

Sort using the For Purchase category (Figure 5-4) to display only the packages that require payment. Most of these are digital versions of books and magazines, although some professional software packages are also available, such as games and utilities offered by Canonical partners (Figure 5-8). These are marked differently, with a price in the spot where others are marked Free and a Buy button where others are marked Install. Also, many of these come with proprietary software licenses, so do not assume you can legally share packages you pay for.

You need to create an Ubuntu Software Center account to use this feature.

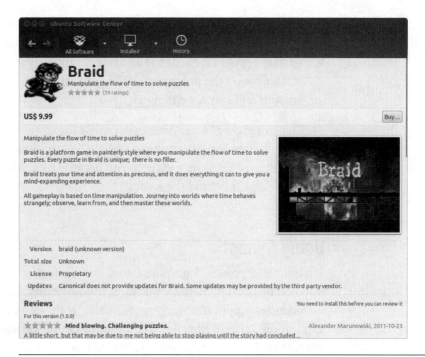

Figure 5-8 Compare this package information screen with Figure 5-6.

Learning Terminology and Foundations

You might want to know a few terms before we continue. These are words used to describe how the software gets installed on your machine as well as how the system works.

- **APT:** Advanced Package Tool, or APT, describes the entire system of online repositories and the parts that download them and install them. This is not highly visible when using graphic interface–based systems like Ubuntu Software Center but very clear when using command-line tools like apt-get, which is described in greater depth in Chapter 8. Whether you use a graphical interface or the command line to deal with Ubuntu software packages, APT is at work.

- **Repositories or software channels:** In the Ubuntu world, these giant online warehouses of software are divided between official Ubuntu repositories and unofficial ones.

- **Packages:** Applications are stored in packages that not only describe the program you want to install but also tell your package manager what the program needs to run and how to safely install and uninstall it. This makes the process of dealing with software dependencies smooth and easy for end users.

- **Dependencies:** Dependencies comprise the software that is needed as a foundation for other software to run. For example, APT is needed for Ubuntu Software Center to run because APT takes care of many of the details behind the scenes.

Using Synaptic

Synaptic is a powerful graphical tool for managing packages. It is not installed by default. While Ubuntu Software Center deals with packages that contain applications, Synaptic deals with all packages, including applications, system libraries, and other pieces of software. Changing the system on this level is more complicated but also allows more detailed control. For instance, you can choose to install a specific library if you need it for a program that is not available in a package format.

TIP   **What's a Library?**
In this context, a library is a collection of software functions that may be useful to more than one program. This collection is put into a separate package to save space by not forcing multiple programs to include the same code but instead simply refer to the library when a certain function the library contains is needed. It also makes updates easier, such as when a security issue is fixed, because the programming code may be changed in one place while benefiting all programs that use the function. Libraries streamline software support to be more efficient.

Synaptic may be installed from the Ubuntu Software Center and then found by searching in the Dash for Synaptic Package Manager. Launch it and you will see the main window, as shown in Figure 5-9.

TIP   **What's in a Name?**
Why the name Synaptic? *Synaptic* is a play on words based on your brain's synapses and the word APT.

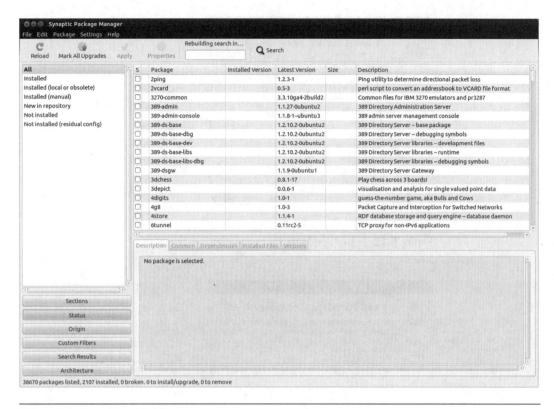

Figure 5-9 Synaptic main window

Installing a Package

As with Ubuntu Software Center, installing packages with Synaptic is fairly easy. After you find the package you wish to install, click the checkbox to the right of the name of the package and select Mark for Installation. A dialog box may pop up (Figure 5-10) showing you what dependencies need to be installed—if any—which you can accept by clicking the Mark button. After you have selected all the packages you wish to install, click Apply on the Synaptic toolbar to begin installation.

Removing a Package

To remove a package, click on the box next to the name of an installed package, and choose Mark for Removal. As with installing a package, you may be asked to mark additional packages for removal (Figure 5-11).

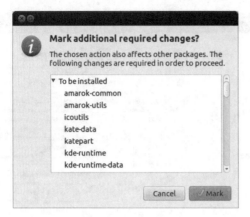

Figure 5-10 Pop-up on Mark for Installation

Figure 5-11 Pop-up on Mark for Removal

These are generally packages that depend on the presence of the main package you are marking for removal. If you wish to remove all the configuration files too, choose Mark for Complete Removal. After you have selected the packages you wish to remove, click Apply on the toolbar to start the process of removing the package.

Finding That Package

So you are looking for a package but don't know where to start? The fastest and easiest way is to enter a word in the Quick Search box at the top center of the Synaptic window. You can also click the Search button on the toolbar. By default, the regular search looks at both the package name and the description, but it can also search just by name or a number of other fields.

If you know what section the package is in, select it in the left pane (you may need to go back to the Sections pane). Select the button in the lower left labeled Sections, and browse through the packages in that section.

In addition to Sections, other package listing and sorting options are worth exploring. You can access them using the buttons at the bottom left of the Synaptic window. Status lets you sort according to installation status. Origin sorts according to the repository from which the software was installed (or no repository for manually installed software; see the section later in this chapter on installing software that is not in a repository). You can even make custom filters to aid your search.

Useful Software Packages to Explore

The software discussed in this section of the chapter is not installed by default but is known to be useful and well respected. These are given here as recommendations to help those who have specific needs narrow their search for programs that meet their requirements.

Creating Graphics with GIMP and Inkscape

GIMP

Package name: gimp
Windows equivalent: Adobe Photoshop or GIMP

The GNU Image Manipulation Program, affectionately known as GIMP to its friends, is a powerful graphics package. GIMP provides a comprehensive range of functionality for creating different types of graphics. It includes tools for selecting, drawing, paths, masks, filters, effects, and more. It also includes a range of templates for different types of media such as Web banners, different paper sizes, video frames, CD covers, floppy disk labels, and even toilet paper. Yes, toilet paper.

Unlike Adobe Photoshop, GIMP does not place all of its windows inside a single large window; instead, GIMP has a number of separate child windows. This can be a little confusing at first for new users—especially those used to Photoshop. To get you started, let's run through a simple session in GIMP.

An Example   Start GIMP by searching for it in the Dash.

When GIMP loads, you will see a collection of different windows, as shown in Figure 5-12.

Close the Tip of the Day window, and you are left with two other windows. The one on the left in the screenshot is the main tool palette. This window

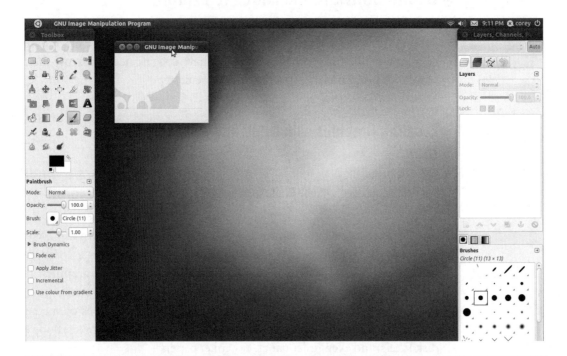

Figure 5-12 GIMP does not put everything in one window like Adobe Photoshop.

provides you with a range of different tools that can be used to create your images. The window on the right provides details of layers, brushes, and other information. GIMP provides a huge range of different windows that are used for different things, and these are just two of them.

To create a new image, click File > New. The window shown in Figure 5-13 will appear.

The easiest way to get started is to select one of the many templates. Click the Template combo box and select 640 × 480. If you click the Advanced Options expander, you can also select whether to use RGB or grayscale with the Colorspace box. You can also choose a background fill color or having a transparent background.

Click OK, and you will see your new image window (Figure 5-14).

To work on your image, use the tool palette to select which tool you want to use on the new image window. Each time you click on a tool in the palette, you see options for the tool appear at the bottom half of the palette window.

When you click the button that looks like an A in the toolbox, it selects the text tool. At the bottom of the toolbox, you will see the different options. Click the Font button that looks like an uppercase and a lowercase case A (like Aa) and select the Sans Bold font. Now click the up arrow on the Size box, and select the size as 60 px. Move your mouse over to the empty

Figure 5-13 Lots of templates are available, including one for toilet paper!

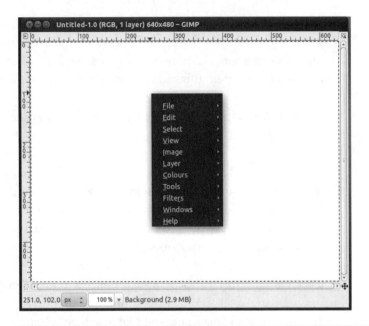

Figure 5-14 Use the right mouse button on the image to access lots of GIMP options and features.

image window, and you will see the mouse pointer change to a text carat. Click in the image, and a box pops up in which you can enter the text to add to the image. Type in *Ubuntu*. With the text entry still open, click the up arrow on the Size box so the text fills most of the window. As you can see, you can adjust the text while it is in the image. When you are happy with the formatting, click Close on the text entry box. Your image should look a little like Figure 5-15.

Now in the toolbox, click the button that has a cross with an arrow on each end. You can use this tool to move the text around. Click the black text, and move the mouse.

Let's now add an effect filter. GIMP comes with a range of different filters built in. You can access these by right-clicking the image and selecting the Filters submenu.

For our image, right-click the image and select Filters > Blur > Gaussian Blur. In the Horizontal and Vertical boxes, select 5 as the value. Click OK,

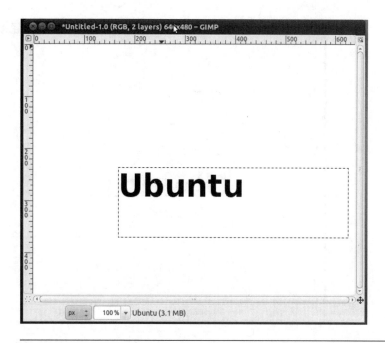

Figure 5-15 Ubuntu comes with a range of attractive fonts for use in your images.

and the blur is applied to your text. Anything in GIMP can be undone by clicking Edit > Undo or typing Ctrl-Z. Your image should now look like Figure 5-16. Now we are going to create another layer and put some text over our blurred text to create an interesting effect. If the Layers window isn't open yet, open it with Windows > Dockable Dialogues > Layers. The Layers window will now appear.

Layers are like clear plastic sheets that can be stacked on top of each other. They allow you to create some imagery on one layer and then create another layer on top with some other imagery. When combined, layers can create complex-looking images that are easily editable because you can edit layers individually. Currently, our blurred text is one layer. We can add a new layer by clicking the paper icon in the Layers dialog box. Another window appears to configure the layer. The defaults are fine (a transparent layer the size of your image), so click OK.

Now double-click the black color chip in the toolbox window and select a light color. You can do this by moving the mouse in the color range and

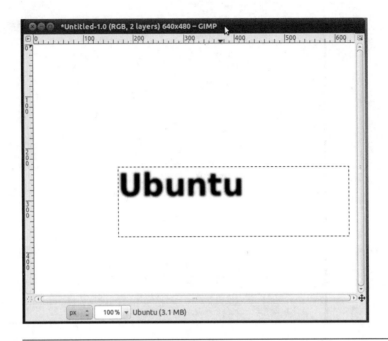

Figure 5-16 Several filters and effects are bundled with GIMP in Ubuntu.

then clicking OK when you find a color you like. Now click the text button from the palette and again add the *Ubuntu* text. When the text is added, it will be the same size as before. Now use the move tool and position it over the blurred text. Now you have the word "Ubuntu" with a healthy glow, as shown in Figure 5-17!

The final step is to crop the image to remove the unused space. Click Tools > Transform Tools > Crop, and use the mouse to draw around the Ubuntu word. You can click in the regions near the corners of the selection to adjust the selection more precisely. Click inside the selection, and the image will be cropped. To save your work, click File > Save, and enter a file-name. You can use the Select File Type expander to select from one of the many different file formats.

Further Resources   A great start is GIMP's own help, which is not installed by default, but if you are on the Internet, the help viewer will download it automatically. You can also install it by searching for gimp

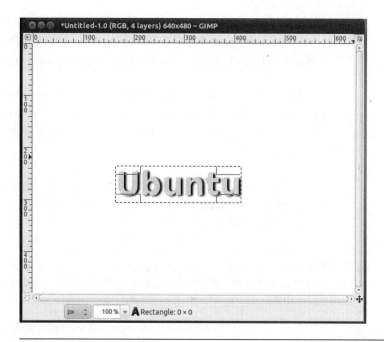

Figure 5-17 Combining steps as we have done can result in interesting effects such as this.

help in the Software Center. The GIMP's own Web site at www.gimp.org has all the help plus tutorials and more.

Inkscape

Package name: inkscape
Windows/OS X equivalents: Adobe Illustrator, Inkscape, Macromedia Freehand

Inkscape is also a drawing and graphic creation tool, much like GIMP, but one that has a slightly different focus. Unlike GIMP, which works with raster graphics, Inkscape is a vector drawing tool. This means rather than a grid of pixels, each assigned a color, drawings are mathematically described using angles and arbitrary units.

To get started with Inkscape, launch it by searching for it in the Dash, and very shortly you will see the default window with the basic canvas of either Letter or A4 depending on where in the world you live. At the top of the screen, below the menus, are three sets of toolbars. The topmost contains common tools like save and zoom, the second a series of snapping options, and the third is changeable depending on the tool selected.

All the tools are listed on the left-hand side of the menu, starting with the selection tool and running down to the eyedropper or paint color selector tool. Let's get started by drawing a simple shape and coloring it in (Figure 5-18).

First, select the rectangle tool on the left, just below the zoom icon. Draw a rectangle anywhere on the screen. Now let's change the color of the fill and outside line or stroke.

NOTE With any of the drawing tools, the Shift key will cause objects to grow from the center of where you clicked and Ctrl will allow you to constrain dimensions and rotation.

With your rectangle still selected, go to the Object menu and choose Fill and Stroke. Over on the right, you will see the window appear, with three different tabs: Fill, Stroke Paint, and Stroke Style. Let's fill that rectangle with a gradient from orange to white. Immediately below the Fill tab, change from Flat color to Linear Gradient (Figure 5-19).

Look back at your rectangle and see the gradient and a new line running horizontally across the rectangle. Moving either the square or the circle allows you to define where the gradient starts and stops. To change the colors, click the Edit... button. Once the Edit dialog is up, each end of the gradient is called a stop and can be edited separately (Figure 5-20).

Now that we have a rectangle, let's add some text to our image. Select the Text tool, which is right near the bottom on the left, and click anywhere. A cursor appears, and you can start typing. Type "Ubuntu," and then we are going to change the color and size of the text. Let's

Figure 5-18
Inkscape's toolbar

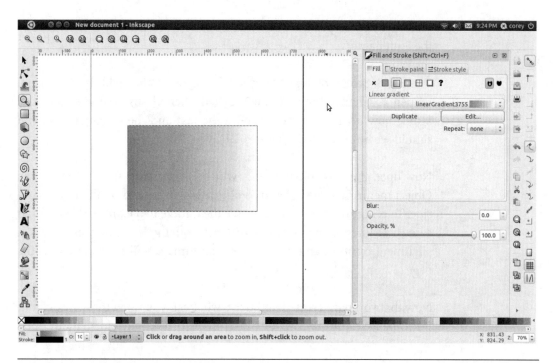

Figure 5-19 Your rectangle, now with gradient-filled goodness

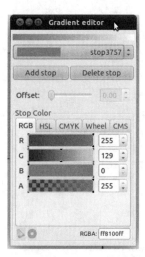

Figure 5-20 Gradient editing dialog

make the text 56 points, which can be selected in the upper right, beside the Font name.

The Fill & Stroke dialog should still be open on the right, but if it isn't, reopen it. Change the text color to Red, then choose the selection tool again. Now drag a box around both the text and the rectangle, and you should see both selected (Figure 5-21).

Now open the Alignment dialog, which is right near the bottom of the Object menu. Like the Fill and Stroke dialog, it appears on the right-hand side. To center the text in the box, see the middle two icons with a line and some blue lines on the side of them. Click both the Horizontal and Vertical alignment options, and both the text and image will be centered on the page (Figure 5-22).

Now that you have created an image, what can you do with it? By default, Inkscape saves in the SVG or Scalable Vector Graphics format, an open

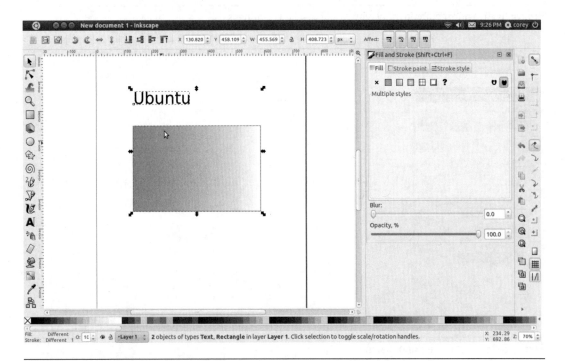

Figure 5-21 Text and rectangle selected

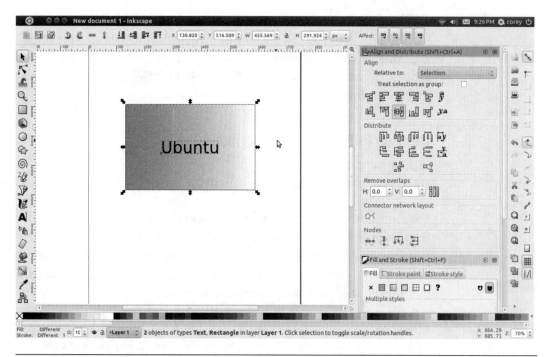

Figure 5-22 Your final drawing

standard for vector graphics. If you want to take your work elsewhere for showing on another computer or printing, Inkscape can also save into PDF format, although if you choose to do so, make certain you also save a copy as an SVG so you can edit the image later if you wish. Both SVG and PDF are options in the Save dialog. One key advantage for PDF is that it embeds fonts and graphics, meaning your image looks the same on nearly any computer you show it on. You can also export your image as a PNG for embedding in a text document or uploading to the Web, although many modern Web browsers such as Firefox and Chrome can display SVG directly, although most don't support the full SVG standard. To export, go to File > Export, which allows you to choose to export just the objects selected, the whole document, or some portion.

Hopefully, you have seen just how powerful Inkscape can be. There are many more things you can do with Inkscape, so play around with the various options, dialogs, and shapes.

Further Resources A good start is always Inkscape's own help, which is in SVG format, so you can see how the original authors created the tutorials. Inkscape's Web site at http://inkscape.org has some great tutorials and articles. If you want a book, Tav Bah's *Inkscape: Guide to Vector Drawing Program, Third Edition*, is a good place to start.

Desktop Publishing with Scribus

Package name: scribus
Windows equivalents: Adobe InDesign, Scribus

For more powerful document creation than LibreOffice can allow, Scribus is just the ticket. A desktop publishing application, Scribus is built for designing and laying out documents of various sizes and sorts. As such, it makes a few different assumptions that might catch you up if you are used to using LibreOffice to create your documents.

When you first launch Scribus, it asks you what kind of document you want to create or if you want to open an existing document. Let's create a one-page document and take Scribus for a spin (Figure 5-23).

The first thing to remember about Scribus is that as a desktop publishing program, it is not designed for the direct editing of images and text. You

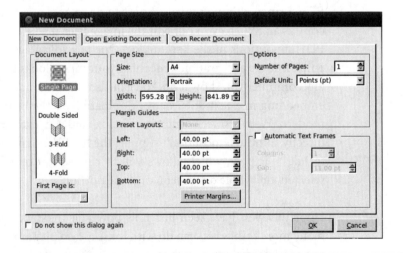

Figure 5-23 Scribus's opening dialog with lots of options

edit and create your images in applications like GIMP or Inkscape and your text in word processors like LibreOffice and then import them.

For starters, let's create a pair of text frames. For our example, we are using a document titled Welcome_to_Ubuntu.odt. To create a text frame, you need to use the Insert Text Frame tool, which can be found near the middle of the toolbar. After you draw the text frame, you need to add text to it. Right-click on the frame and choose Get Text. A dialog very similar to the Open dialog appears. Choose the Welcome_to_Ubuntu.odt file, and then select OK. You will be asked a few options; for now, accept the defaults. You should see the text appear on the screen (Figure 5-24).

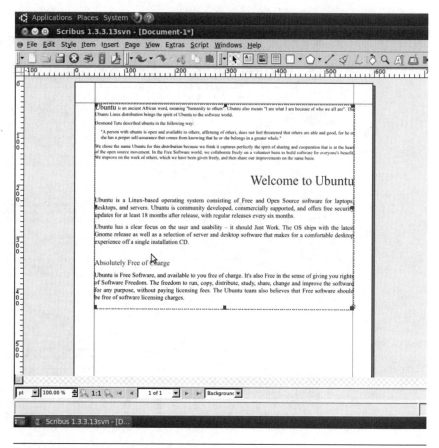

Figure 5-24 The imported text in a frame

NOTE   Scribus currently cannot import Microsoft Word documents, so you need to open them in LibreOffice.org and convert them to .odt files so Scribus can import them.

But as you can see, the text overflows the frame. In order for the rest of the text to show up, you need to create another text frame and then link the two, allowing the overflow to appear in the second frame. Go up to the toolbar again, select the Insert Text Frame, and draw another frame roughly on the bottom of the page. Then select the first frame and choose the Link Text Frames icon on the toolbar, which looks like two columns with an arrow between them. After you have selected that, click on the second text box and you should see an arrow appear and, more importantly, your text will now flow from one frame to the next (Figure 5-25).

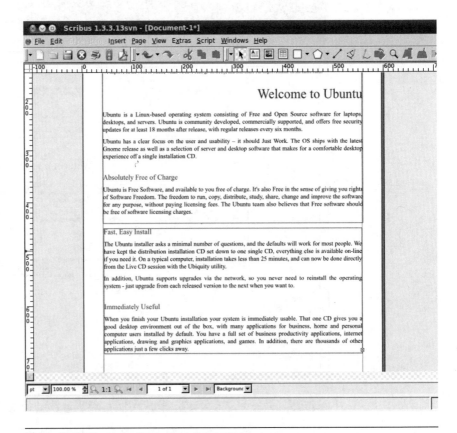

Figure 5-25 Text now flows from frame to frame.

Next let's insert an image at the bottom of the screen. As with text, you need to create an image frame, then add the image to that frame. Draw the image frame below the two text frames, and then right-click and choose Get Image. Just as with the text import, choose your file, this time an image file, in the Open dialog, and it will appear in the frame. Let's choose the Ubuntu logo, under the Logo folder in Example Content. It will appear in your image frame (Figure 5-26).

NOTE   Scribus can import gif, jpg, png, xpm, psd, tiff, eps, and pdf. It cannot yet import GIMP's XCF, so you will need to save any images you create in the GIMP in one of the supported formats.

Now that you have added some text and an image, let's export to PDF so you can share your creation with the world. On the toolbar near the left-hand

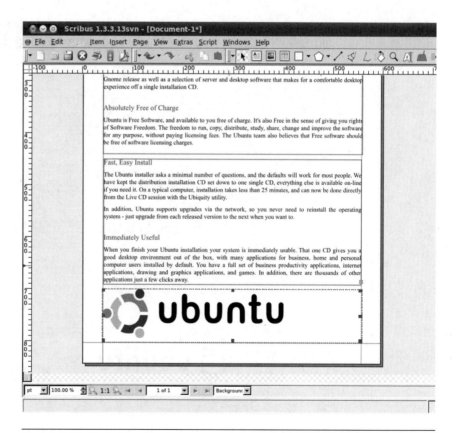

Figure 5-26 Your document with an image added

edge, you will see the PDF logo, just to the left of the traffic light icon. Select that, and don't worry about the error about the DPI of the image. Select Ignore Errors, and you will see a large dialog with many options for embedding fonts and the like. Don't worry too much about them right now, as the document you have created isn't that complicated. Choose a good name for your document, and then save it to your Documents folder. Now let's take a look at your creation in the Document Viewer. Open the File Manager and load your new document (Figure 5-27).

Now let's go back to Scribus and save the image in Scribus's own SLA format so that you can edit it later if you wish. Enter the name you chose for the PDF name and save it in the Documents folder as well. You have now created your first document in Scribus. There is a lot more to explore, so go and try things out. Just remember to save every now and again.

Figure 5-27 Your document as a PDF

Further Resources   As always, Scribus's own help is a great place to start. The Scribus Web site at www.scribus.net has a help wiki, further documentation, and more. There is also an official book, which isn't out as of this writing but should be very shortly. Information about it can also be found on the Scribus Web site.

Creating Music with Jokosher

Package name: jokosher
Windows/OS X equivalents: Garage Band

Musicians abound in the Ubuntu community and the wider world, but until Jokosher came along, there wasn't an easy-to-use and simple program for creating that music. Founded by Ubuntu's own Jono Bacon and named after a kosher joke about the food that is Jono's name, Jokosher makes creating music or other audio recordings a breeze.

To get started in Jokosher, you first need to create a project to hold the various audio tracks that make up the end file. For our basic project, we are going to take two of the free culture showcase projects that ship with Ubuntu and combine them together. Click on the Create a New Project button in the welcome screen (Figure 5-28) and then on the next window, enter in Ubuntu combination into the Project Name field.

Figure 5-28 Jokosher's welcome window

NOTE   Jokosher is a nondestructive editor, which means that it doesn't edit the files you add directly; rather, it stores the edits and applies them separately.

Once that is open, you will see a largely blank screen and you need to fill that with sound files. Choose Add Audio File on the upper toolbar and type in /usr/share/example-content in the location bar. Select one of two files in the Ubuntu Free Culture Showcase folder. After that is loaded, select Add Audio File again and select the other audio files. You should see something like in Figure 5-29.

Now that we have both files loaded, let's create some sweet solos so that you can only hear one of the two files. To create a cut in the audio file, simply double-click wherever you want your cut. So anywhere in the How Fast.ogg file, double-click and then drag the second piece to the left.

This will create a very abrupt break in the music, so to make it more pleasing, let's create a pair of fades on either side. While holding the shift key down, click near the end of the first part and drag to the end. Release the mouse and you should see a pair of 100% boxes. Click and drag the right-

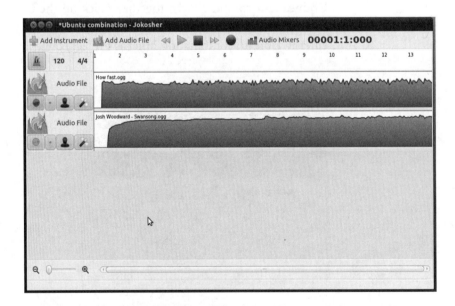

Figure 5-29 The audio files are loaded.

most one down to the bottom where it will read 0%. After you are done, you should have something like Figure 5-30.

Now let's export that file so you can share your awesome creation with your friends. Go to File > Mixdown Project and in the Mixdown Project, create a new profile by clicking the plus icon in the upper right. Name is exported and then click ok. Now you need to add an action, in this case export, so click on the lower right-most plus icon. Select Export File and then select Add Action. Now we need to configure the file name, type of audio file, and where you are going to save it to. Select Export File on the list and click the little configure icon in the lower right, it looks like a wrench and screwdriver. Name your file Ubuntu Combination and then Save it as a FLAC file. In the location bar, click the folder icon and choose your music folder. After you're done, it should look like Figure 5-31. Now click the Mixdown button and your file is created. Go to your Music folder and hit play for the fun to begin.

We have just scratched the surface with Jokosher. We didn't get into adding live instruments and recording them directly, which is where Jokosher

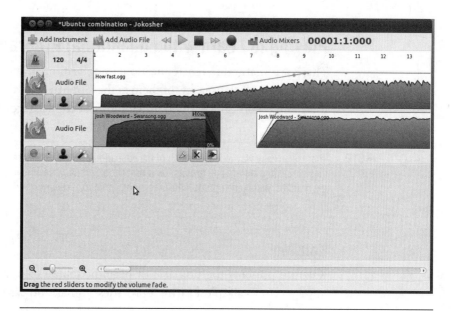

Figure 5-30 Adding some fades and cuts

Figure 5-31 Naming your file and exporting to the right place is easy.

really shines. But we did get a taste of the power of Jokosher even with a few simple audio files that come with Ubuntu. Go out and have fun.

Further Resources   As always, Jokosher's own help is a great place to start. The Jokosher Web site at www.jokosher.org has a help wiki, further documentation, and more.

Playing to Learn with Educational Programs

There are many different educational applications available on Ubuntu. Let's take a look at just a few of them in the Ubuntu Software Center. Most of these and others can be found under the Education category in the center.

NOTE   There is an easy way to install much of the educational software via preselected package bundles aimed at different age groups, be it preschool, primary, secondary, or tertiary. To install the bundles, install the ubuntu-edu-preschool, -primary, -secondary, or -tertiary package.

Kalzium

Kalzium presents the pinnacle of periodic table exploration for users of any ages. In its simplest form, it provides a quick and easy reference to the periodic table. Kalzium includes 105 of the naturally occurring elements, many of which are accompanied by sample pictures. If the user hovers the mouse pointer over an element symbol in the periodic table, a balloon appears showing the selected element's name, atomic number, and mass (Figure 5-32).

For more advanced users, Kalzium provides a fascinating way to explore the periodic table. Using the left-hand panel, users have access to the timeline, boiling point, and melting point sliders. When users move these sliders, the elements on the periodic table change color according to their dates of discovery, boiling points, or melting points respectively. Users can then start to see patterns emerging in the periodic table right in front of their eyes.

As well as presenting the basic information, Kalzium provides very advanced statistics on each of the 105 elements present.

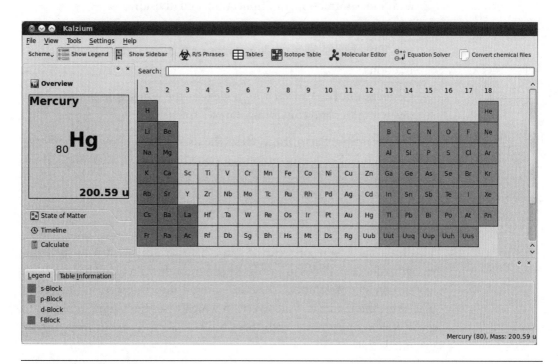

Figure 5-32 Kalzium

Kanagram

Kanagram is a simple package that messes up the letters of a word to create an anagram that children must then unscramble. The package comes with hints, a cheat feature that reveals the word, and built-in word lists, which can be extended.

KBruch

KBruch is a math program to help students practice the use of fractions. It comes with four distinct modes of play.

- **Fraction Task:** In this exercise, the user is given a fraction sum that must be solved by adding the numerator and denominator. The difficulty of the sum can be changed by the user, who has control over the number of fractions to use, the maximum size of the main denominator, and the mathematical operations to use, such as addition, subtraction, multiplication, and division.

- **Comparison:** This exercise is designed to test the user's understanding of fraction sizes by making him or her compare two given fractions.

- **Conversion:** The Conversion mode tests the user's skills at taking a given number and converting it into a fraction.

- **Factorization:** Factorization tests the user in calculating the factors of a given number. Factorization is a key skill in using and manipulating fractions.

KHangman

This modern version of a classic game helps children learn to spell and recognize letter patterns in words. KHangman shows a blank base to start; as the user chooses letters, they are entered into the word if correct or placed on the tries list if incorrect, in which case the hangman begins to grow. KHangman comes with three built-in word lists, but these can be extended easily.

Kig

For people wishing to learn about geometrical construction in mathematics, Kig is a must. It is an extremely powerful package but very simple to use. Kig allows users to create complex geometrical abstractions from over thirty simple tools, such as points, parallel and perpendicular lines, arcs, bisectors, circles, and hyperbola (Figure 5-33). When creating abstractions, Kig uses other lines and points already on the diagram to lock onto, making it easy to achieve high precision.

Kig also includes some testing tools. Once a geometrical diagram has been drawn, it is often required to prove a concept by showing that two lines are indeed parallel or perpendicular. Kig offers these tools and more in an easy-to-use manner. Just clicking on the tool prompts the user to choose the item to test against. Then, each time the user hovers over another item while moving the cursor around, Kig will pop up with a message to tell whether or not it satisfies the test case.

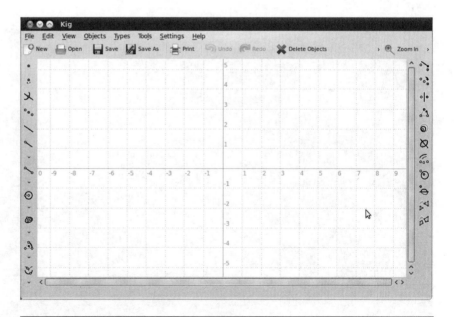

Figure 5-33 Kig

KmPlot

KmPlot is a mathematical function–graphing program for Edubuntu. The package has a powerful expression parser built in and can plot different functions simultaneously and combine their function terms to build more complex mathematical functions. KmPlot also supports functions with parameters and functions in polar coordinates. KmPlot can create graphs to a very high precision, making it excellent for teaching purposes.

Stellarium

With a default catalog of over 600,000 stars, Stellarium is a powerful planetarium designed to show you exactly what you would see with the naked eye, binoculars, or telescope.

In keeping with the multicultural nature of Ubuntu and Open Source, Stellarium can show you not only the constellations from the Greek and Roman traditions (Figure 5-34) but also those of other "sky cultures," as

Figure 5-34 Stellarium

Stellarium describes them, such as the various Chinese, Ancient Egyptian, and Polynesian traditions.

Stellarium is even capable of driving a dome projector, like you would see at a large-scale, purpose-built planetarium as well as controlling a wide variety of telescopes directly.

KTouch

In this day and age, typing is an everyday occurrence for most people. KTouch is a tutor that gives help and support to those wishing to learn the art of touch typing. With fifteen levels and automatic level progression, KTouch is a fairly advanced tutor program, offering statistics and alternative language options, too.

KTurtle

KTurtle is a Logo programming language interpreter for Edubuntu. The Logo programming language is very easy to learn, and thus young children can use it. A unique quality of Logo is that the commands or instructions can be translated, so the user can program in his or her native language. This makes Logo ideal for teaching children the basics of programming, mathematics, and geometry. One of the reasons many children warm to Logo is that the programmable icon is a small turtle, which can be moved around the screen with simple commands and can be programmed to draw objects (Figure 5-35).

By typing in commands such as `turnleft 90`, `forward 4`, children are using a language native to themselves while also learning procedural logic. KTurtle can even handle simple subroutines, so it's easy to extend the programming onward and upward.

With the introduction of KDE 4, Edubuntu includes a group of brand new educational packages. Next is a brief summary of each new application.

Marble

Marble, the desktop globe, is a virtual globe and world atlas, which can be utilized to learn more about the Earth. With the ability to pan and zoom,

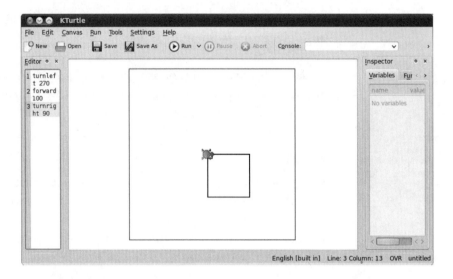

Figure 5-35 KTurtle

click on a label to open a corresponding Wikipedia article, and view the globe and maps with various projections, Marble is a welcome addition to Edubuntu's educational packages.

Parley

Parley, the digital flash card, allows you to easily remember things utilizing the spaced repetition learning method, otherwise known as flash cards. Features include different testing types, fast and easy setup, multiple languages, the ability to share and download flash cards, and much more.

Step

Step is an interactive physics simulator that allows you not only to learn but to feel how physics works. By placing bodies on the scene and adding some forces such as gravity or springs, you can simulate the law of physics, and Step will show you how your scene evolves.

Blinken

Blinken takes you back, back to the 1970s, as a digital version of the famous Simon Says game. Watch the lights, listen to the sounds, and then try to complete the sequence in order. Blinken provides hours of fun with the added benefit of learning.

Others Not on the Education Menu

Some educational applications are not located in the Education menu in the software center. Here are brief descriptions of two of them.

- **Tux Paint:** Tux Paint is a drawing package for younger children. Although geared toward a younger audience, Tux Paint still packs in some of the more advanced features of drawing packages and can draw shapes, paint with different brushes, use a stamp, and add text to the image. The Magic feature allows many of the more advanced tools normally found in full-fledged photo editors to be used, such as smudge, blur, negative, tint, and many more. There is also the facility to save as well as print.

- **GCompris:** GCompris is a set of small educational activities aimed at children between two and ten years old and is translated into over forty languages. Some of the activities are game oriented and at the same time educational. Among the activities, there are tasks to educate children in computer use, algebra, science, geography, reading, and more. More than eighty activities are available in the latest release.

Summary

In this chapter, you learned how to install and use just a few of the additional applications available for Ubuntu. Although this chapter only scratched the surface of what each application can do, you should have enough of an understanding of each to get started with them, and the Further Resources sections should help you become an expert. But beyond what is in this chapter, the vast universe of new programs is available. Go and explore—try out something new. At worst, you will have wasted a few hours, but you might find something that will change your life.

Always remember that there is a wealth of help and documentation available online. If you ever find yourself stuck, take a look at the Ubuntu Web site at www.ubuntu.com or the Ubuntu documentation at http://help.ubuntu.com and make use of the forums, wiki, mailing lists, and IRC channels.

CHAPTER 6

Customizing Ubuntu for Performance, Accessibility, and Fun

- **Unity Terminology**
- **Appearance Tool**
- **MyUnity**
- **Compiz Config Settings Manager**
- **Unity Lenses and Scope**
- **Additional Resources**
- **Summary**

ONE OF THE MOST APPEALING ARGUMENTS FOR the adoption and use of Linux is the fact it can be customized according to personal preferences, and in this chapter we look at the many ways the Unity desktop can be adapted to different users. Unity is a relatively new desktop, so we start by reviewing the terminology for the desktop, then look at the default settings, and various ways to tweak them. Lenses were introduced in the Ubuntu 11.04 release, and now in the 12.04 LTS, a wide variety of Lenses are available. We examine some popular Lenses and how to use them. Different people use their computers in different ways, and for that reason we want to help you discover how to tweak your Unity desktop for your needs.

While tweaking your desktop is a fun way to personalize your desktop experience, we also want to caution you about making changes without understanding what those changes will do. If you are unsure about making those changes, take some time to research the changes you want to make. At the end of this chapter, we give you some more resources to further your understanding about the Unity desktop.

In this chapter, we show you just a few of the Lenses that are available and how you can install them. At the end, we show you the resources to get you started writing those Lenses as you go from novice to superuser. Let's get ready to supercharge your Unity desktop!

Unity Terminology

When the Unity launcher was introduced in the Ubuntu 11.04 release, a number of design goals were set out. The icons needed to be easy to find, running applications needed to be always visible, the focused application needed to be easily accessible, and the interface needed to be touch friendly. The Unity desktop has certainly been met with a mixed range of highly charged emotions from early adopters, and due to their passion and feedback, the desktop and its functionality have improved. Providing user feedback is one of the most important things an Ubuntu user can do for the project. At the end of this chapter, you'll be given a list of resources to get you started on providing the developers with feedback.

In Ubuntu 12.04 Unity desktop are two new Unity Lenses installed by default. These new Lenses, which we talk about later in this chapter, are the home and video Lenses.

Also new to the desktop is the HUD (Heads Up Display) that users can use to search the menus of a focus (active) window or full application. HUD doesn't replace your global menu, but it is a feature that can be accessed by tapping the Alt key.

As we look at the parts that make up the Unity desktop, we also explore the MyUnity tool (Figure 6-1). MyUnity is a third-party tool that allows users to configure and tune their Unity desktops. It also allows users to return to the default desktop settings. To install MyUnity through the software center, you need to click on the Ubuntu Software Center icon located in the launcher. Once the software center opens, type *MyUnity* into the search box and click Install (Figure 6-2).

Figure 6-1 MyUnity tool

Figure 6-2 Installing MyUnity from the software center

You can also install the MyUnity tool from the command line with the command sudo apt-get install myunity.

Following is the list of user interface (UI) terms for the parts of your Unity desktop; numbers 1 to 7 correspond to the numbers in Figure 6-3 and the words in Figure 6-4, number 8 is shown at the top right of Figure 6-5, which also shows the HUD.

1. Windows Tile

2. Application Menu

3. Dash Icon, which opens what is shown in 6-4, including:

   a. Application Lens

   b. File Lens

   c. Music Lens

4. Launcher Icons

5. Workspace Switcher

6. Launcher

7. Trash

8. Indicators

9. HUD

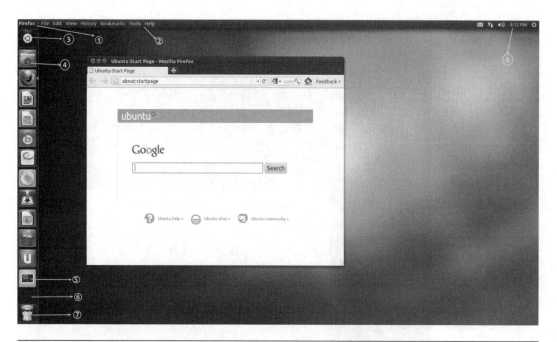

Figure 6-3 Diagram of the Unity Desktop

Figure 6-4 Diagram of the Dash

Figure 6-5 Diagram of the HUD

Now that we have reviewed the terminology for your desktop, let's look at those default settings.

The Ubuntu 12.04 release uses the 3.2.0 kernel and is based on the 3.2.6 upstream stable kernel and Xorg server 1.11.4.

The applications included by default and not necessarily locked to the launcher are Nautilus, Ubuntu Software Center Firefox, Thunderbird, LibreOffice, Rhythmbox, Deja Dup Backup Tool, Gwibber, Empathy,

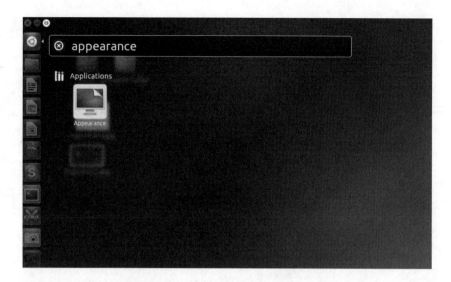

Figure 6-6 Locating the Appearance icon from the Dash

Shotwell, Transmission, Remmina (remote desktop client), GNOME Control Center (system settings), Gedit, Brasero, and Totem.

As mentioned earlier, tweaking your Unity desktop can be done easily with tools like MyUnity, and some tweaks can be made using the Appearance tool. To get to the Appearance tool, tap the Alt key once and the dash will open, in the search box type Appearance, then click on the Appearance icon to open this tool (Figure 6-6).

Appearance Tool

The Appearance tool is available by default and allows users to change the look and behavior of their Unity desktop. It opens to the Look tab (Figure 6-7) and allows you to change the background, theme, and launcher icon size. The Behavior tab (Figure 6-8) allows you to change whether or not the launcher will autohide, the reveal location (where you need to put your mouse in order for the launcher to reappear), and the reappear sensitivity levels.

Figure 6-7 Appearance tool; Look tab

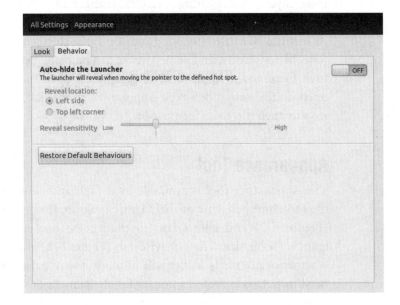

Figure 6-8 Appearance tool; Behavior tab

MyUnity

As mentioned earlier, MyUnity is a third-party tool, which uses Gambas, and was created by the MyUnity team. To find out more about the team, go to http://uielinux.org/myunity.

If you followed the instructions to get the MyUnity tool early in the chapter, great; if not, you may want to do that now. This tool allows users to tweak six areas of the Unity desktop. Now let's look at those areas.

The Launcher (Figure 6-9) allows you to change the color, transparency, size, backlight, display, and behavior and to select what devices, if any, will show.

The Dash (Figure 6-10) allows you to change what applications you see when you search. You can display available applications or most recent applications by simply choosing yes or no from this tab. You can also change the blur settings and the Dash size.

The Panel (Figure 6-11) allows you to change the transparency settings.

Figure 6-9 MyUnity Launcher

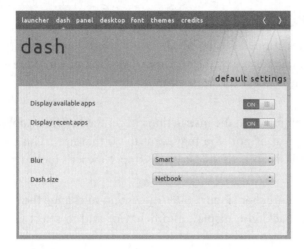

Figure 6-10 MyUnity Dash

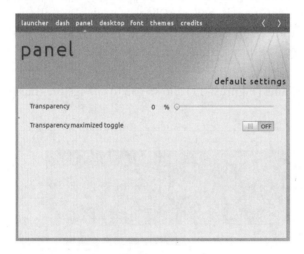

Figure 6-11 MyUnity Panel

The Desktop (Figure 6-12) allows you to decide what icons you want showing on your desktop. You can decide to turn on or off the Home icon, Networking icon, Devices icon, Trash icon, and more.

The Font (Figure 6-13) allows you to decide which fonts you want to use for the window title, documents, desktop, system, and monospace and allows you to set the hinting and antialiasing.

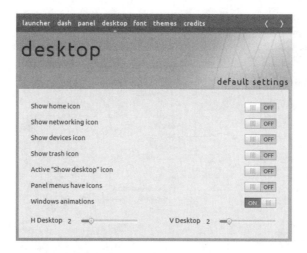

Figure 6-12 MyUnity Desktop

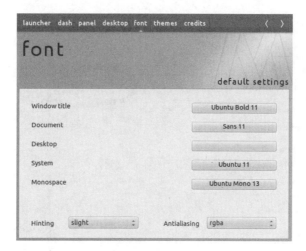

Figure 6-13 MyUnity Font

The Themes (Figure 6-14) allows you to mix and match various themes and icons.

Play around with these settings. MyUnity is a very forgiving tool. If you don't like the tweaks you are making, simply click the default settings area (Figure 6-15) found on every tab, and you'll be able to start your tweaking adventure all over again.

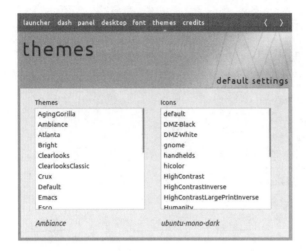

Figure 6-14 MyUnity Themes

Figure 6-15 MyUnity Default Settings

Compiz Config Settings Manager

Compiz Config Settings Manager is a configuration tool for Compiz that you may want to become familiar with. To get started with the Compiz Config Settings Manager, you will need to install it from the Ubuntu Software Center, then launch it from the Launcher by tapping the Super key to bring up the Dash, and type *Compiz*. Click on the Compiz Config Settings

Manager icon to launch. The first time you open this manager, you will get a warning (Figure 6-16). Although it is an incredible tool, Compiz Config Settings Manager is not as forgiving as the Appearance and MyUnity tools. Users are cautioned to use Compiz (Figure 6-17) with care, as it is possible to be left with an unusable desktop.

When you open Compiz Config Settings Manager, you'll notice that some of the categories have the boxes beside them checked. This is because those areas have been integrated with the Unity desktop.

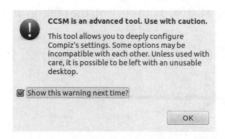

Figure 6-16 Compiz Config Settings Manager warning

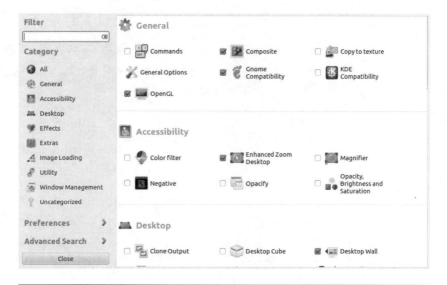

Figure 6-17 Compiz Config Settings Manager main view

Let's take a closer look at the features offered with Compiz Config Settings Manager.

In the upper left corner of the Main view, you'll notice a search box (Figure 6-18). It can be used for quick and easy filtering of the plug-ins list using the text you type in the search box. The search box can also be used like a filter for the options on various plug-in pages.

The Advanced Search button at the bottom left corner of the Main view (as seen in Figure 6-19) allows you to filter through all the options of all the plug-ins. Please note this may take a while to load. Advanced Search allows you to search by name, long description, and the values you have set. Once you have a list, you can click on the plug-in and see which groups contain the option you searched for.

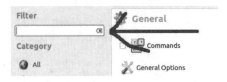

Figure 6-18 Compiz Config Settings Manager search box

Figure 6-19 Compiz Config Settings Manager General category

The plug-ins for the Compiz Config Settings Manager are divided into eight categories:

1. **General:** Contains the core plug-ins (Figure 6-19).

2. **Accessibility:** Contains plug-ins to make your desktop easier to use, especially for those who have a reading or viewing disability (Figure 6-20). The Color Filter has some interesting settings to allow you to adjust your screen so that it looks as it would be perceived by a person with colorblindness, great for checking that you have not used a poor choice of colors in a document or Web page. The Enhanced Zoom plug-in magnifies the whole screen on demand, and the Show Mouse plug-in shows pretty stars moving around the mouse cursor so you will never lose it again!

3. **Desktop:** Contains plug-ins to configure how your desktop behaves (Figure 6-21).

4. **Effects:** Contains plug-ins to configure various animations and effects, such as Wobbly Windows (Figure 6-22).

5. **Extras:** Contains plug-ins that serve a minor or ambiance purpose like annotate.

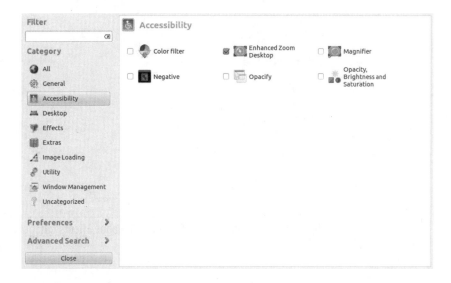

Figure 6-20 Compiz Config Settings Manager Accessibility category

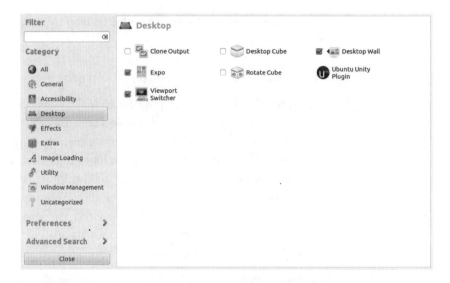

Figure 6-21 Compiz Config Settings Manager Desktop category

Figure 6-22 Compiz Config Settings Manager Effects category

6. **Image Loading:** Contains plug-ins that allow various image formats to be loaded (Figure 6-23).

7. **Utility:** Contains plug-ins that provide internal functionality like D-Bus (Figure 6-24).

8. **Window Management:** Contains plug-ins that provide basic to advanced window treatment functionality, like moving windows (Figure 6-25).

NOTE   Use caution when working with Compiz Config Settings Manager because you can render your desktop unusable. Make sure you are familiar with how to recover your desktop from the command line.

To become more familiar with Compiz and the Compiz Config Settings Manager, go to www.compiz.org.

Figure 6-23 Compiz Config Settings Manager Image Loading category

Figure 6-24 Compiz Config Settings Manager Utility category

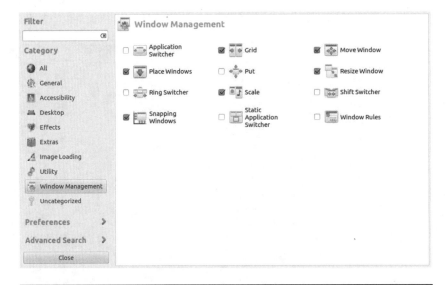

Figure 6-25 Compiz Config Settings Manager Window Management category

Unity Lenses and Scopes

The Dash is one of Unity's main features. It allows users to search for information both locally and remotely using Lenses. Each Lens is responsible for one category of search results for the Dash.

The Lens alone is not very useful, because the Lens doesn't perform the search. Instead, it relies on one or more *scopes*, which are the actual search engines, to return the search results.

In the terminology section of this chapter, we looked at the music Lens. This Lens has two scopes, which means that four processes are involved in searching the music category for content: the Dash, the Lens daemon, first Scope daemon, and second Scope daemon.

As a user, you won't even notice the complex process the Lens performs to keep everything in sync. You can just enjoy the benefits of being able to quickly search various categories of information.

NOTE   For more information on how Lenses work and are created, see the Lens Guidelines wiki at https://wiki.ubuntu.com/Unity/Lenses/Guidelines.

It seems that everyone has a favorite Unity Lens. By default, Unity comes with the following Lenses: Applications, Files, Music, and Video.

Additional Resources

In this chapter, we looked at three tools you can use to tweak your Unity desktop: Appearance, MyUnity, and Compiz Config Settings Manager. Other tools and resources are available to help you personalize your desktop environment.

Remember that there is a wealth of help and documentation available online. If you ever find yourself stuck, take a look at the Ubuntu Web site at www.ubuntu.com or the Ubuntu documentation at https://help.ubuntu.com, and make use of the forums, wiki, mailing lists, and IRC channels.

Summary

In this chapter we outlined several ways to customize your Ubuntu experience. Changing the Unity desktop from its default settings is not something everyone will want or need to do, but knowing how to do so is both useful and sometimes necessary.

CHAPTER 7

Welcome to the Command Line

- Starting Up the Terminal
- Getting Started
- Building Pipelines
- Running Commands as Superuser
- Finding Help
- Moving around the Filesystem
- Manipulating Files and Folders
- System Information Commands
- Searching and Editing Text Files
- Dealing with Users and Groups
- Getting Help on the Command Line
- Searching for Man Files
- Using Wildcards
- Executing Multiple Commands
- Moving to More Advanced Uses of the Command Line

ONE OF THE MOST powerful parts of any Ubuntu system is the command line. It can also be one of the most daunting to dive into. It seems there is often little help, and that the commands are not easy to find or figure out. If you are willing to learn, the power of the command line will speed up your work and will be a great education that serves you for years by increasing your ability to do exactly what you want to do with your computer with greater efficiency.

While the command line is a nice addition to a desktop user's life, it is completely invaluable if you run a server. The Ubuntu server installs without any GUI, so the tools explained in this chapter and other books are absolutely critical to success. And hey, remember to have fun!

Starting Up the Terminal

The terminal can be found by clicking the tooltip or Dash Home icon (Figure 7-1)—it has the Ubuntu symbol on it and should be the first icon found at the top of your Launcher. This opens the Dash, and in the dash, type *terminal* to find Terminal (Figure 7-2). When it first launches, you will see something similar to what Figure 7-3 shows.

You will see a blinking cursor immediately preceded by some letters, and perhaps numbers and symbols, ending with a $. The first word in that string of characters is your username, followed by the @ symbol. After the @, the hostname of your computer is listed, followed by a colon and the name of the directory you are currently in (you always start in your home directory, which is represented by a ~ symbol).

There are many dozens of commands. This chapter presents just a few useful ones in a narrative style to get you started, then lists some more with just a basic description and broken down by category.

Figure 7-1 The Dash Home icon

Figure 7-2 The Dash with the Terminal search

Figure 7-3 The Terminal window

Getting Started

First have a look at the files in your home folder by running the following command:

```
username@computer:~$ ls
```

The ls command lists the files in your current folder. The default command just displays a collection of items that are in your current directory, or location in the filesystem. To make `ls` more useful, you can type it with options:

```
username@computer:~$ ls -al
```

The `-al` parts are options that can be passed to the command. In this example, two options, a (list all files) and l (use a long display format to display file permissions, dates, sizes, and more), are used with `ls` to display all of the files (including hidden files) and their details.

TIP   **To Dash or Not to Dash?**
In many command-line tools, options are added after a dash (-). Some tools, however, don't need the dash. It isn't particularly consistent, so you must pay attention as you learn new commands.

Now move to a different directory:

```
username@computer:~$ cd Desktop
```

The `cd` command changes the directory to the place you specify after the command (in this case, the desktop directory). A nice shortcut that you can use when typing files and folders is to type the first few letters and then press the Tab key to fill in the remainder of the file/folder name. As an example, in the previous command, you could type cd Des and press the Tab key to fill in the rest of Desktop (with the / added automatically because it is a directory).

When inside a directory, you may want to have a quick look at the contents of a text file. To do this, use the `cat` command:

```
username@computer:~$ cat myfile.txt
```

This command prints the contents of the file on the screen (a more correct way to say this in computer geek jargon would be "outputs to the screen").

Building Pipelines

The power of the command line really comes into its own when you start to pass the output of one command so that it goes to the input of the next, combining commands by using pipelines. A pipeline uses the pipe symbol

(|) to string together a number of commands to perform a specific task. As an example, if you use the cat command to display the contents of a file to the screen, but the file scrolls past you, create a pipeline and use the less command so you can browse the file:

```
username@computer:~$ cat foo.txt | less
```

To see how this works, break the command into parts, each separated by the pipe. The output of the part on the left (cat'ing the file) is fed into the less command on the right, which allows you to browse the file with the arrow keys.

Pipelines can be useful for finding specific information on the system. As an example, if you want to find out how many particular processes are running, you could run a command like this:

```
username@computer:~$ ps ax | grep getty | wc -l
```

Here you count how many getty processes are running (getty is the software that runs a console session). The ps ax command on the left lists the processes on the system, and then the grep command searches through the process list and returns only the lines that contain the text "getty." Finally, these lines are fed into wc, which is a small tool that counts the number of words or lines. The -l option specifies that the number of lines should be counted. Cool, huh?

Running Commands as Superuser

When you log in to your computer, the account you use is a normal user account. This account is restricted from performing various system administration tasks. The security model behind Ubuntu has you run as a normal user all the time and dip into the system administrator account only when you need to. This prevents accidental changes or malicious installation of unwanted programs and similar things.

To jump to this superuser account when using the terminal, put the sudo command before the command you want to run. As an example, if you want to restart the networking system from the command line, run:

```
username@computer:~$ sudo apt-get install byobu
```

The command to the right of sudo is the command that should be run as the administrator, but sudo lets you run the command as the current user. When you run the above command, you are asked for the administrator password. This is the same password as the one you established for the first user you added when you installed Ubuntu on the computer. If you are using that user's account, just enter your normal password. In this instance, you are installing byobu, which you can use to make your life in the terminal easier.

TIP   **Byobu**
Byobu is a Japanese term for decorative, multipanel screens that serve as folding room dividers. As an open source project, byobu is an elegant enhancement of the otherwise functional, plain, practical GNU screen. Byobu includes an enhanced profile and configuration utilities for the GNU screen window manager, such as toggle-able system status notifications. More about byobu can be found at http://manpages.ubuntu.com/manpages/precise/en/man1/byobu.1.html.

When you have authenticated yourself to sudo using the terminal, you will not be asked for the password again for another 15 minutes.

Finding Help

Each command on your computer includes a manual page—or man page—that contains a list of the options available. Man pages are traditionally rather terse and intended only for referencing the different ways the command should be used. For a friendlier introduction to using commands, we recommend a Google search.

To view a man page (such as the man page for ls), run:

```
username@computer:~$ man ls
```

The man page command itself has a number of options (run man man to see them), and one of the most useful is -k. This option allows you to search the man pages for a particular word. This is useful when you don't remember the command. As an example, you could find all commands related to processes by running:

```
username@computer:~$ man -k processes
```

TIP   **Ubuntu Manpage Repository**
This site contains hundreds of thousands of dynamically generated manuals from every package of every supported version of Ubuntu, and it's updated on a daily basis. Manpages as described earlier are traditionally viewed from the command line, but thanks to Dustin Kirkland, Ubuntu users now have all the manuals included in Ubuntu in an HTML, Web-browsable format. This repository can be found at http://manpages.ubuntu.com.

The remainder of this chapter gives a brief introduction to some of the more common and useful commands you will encounter and want to learn, organized in categories based on how they are used. We end with a short list of some other resources for further research.

Moving around the Filesystem

Commands for navigating in the filesystem include the following.

- **pwd:** The pwd command allows you to know the directory in which you're located (pwd stands for "print working directory"). For example, pwd in the desktop directory will show ~/Desktop. Note that the GNOME terminal also displays this information in the title bar of its window.

- **cd:** The cd command allows you to change directories. When you open a terminal, you will be in your home directory. To move around the filesystem, use cd.
  - Use cd ~/Desktop to navigate to your desktop directory.
  - Use cd / to navigate into the root directory.
  - Use cd to navigate to your home directory.
  - Use cd .. to navigate up one directory level.
  - Use cd - to navigate to the previous directory (or back).
  - If you want to go directly to a specific, known directory location at once, use cd /directory/otherdirectory. For example, cd /var/www will take you directly to the /www subdirectory of /var.

Manipulating Files and Folders

You can manipulate files and folders with the following commands.

- **cp:** The cp command makes a copy of a file for you. For example, cp *file* foo makes an exact copy of the file whose name you entered and names the copy foo, but the first file will still exist with its original name.

- **mv:** The mv command moves a file to a different location or renames a file. Examples are as follows: mv *file* foo renames the original file to foo. mv foo ~/Desktop moves the file foo to your desktop directory but does not rename it. You must specify a new filename to rename a file. After you use mv, the original file no longer exists, but after you use cp, as above, that file stays and a new copy is made.

- To save on typing, you can substitute ~ in place of the home directory, so /home/username/pictures is the same as ~/pictures.

NOTE   If you are using mv with sudo, which is often necessary outside of your home directory, you will not be able to use the ~ shortcut. Instead, you will have to use the full pathnames to your files.

- **rm:** Use this command to remove or delete a file in your directory, as in rm file.txt. It does not work on directories that contain files, which must first be emptied and may then be deleted using the rmdir command. There are some advanced cases where you may use rm to remove directories, but discussing those are beyond the intent of this chapter.

- **ls:** The ls command shows you the files in your current directory. Used with certain options, it lets you see file sizes, when files where created, and file permissions. For example, ls ~ shows you the files that are in your home directory.

- **mkdir:** The mkdir command allows you to create directories. For example, mkdir music creates a music directory.

- **chmod:** The chmod command changes the permissions on the files listed. Permissions are based on a fairly simple model. You can set permissions for user, group, and world, and you can set whether each can read, write, and/or execute the file. For example, if a file had permission to allow everybody to read but only the user could write, the permissions would read rwxr-r-. To add or remove a permission, you append a + or a - in front of the specific permission. For example, to add the capability for the group to edit in the previous example, you could type chmod g+w file.

- **chown:** The chown command allows the user to change the user and group ownerships of a file. For example, sudo chown jim *file* changes the ownership of the file to Jim.

System Information Commands

System information commands include the following.

- **df:** The df command displays filesystem disk space usage for all partitions. The command df-h is probably the most useful. It uses megabytes (M) and gigabytes (G) instead of blocks to report. (-h means "human-readable.")

- **free:** The free command displays the amount of free and used memory in the system. For example, free -m gives the information using megabytes, which is probably most useful for current computers.

- **top:** The top command displays information on your Linux system, running processes, and system resources, including the CPU, RAM, swap usage, and total number of tasks being run. To exit top, press Q.

- **uname -a:** The uname command with the -a option prints all system information, including machine name, kernel name, version, and a few other details. This command is most useful for checking which kernel you're using.

- **lsb_release -a:** The lsb_release command with the -a option prints version information for the Linux release you're running. For example:

```
username@computer:~$ lsb_release -a

No LSB modules are available.
Distributor ID: Ubuntu
Description:    Ubuntu 12.04
Release:        12.04
Codename:       precise
```

- **ifconfig:** This reports on your system's network interfaces.

- **iwconfig:** The `iwconfig` command shows you any wireless network adapters and the wireless-specific information from them, such as speed and network connected.

- **ps:** The `ps` command allows you to view all the processes running on the machine.

The following commands list the hardware on your computer, either of a specific type or with a specific method. They are most useful for debugging when a piece of hardware does not function correctly.

- **lspci:** The `lspci` command lists all PCI buses and devices connected to them. This commonly includes network cards and sound cards.

- **lsusb:** The `lsusb` command lists all USB buses and any connected USB devices, such as printers and thumb drives.

- **lshal:** The `lshal` command lists all devices the hardware abstraction layer (HAL) knows about, which should be most hardware on your system.

Searching and Editing Text Files

Search and edit text files by using the following commands.

- **grep:** The `grep` command allows you to search inside a number of files for a particular search pattern and then print matching lines. For example, `grep blah` *file* will search for the text "blah" in the file and then print any matching lines.

- **sed:** The `sed` (or Stream EDitor) command allows search and replace of a particular string in a file. For example, if you want to find the string "cat" and replace it with "dog" in a file named pets, type `sed s/cat/dog/g pets`.

Both `grep` and `sed` are extremely powerful programs. There are many excellent tutorials available on using them, but here are a couple of good Web sites to get you started:

- https://help.ubuntu.com/community/grep

- http://manpages.ubuntu.com/manpages/precise/man1/
  9base-sed.1.html

Five other commands are useful for dealing with text.

- **cat:** The cat command, short for concatenate, is useful for viewing
  and adding to text files. The simple command cat *FILENAME* displays
  the contents of the file. Using cat *FILENAME* file adds the contents of
  the first file to the second and displays both on the screen, one after
  the other. You could also use cat file1 >> file2 to append the
  contents of file1 to the end of file2.

- **nano:** Nano is a simple text editor for the command line. To open a
  file, use nano *filename*. Commands listed at the bottom of the screen
  are accessed via pressing Ctrl followed by the letter. To close and save
  a file you are working on, use Ctrl-X.

- **less:** The less command is used for viewing text files as well as
  standard output. A common usage is to pipe another command
  through less to be able to see all the output, such as ls | less.

- **head:** The head command is used for viewing the first 10 lines of text
  files as well as standard output. A common usage is to pipe another
  command through head to be able to see varying lines of output, such
  as ls | head.

- **tail:** The tail command is used for viewing the last 10 lines of text files
  as well as standard output. A common usage is to pipe another
  command through tail to be able to see varying lines of output, such
  as ls | tail.

Dealing with Users and Groups

You can use the following commands to administer users and groups.

- **adduser:** The adduser command creates a new user. To create a new
  user, simply type sudo adduser *loginname*. This creates the user's home
  directory and default group. It prompts for a user password and then
  further details about the user.

- **passwd:** The `passwd` command changes the user's password. If run by a regular user, it will change his or her password. If run using `sudo`, it can change any user's password. For example, `sudo passwd joe` changes Joe's password.

- **who:** The `who` command tells you who is currently logged into the machine.

- **addgroup:** The `addgroup` command adds a new group. To create a new group, type `sudo addgroup groupname`.

- **deluser:** The `deluser` command removes a user from the system. To remove the user's files and home directory, you need to add the `-remove-home` option.

- **delgroup:** The `delgroup` command removes a group from the system. You cannot remove a group that is the primary group of any users.

- **chgrp:** The `chgrp` command changes group ownership of files and directories.

Getting Help on the Command Line

This section provides you with some tips for getting help on the command line. The commands `-help` and `man` are the two most important tools at the command line.

Virtually all commands understand the `-h` (or `-help`) option, which produces a short usage description of the command and its options, then exits back to the command prompt. Try `man -h` or `man -help` to see this in action.

Every command and nearly every application in Linux has a man (manual) file, so finding such a file is as simple as typing `man command` to bring up a longer manual entry for the specified command. For example, `man mv` brings up the `mv` (move) manual.

Some helpful tips for using the `man` command include the following.

- **Arrow keys:** Move up and down the man file by using the arrow keys.

- **q:** Quit back to the command prompt by typing `q`.

- **man man:** man man brings up the manual entry for the man command, which is a good place to start!

- **man intro:** man intro is especially useful. It displays the Introduction to User Commands, which is a well-written, fairly brief introduction to the Linux command line.

There are also info pages, which are generally more in-depth than man pages. Try info info for the introduction to info pages.

Searching for Man Files

If you aren't sure which command or application you need to use, you can try searching the man files.

- **man -k foo:** This searches the man files for *foo*. Try man -k nautilus to see how this works.

NOTE   man -k foo is the same as the apropos command.

- **man -f foo:** This searches only the titles of your system's man files. Try man -f unity, for example.

NOTE   man -f foo is the same as the whatis command.

Using Wildcards

Sometimes you need to look at or use multiple files at the same time. For instance, you might want to delete all .rar files or move all .odt files to another directory. Thankfully, you can use a series of wildcards to accomplish such tasks.

- * matches any number of characters. For example, *.rar matches any file with the ending .rar.

- ? matches any single character. For example, ?.rar matches a.rar but not ab.rar.

- **[*characters*]** matches any of the characters within the brackets. For example, [ab].rar matches a.rar and b.rar but not c.rar.
- ***[!*characters*]** matches any characters that are not listed. For example, *[!ab].rar matches c.rar but not a.rar or b.rar.

Executing Multiple Commands

Often you may want to execute several commands together, either by running one after another or by passing output from one to another.

Running Sequentially

If you need to execute multiple commands in sequence but don't need to pass output between them, there are two options based on whether or not you want the subsequent commands to run only if the previous commands succeed or not. If you want the commands to run one after the other regardless of whether or not preceding commands succeed, place a ; between the commands. For example, if you want to get information about your hardware, you could run lspci ; lsusb, which would output information on your PCI buses and USB devices in sequence.

However, if you need to conditionally run the commands based on whether the previous command has succeeded, insert && between commands. An example of this is building a program from source, which is traditionally done with ./configure, make, and make install. The commands make and make install require that the previous commands have completed successfully, so you would use ./configure && make && make install.

Using Byobu to Manage Your Terminal

One of the challenges of using the terminal is the difficulty of managing multiple screens. If you are in a desktop environment, you can launch another terminal window or use GNOME terminal's tabs, but if you are on a server or another machine that doesn't have a desktop environment installed, that doesn't work.

Thankfully, such a tool to help you does exist: byobu. Japanese for *screen*, byobu is a set of default configurations for the GNU screen command. Essentially, screen is a window manager for the command line. To install byobu, type sudo apt-get install byobu.

After it is started, you will notice you are back at a terminal prompt, but with a few differences. At the bottom are two lines of information. From the left to the right, the bottom line shows you the version of Ubuntu you are currently running, number of packages to update (if there are none, this won't appear), how long the system has been running, the system load, the CPU speed, the current memory usage, and the current date and time. The upper bar shows the list of open windows, the current logged in user, the system name, and the menu option (Figure 7-4).

You can now use your terminal exactly as you normally would, just with a few added pieces of information. Advanced use of byobu (and screen) is a topic too large for this chapter, but following are a few commands to get you started:

F2:   Open new terminal window.

F3/F4: Move backward/forward through the list of windows.

F6:   Detach from current byobu session. To reattach, use byobu -x.

F7:   Scroll back through the output. Hit Esc to exit this mode and return to the command prompt.

F8:   Set the window title to a custom title.

F9:   Launch the menu.

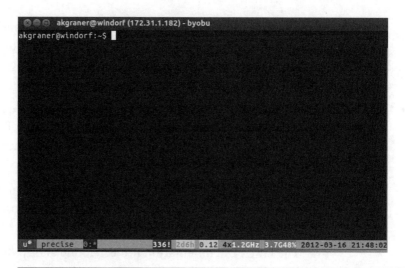

Figure 7-4 Byobu in GNOME terminal

Using Byobu by Default in GNOME Terminal

To have GNOME terminal launch byobu by default when it starts, you need to edit the preferences, which can be found at Edit > Profile Preferences under the Title and Command tab. Tick the box Run a Custom Command Instead of My Shell, and enter byobu in the line below. Now when you launch GNOME terminal, byobu will launch with it, and closing byobu will close GNOME terminal as well.

Moving to More Advanced Uses of the Command Line

There are a great number of good books out there for working the command line. In addition, because most of the command line has not changed in many years, a large body of information is available on the Internet. If you need help with something, often simply searching for the command will turn up what you need.

As you can imagine, there are hundreds and hundreds of different commands available on the system, and we don't have the space to cover them here. A number of superb Web sites and books can help you find out about the many different commands.

To get you started, here are some recommendations.

- *The Official Ubuntu Server Book* by Kyle Rankin and Benjamin Mako Hill (Prentice Hall, 2009) is an excellent resource for learning all things server related, including the effective use of the command line to accomplish administration tasks.

- *A Practical Guide to Linux® Commands, Editors, and Shell Programming, Second Edition*, by Mark G. Sobell (Prentice Hall, 2009) is a good book for any user of the shell in Linux to have on his or her bookshelf.

- **LinuxCommand.org**, found at http://linuxcommand.org, is an excellent Web site designed to help people new to using the command line.

- **The Linux Documentation Project**, found at http://www.tdlp.org, is another excellent and free resource.

CHAPTER 8

The Ubuntu Server

- What Is Ubuntu Server?
- Installing Ubuntu Server
- Ubuntu Package Management
- Ubuntu Server Security
- Advanced Topics
- Summary

UBUNTU 4.10, LOVINGLY KNOWN AS WARTY WARTHOG, was the first public version of Ubuntu. Its installation media provided no obvious way to install the bare-bones OS without a full desktop environment. The system administrator crowds, easily irritable and feisty by nature, were greatly annoyed: They proclaimed Ubuntu was just a desktop distribution and sauntered back to their caves in contempt.

The next release of Ubuntu that came out, Hoary Hedgehog, rectified the problem and allowed for trivial installation of a minimal Ubuntu version suitable for servers. Yet the myth of Ubuntu as a purely desktop-oriented distribution stuck.

Luckily, the sentiment is just that—a myth. Ubuntu is a world-class server platform today, providing everything you'd expect from a server OS and with the human flavor that makes Ubuntu different. The dedicated hackers on the Ubuntu Server Team tend to the minutiae of hardware support and testing, mercilessly beat on the latest version of server software to make sure it's up to snuff for inclusion in the distribution, look for ways to push innovation into the server field, and are available to users like you to field feedback, questions, and cries of anguish.

That said, setting up a server is no small task. Server administrators constantly deal with complex issues such as system security, fault tolerance, and data safety, and while Ubuntu makes these issues more pleasant to deal with, they're not to be taken lightly. The aim of this chapter is thus not to teach you how to be a system administrator—we could easily fill a dozen books attempting to do that—but to give you a quick crash course. We also highlight the specific details that set Ubuntu Server apart from other server platforms, offer tips on some of the most common server uses, and give you pointers on where to find other relevant information.

What Is Ubuntu Server?

By far the most common reaction from users first encountering Ubuntu Server is one of utter and hopeless confusion. People are foggy on whether Ubuntu Server is a whole new distribution or an Ubuntu derivative like Kubuntu (only for servers) or perhaps something else entirely.

Let's clear things up a bit. The primary software store for Ubuntu and official derivatives is called the Ubuntu archive. The archive is merely a collection of software packages in Debian "deb" format, and it contains every single package that makes up distributions such as Ubuntu, Edubuntu, Xubuntu, Kubuntu, and Ubuntu Server. What makes Kubuntu separate from Ubuntu, then, is only the set of packages from the archive that its installer installs by default and that its CDs carry.

Ubuntu Server is no different. It depends on the very same archive as the standard Ubuntu distribution, but it installs a distinctive set of default packages. Notably, the set of packages comprising Ubuntu Server is very small. The installer will not install things such as a graphical environment or many user programs by default. But since all the packages for Ubuntu Server come from the same official Ubuntu archive, you can install any package you like later. In theory, there's nothing stopping you from transforming an Ubuntu Server install into a regular Ubuntu desktop installation or vice versa (in practice, this is tricky, and we don't recommend you try it). You can even go from running Kubuntu to running Ubuntu Server. The archive paradigm gives you maximum flexibility.

We've established that Ubuntu Server just provides a different set of default packages than Ubuntu. But what's important about that different set? What makes Ubuntu Server a server platform?

The most significant difference is a custom server kernel. This kernel employs an internal timer frequency of 100Hz instead of the desktop default of 250Hz, uses the deadline I/O scheduler instead of the desktop's CFQ scheduler, and contains a batch of other minor tweaks for virtualization, memory support, and routing. We'll spare you the OS theory: The idea is to offer some extra performance and throughput for server applications. In addition, the server kernel supports basic NUMA, a memory design used in some multiprocessor systems that can dramatically increase multiprocessing performance.

So what else is different in Ubuntu Server? Other than the server kernel and a minimal set of packages, not too much. Though Ubuntu has supported a minimal installation mode for a number of releases, spinning off Ubuntu Server into a separate product that truly stands on its own is still a young effort, but one that's moving along very quickly.

Starting with Ubuntu Server 6.06 LTS, known as Dapper Drake, Ubuntu Server offers officially supported packages for the Red Hat Cluster Suite, Red Hat's Global File System (GFS), Oracle's OCFS2 filesystem, and the Linux Virtual Server utilities: keepalived and ipvsadm. Combined with the specialized server kernel, these bits already let you use your Ubuntu Server for some heavy lifting. And there's a growing lineup of compelling features, including built-in virtualization, interoperability with Windows machines on the network through Samba, automatic version control for configuration files, support for LDAP directory services, hard drive replication over the network, and even a healthy dose of the latest buzzword—cloud computing.

Installing Ubuntu Server

So you've downloaded your Ubuntu Server CD from http://releases.ubuntu.com/12.04/ and burned it, eagerly placed it in your CD drive, and rebooted the machine to be greeted by the friendly Ubuntu menu. The first option, Install Ubuntu Server, marks the beginning of a journey toward your very own system administrator cave.

Until recently, the process of installing Ubuntu Server was identical to installing a desktop. Both installations were performed with a textual installer, a charmingly quaint combination of red and blue screens with text all over. Since then, the desktop version's installer has been replaced by a beautiful graphical environment that lets you play with a fully usable Ubuntu setup right off the install CD. But the Server CD retained its red and blue colors; because the textual installer doesn't rely on automatically detecting finicky graphics cards, it's just about certain to work on most any piece of hardware you can get your hands on. And when you're installing a server, that's worth more than all the eye candy in the world.

Here, we look at some of the advanced textual installer gadgetry that is particularly geared toward server users.

The neat stuff begins when you arrive at the partitioning section of the installer. With a desktop machine, you'd probably let the installer configure a basic set of partitions by itself and go on its merry way. But with servers, things get a bit more complicated.

A Couple of Installer Tricks

As we'll explore below, in terms of partitioning and storage, server installations can be quite a bit more complex than desktop ones. There's a small bag of useful tricks with the installer that can help when things get hairy.

The installer itself runs on virtual console 1. If you switch to console 2 by pressing Alt-F2, you'll be able to activate the console by hitting Enter and land in a minimalistic (busybox) shell. This will let you explore the complete installer environment and take some matters into your own hands if necessary. You can switch back to the installer console by pressing Alt-F1. Console 4 contains a running, noninteractive log file of the installation, which you can inspect by pressing Alt-F4. Finally, it's sometimes useful to be able to connect to another server during installation, perhaps to upload a log file or to gain access to your mailbox or other communication. By default, the shell on console 2 will not provide you with an ssh client, but you can install one by running `anna-install openssh-client-udeb` after the installer has configured the network. Now you can use the `ssh` and `scp` binaries to log in or copy data to the server of your choice.

Partitioning Your Ubuntu Server

Deciding how to partition the storage in your server is a tricky affair and certainly no exact science. Generally, it's a good idea to have at least three partitions separate from the rest of the system:

- /home: where all the user files will live

- /tmp: temporary scratch space for running applications

- /var: mail spools and log files

TIP   **Partition Security and Separating Logs and Spools**
There are several options that you can turn on for specific system partitions that afford you extra security. We explain them later in this chapter, in the section dealing with security.

As an aside, if your server will keep extensive mail and news spools, you might want to further separate /var into partitions for /var/log and /var/spool. Having them both on the same partition might cause severe I/O congestion under heavy use.

Keeping data on separate partitions gives you, the administrator, an expansive choice of filesystems you use for particular purposes. For instance, you might choose to put /tmp on ReiserFS for its superior handling of many files in a directory and excellent performance on small files, but you might keep /home and /var on ext3 for its rock-solid robustness or on the default ext4 filesystem as a good compromise between the two.

In addition, a dedicated /home partition lets you use special options when mounting it to your system, such as imposing disk space quotas or enabling extended security on user data. The reason to keep /tmp and /var separate from the rest of your system is much more prosaic: These directories are prone to filling up. This is the case with /tmp because it's a scratchpad, and administrators often give users very liberal quotas there (but have a policy, for example, of purging all user data in /tmp older than two days), which means /tmp can easily get clogged up. /var, on the other hand, stores log files and mail spools, both of which can take up massive amounts of disk space either as a result of malicious activity or due to a significant spike in normal system usage.

Becoming a system administrator means you have to learn how to think like one. If /tmp and /var are easy to fill up, you compartmentalize them so that they can't eventually consume all the disk space available on your server.

The Story of RAID

If you've got only one hard drive in your server, feel free to skip ahead. Otherwise, let's talk about putting those extra drives to use. The acronym RAID stands for redundant array of inexpensive disks, although if you're a businessperson, you can substitute the word *independent* for *inexpensive*. We forgive you. And if you're in France, RAID is short for *recherche* assistance intervention dissuasion, which is an elite commando unit of the National Police—but if that's the RAID you need help with, you're reading the wrong book. We think RAID is just a really awesome idea for data: When dealing with your information, it provides extra speed, fault tolerance, or both.

At its core, RAID is just a way to replicate the same information across multiple physical drives. The process can be set up in a number of ways, and specific kinds of drive configurations are referred to as RAID levels. These days, even low- to mid-range servers ship with integrated hardware RAID controllers, which operate without any support from the OS. If your new server doesn't come with a RAID controller, you can use the software RAID functionality in the Ubuntu kernel to accomplish the same goal.

Setting up software RAID while installing your Linux system was difficult and unwieldy only a short while ago, but it is a breeze these days: The Ubuntu installer provides a nice, convenient interface for it and then handles all the requisite backstage magic. You can choose from three RAID levels: 0, 1, and 5.

RAID 0   A so-called striped set, RAID 0 allows you to pool the storage space of a number of separate drives into one large, virtual drive. The important thing to keep in mind is that RAID 0 does not actually concatenate the physical drives—it actually spreads the data across them evenly, which means that no more space will be used on each physical drive than can fit on the smallest one. In practical terms, if you had two 250GB drives and a 200GB drive, the total amount of space on your virtual drive would equal 600GB; 50GB on each of the two larger drives would go unused. Spreading data in this fashion provides amazing performance but also significantly decreases reliability. If any of the drives in your RAID 0 array fail, the entire array will come crashing down, taking your data with it.

RAID 1   This level provides very straightforward data replication. It will take the contents of one physical drive and multiplex it to as many other drives as you'd like. A RAID 1 array does not grow in size with the addition of extra drives—instead, it grows in reliability and read performance. The size of the entire array is limited by the size of its smallest constituent drive.

RAID 5   When the chief goal of your storage is fault tolerance, and you want to use more space than provided by the single physical drive in RAID 1, this is the level you want to use. RAID 5 lets you use n identically sized physical drives (if different-sized drives are present, no more space than the size of the smallest one will be used on each drive) to construct an array whose total available space is that of $n-1$ drives, and the array tolerates the failure of any one—but no more than one—drive without data loss.

TIP   **The Mythical Parity Drive**
If you toss five 200GB drives into a RAID 5 array, the array's total usable size will be 800GB, or that of four drives. This makes it easy to mistakenly believe that a RAID 5 array "sacrifices" one of the drives for maintaining redundancy and parity, but this is not the case. Through some neat mathematics of polynomial coefficients over Galois fields, the actual parity information is striped across all drives equally, allowing any single drive to fail without compromising the data. Don't worry, though. We won't quiz you on the math.

Which RAID to Choose?   If you're indecisive by nature, the past few paragraphs may have left you awkwardly hunched in your chair, mercilessly chewing a No. 2 pencil, feet tapping the floor nervously. Luckily, the initial choice of RAID level is often a no-brainer, so you'll have to direct your indecision elsewhere. If you have one hard drive, no RAID for you. Do not pass Go, do not collect $200. Two drives? Toss them into RAID 1, and sleep better at night. Three or more? RAID 5. Unless you really know what you're doing, avoid RAID 0 like the plague. If you're not serving mostly read-only data without a care about redundancy, RAID 0 isn't what you want.

TIP   **Other RAID Modes**
Though the installer offers only the most common RAID modes—0, 1, and 5—many other RAID modes exist and can be configured after the installation. Take a look at http://en.wikipedia.org/wiki/RAID for a detailed explanation of all the modes.

Setting Up RAID

After carefully studying the last section, maybe reading a few books on abstract algebra and another few on finite field theory, you finally decided on a RAID level that suits you. Since books can't yet read your mind, we'll assume you chose RAID 1. So how do you set it up?

Back to the installer. When prompted about partitioning disks, you'll want to bravely select the last option, Manually Edit Partition Table.

Below the top two options on the screen (Guided Partitioning and Help), you'll find a list of the physical drives in your server that the Ubuntu installer detected.

TIP   **Avoiding the "Oh, No!" Moment**
We've said this before, and we'll say it again: It's very easy to mistakenly erase valuable data when partitioning your system. Since you're installing a server, however, we'll assume you're comfortable deleting any data that might already exist on the drives. If this is not the case, back up all data you care about now! We mean it.

Indented below each drive, you'll find the list of any preexisting partitions, along with their on-disk ordinal number, size, bootable status, filesystem type, and, possibly, their mount point. Using the arrow keys, highlight the line summarizing a physical drive (not any of its partitions), and hit Enter—you'll be asked to confirm replacing any existing partition table with a new one. Select Yes, and the only entry listed below that drive will be FREE SPACE. In our fictional server, we have two 80GB drives—hda and hdb—so we'd follow this process for both drives, giving each a fresh partition table. Say we've decided on a 20GB /home partition. Arrow over to FREE SPACE, hit Enter, and create the partition. Once you've entered the size for the new partition, you'll be brought to a dialog where you can choose the filesystem and mount options. Instead of plopping a filesystem on the raw partition, however, you'll want to enter the Use As dialog and set the new partition to be a physical volume for RAID.

Still with us? Now rinse and repeat for the other drive—create the exact same partition, same size, and set it as a RAID volume. When you're done, you should be back at the initial partitioning screen, and you should have an identically sized partition under each drive. At this point, choose Configure Software RAID at the top of the screen, agree to write out changes to the storage devices if need be, and then choose to create an MD (multidisk) device. After selecting RAID 1, you'll be asked to enter the number of active devices for the array. In our fictional two-drive server, it's two. The next question concerns the number of spare devices in the array, which you can leave at zero. Now simply use the spacebar to put a check next to both partitions that you've created (hda1 and hdb1), and hit Finish in the Multidisk dialog to return to the basic partitioner.

If you look below the two physical drives that you used to have there, you'll notice a brand new drive, the Software RAID device that has one partition below it. That's your future /home partition, sitting happily on a RAID array. If you arrow over to it and hit Enter, you can now configure it just as you would a real partition.

The process is the same for any other partitions you want to toss into RAID. Create identical-sized partitions on all participating physical drives, select to use them as RAID space, enter the multidisk configurator (software RAID), and finally, create an array that uses the real partitions. Then create a filesystem on the newly created array.

TIP   Array Failure and Spare Devices

When a physical drive fails in a RAID array that's running in a level that provides redundancy—such as 1 or 5—the array goes into so-called degraded mode (never verbally abuse or be cruel to your RAID arrays!). Depending on the number of devices in the array, running in degraded mode might just have performance downsides, but it might also mean that another physical drive failure will bring down the whole array and cause total data loss. To recover the array from degraded mode, you need to add a working physical drive to the system (the old one can be removed) and instruct the array to use the new device to "rebuild."

In order to minimize the amount of time an array spends in degraded mode, and to prevent having to power off the machine to insert new physical drives if the server doesn't support hot-swapping, you can put extra physical drives into the machine and flag them as hot spares, which means the system will keep them active but unused until there's a drive failure. Cold spares, as the name implies, are just extra drives that you keep around on a shelf until there's a failure, at which point you manually add them to the array.

That's it! The Ubuntu installer will take care of all the pesky details of configuring the system to boot the RAID arrays at the right time and use them, even if you've chosen to keep your root partition on an array. Now let's look at another great feature of the Ubuntu installer: logical volume management (LVM).

The Story of the Logical Volume Manager

Let's take a step back from our RAID adventure and look at the bigger picture in data storage. The entire situation is unpleasant. Hard drives are slow and fail often, and though abolished for working memory ages ago, fixed-size partitions are still the predominant mode of storage space allocation. As if worrying about speed and data loss weren't enough, you also have to worry about whether your partition size calculations were just right when you were installing a server or whether you'll wind up in the unenviable position of having a partition run out of space, even though another partition is maybe mostly unused. And if you might have to move a partition across physical volume boundaries on a running system, well, woe is you.

RAID helps to some degree. It'll do wonders for your worries about performance and fault tolerance, but it operates at too low a level to help with the partition size or fluidity concerns. What we'd really want is a way to push the partition concept up one level of abstraction, so it doesn't operate directly on the underlying physical media. Then we could have partitions that are trivially resizable or that can span multiple drives, we could easily take some space from one partition and tack it on another, and we could juggle partitions around on physical drives on a live server. Sounds cool, right?

Very cool, and very doable via LVM, a system that shifts the fundamental unit of storage from physical drives to virtual or logical ones (although we harbor our suspicions that the term *logical* is a jab at the storage status quo, which is anything but). LVM has traditionally been a feature of expensive, enterprise UNIX operating systems or was available for purchase from third-party vendors. Through the magic of free software, a guy by the name of Heinz Mauelshagen wrote an implementation of a logical volume manager for Linux in 1998. LVM has undergone tremendous improvements since then and is widely used in production today, and just as you expect, the Ubuntu installer makes it easy for you to configure it on your server during installation.

LVM Theory and Jargon   Wrapping your head around LVM is a bit more difficult than with RAID because LVM rethinks the whole way of dealing with storage, which expectedly introduces a bit of jargon that you need to learn. Under LVM, physical volumes, or PVs, are seen just as providers of disk space without any inherent organization (such as partitions mapping to a mount point in the OS). We group PVs into volume groups, or VGs, which are virtual storage pools that look like good old cookie-cutter hard drives. We carve those up into logical volumes, or LVs, that act like the normal partitions we're used to dealing with. We create filesystems on these LVs and mount them into our directory tree. And behind the scenes, LVM splits up physical volumes into small slabs of bytes (4MB by default), each of which is called a physical extent, or a PE.

Okay, so that was a mouthful of acronyms, but as long as you understand the progression, you're in good shape. You take a physical hard drive and set up one or more partitions on it that will be used for LVM. These partitions are now physical volumes (PVs), which are split into physical extents (PEs) and then grouped in volume groups (VGs), on top of which you finally create logical volumes (LVs). It's the LVs, these virtual partitions, and not the ones on the physical hard drive, that carry a filesystem and are mapped and mounted into the OS. And if you're really confused about what possible benefit we get from adding all this complexity only to wind up with the same fixed-size partitions in the end, hang in there. It'll make sense in a second.

The reason LVM splits physical volumes into small, equally sized physical extents is that the definition of a volume group (the space that'll be carved into logical volumes) then becomes "a collection of physical extents" rather than "a physical area on a physical drive," as with old-school partitions. Notice that "a collection of extents" says nothing about where the extents are coming from and certainly doesn't impose a fixed limit on the size of a volume group. We can take PEs from a bunch of different drives and toss them into one volume group, which addresses our desire to abstract partitions away from physical drives. We can take a VG and make it bigger simply by adding a few extents to it, maybe by taking them from another VG, or maybe by tossing in a new physical volume and using extents from there. And we can take a VG and move it to different physical storage simply by telling it to relocate to a different collection of extents. Best of all, we can do all this on the fly, without any server downtime.

Do you smell that? That's the fresh smell of the storage revolution.

Setting Up LVM

By now, you must be convinced that LVM is the best thing since sliced bread. Which it is—and, surprisingly enough, setting it up during installation is no harder than setting up RAID. Create partitions on each physical drive you want to use for LVM just as you did with RAID, but tell the installer to use them as physical space for LVM. Note that in this context, PVs are not actual physical hard drives; they are the partitions you're creating.

You don't have to devote your entire drive to partitions for LVM. If you'd like, you're free to create actual filesystem-containing partitions alongside the storage partitions used for LVM, but make sure you're satisfied with your partitioning choice before you proceed. Once you enter the LVM configurator in the installer, the partition layout on all drives that contain LVM partitions will be frozen.

Let's look back to our fictional server, but let's give it four drives, which are 10GB, 20GB, 80GB, and 120GB in size. Say we want to create an LVM partition, or PV, using all available space on each drive, and then combine the first two PVs into a 30GB volume group and the latter two into a 200GB one. Each VG will act as a large virtual hard drive on top of which we can create logical volumes just as we would normal partitions.

As with RAID, arrowing over to the name of each drive and hitting Enter will let us erase the partition table. Then hitting Enter on the FREE SPACE entry lets us create a physical volume—a partition that we set to be used as a physical space for LVM. Once all three LVM partitions are in place, we select Configure the Logical Volume Manager on the partitioning menu.

After a warning about the partition layout, we get to a rather spartan LVM dialog that lets us modify VGs and LVs. According to our plan, we choose the former option and create the two VGs we want, choosing the appropriate PVs. We then select Modify Logical Volumes and create the LVs corresponding to the normal partitions we want to put on the system—say, one for each of /, /var, /home, and /tmp.

You can already see some of the partition fluidity that LVM brings you. If you decide you want a 25GB logical volume for /var, you can carve it out of the first VG you created, and /var will magically span the two smaller hard drives. If you later decide you've given /var too much space, you can shrink the filesystem and then simply move over some of the storage space from the first VG to the second. The possibilities are endless.

Last but not least, recent Ubuntu versions support encrypting your LVM volumes right from the installer, which is music to paranoid ears: It means you can now have full-disk encryption from the moment you install your machine. Encrypted LVM is offered as one of the "guided" options in the partitioning menu, but you can also accomplish the same result by hand.

TIP   **LVM Doesn't Provide Redundancy**

The point of LVM is storage fluidity, not fault tolerance. In our example, the logical volume containing the /var filesystem is sitting on a volume group that spans two hard drives. Unfortunately, this means that either drive failing will corrupt the entire filesystem, and LVM intentionally doesn't contain functionality to prevent this problem.

Instead, when you need fault tolerance, build your volume groups from physical volumes that are sitting on RAID! In our example, we could have made a partition spanning the entire size of the 10GB hard drive and allocated it to physical space for a RAID volume. Then, we could have made two 10GB partitions on the 20GB hard drive and made the first one also a physical space for RAID. Entering the RAID configurator, we would create a RAID 1 array from the 10GB RAID partitions on both drives, but instead of placing a regular filesystem on the RAID array as before, we'd actually designate the RAID array to be used as a physical space for LVM. When we get to LVM configuration, the RAID array would show up as any other physical volume, but we'd know that the physical volume is redundant. If a physical drive fails beneath it, LVM won't ever know, and no data loss will occur. Of course, standard RAID array caveats apply, so if enough drives fail and shut down the array, LVM will still come down kicking and screaming.

Encrypted Home and Software Selection

After you have partitioned the disk, the installer will install the base system and ask you for user information, much like with the desktop install. You'll then be asked a question you might not have seen before: Do you wish to encrypt your home directory?

If you answer in the affirmative, your account password will take on a second purpose. Rather than just allowing you to log in, it will also be used to transparently encrypt every file in your home directory, turning it into gibberish for anyone without the password. This means that if your computer gets stolen, your data remains safe from prying eyes as long as your password isn't too easy to guess. If this sounds familiar, it's because this functionality exists as FileVault on Apple's Mac OS X and is also a subset of the BitLocker system that debuted in Windows Vista. (The directory encryption system used in Ubuntu is called ecryptfs, which is a decidedly less punchy name. We're working on it.)

TIP   **Encrypted Swap and Remote Login**

If you use a swap partition, protecting your home directory isn't enough; sensitive data can get swapped out to disk in the clear. The solution is to use encrypted swap, which you can manually enable with the `ecryptfs-setup-swap` command, but this will presently take away your computer's ability to enter the hibernate power-saving mode. Suspend mode is unaffected.

Note also that encrypting your home directory makes all the data in it, including special directories such as .ssh, unavailable until after you log in. If you're logging into a machine where your home directory is encrypted and hasn't yet been unlocked, and the machine only allows SSH public key authentication, there is no way for the system to consult your authorized_keys file, and you're locked out. You can fix this by physically logging in, unmounting your encrypted home directory with `ecryptfs-umount-private`, then creating a .ssh directory in your "underlying" home directory left behind by ecryptfs. Stick your public keys into an authorized_keys file under that .ssh directory as normal, and you'll be all set to log in remotely, at which point you can use `ecryptfs-mount-private` to enter your password and unlock your actual home directory.

After the installer downloads some updated software sources, though, you will see a new menu that lists a number of common server types, including DNS, LAMP, Mail, OpenSSH, PostgreSQL, Print, and Samba servers. Select one or more of these options and the installer will automatically download the standard set of packages you will need for that server as well as perform some basic configuration of the services for you. For instance, if you wanted to install a LAMP environment, but you also wanted to make sure you could ssh into the machine from another computer, you could select both LAMP and OpenSSH server from the menu.

TIP   **Software Installer Prompts**

Depending on which servers you select, you may be asked a number of questions as the packages install. For instance, when you select the LAMP environment, the installer will recommend you choose a password for the root MySQL user.

You're Done—Now Watch Out for Root!

Whew. With the storage and software stuff out of the way, the rest of your server installation should go no differently than installing a regular Ubuntu workstation. And now that your server is installed, we can move on to the fun stuff. From this point on, everything we do will happen in a shell.

When your Ubuntu server first boots, you'll have to log in with the user you created during installation. Here's an important point that bites a number of newcomers to Ubuntu: Unlike most distributions, Ubuntu does not enable the root account during installation! Instead, the installer adds the user you've created during installation to the admin group, which lets you use a mechanism called sudo to perform administrative tasks. We'll show you how to use sudo in a bit. In the meantime, if you're interested in the rationale for the decision to disable direct use of the root account, simply run man sudo_root after logging in.

TIP   **Care and Feeding of RAID and LVM Arrays**

If you've set up some of these during installation, you'll want to learn how to manage the arrays after the server is installed. We recommend the respective how-to documents from The Linux Documentation Project at

www.tldp.org/HOWTO/Software-RAID-HOWTO.html and
www.tldp.org/HOWTO/LVM-HOWTO.

The how-tos sometimes get technical, but most of the details should sound familiar if you've understood the introduction to the subject matter that we gave in this chapter.

Ubuntu Package Management

Once your server is installed, it contains only the few packages it requires to boot and run properly plus whatever software you selected at the software select screen. In the comfort of the GNOME graphical environment on an Ubuntu desktop, we could launch Synaptic and point and click our way through application discovery and installation. But on a server, we must be shell samurai.

The Ubuntu Archive

Before we delve into the nitty-gritty of package management, let's briefly outline the structure of the master Ubuntu package archive, which we mentioned in the introduction to this chapter. Each new release has five repositories in the archive, called main, restricted, backports, universe, and multiverse. A newly installed system comes with only the first two enabled plus the security update repository. Here's the repository breakdown.

- **Main:** This includes all packages installed by default; these packages have official support.

- **Restricted:** These are packages with restricted copyright, often hardware drivers.

- **Backports:** These are newer versions of packages in the archive, provided by the community.

- **Universe:** The universe includes packages maintained by the Ubuntu community.

- **Multiverse:** The multiverse includes packages that are not free (in the sense of freedom).

The term *official support* is a bit of a misnomer, as it doesn't refer to technical support that one would purchase or obtain but speaks instead to the availability of security updates after a version of Ubuntu is released. Standard Ubuntu releases are supported for 18 months, which means that Ubuntu's parent company, Canonical, Ltd., guarantees that security updates will be provided, free of charge, for any vulnerabilities discovered in software in the *main* repository for 18 months after a release. No such guarantee is made for software in the other repositories.

Of particular note is that certain Ubuntu releases have longer support cycles. These releases are denoted by the acronym LTS (Long Term Support) in their version number. The latest Ubuntu LTS, version 12.04 (Precise), will be supported for five years on servers.

APT Sources and Repositories

You're now aware of the structure of the Ubuntu archive, but we didn't explain how to actually modify the list of repositories you want to use on your system. In Debian package management parlance, the list of repositories is part of the list of Advanced Package Tool (APT) sources. (Keep your eyes peeled: Many of the package tools we'll discuss below begin with the prefix *apt*.) These sources tell APT where to find available packages: in the Ubuntu archive on the Internet, on your CD-ROM, or in a third-party archive.

The APT sources are specified in the file /etc/apt/sources.list. Let's open this file in an editor. (If you're not used to vim, substitute nano for it, which is an easier-to-use, beginner-friendly editor.)

```
$ vim /etc/apt/sources.list
```

The lines beginning with a hash, or #, denote comment lines and are skipped over by APT. At the top, you'll see the CD-ROM source that the installer added, and following it these two lines (or something very similar):

```
deb http://us.archive.ubuntu.com/ubuntu/ precise main restricted
deb-src http://us.archive.ubuntu.com/ubuntu/ precise main restricted
```

We can infer the general format of the APT sources list by looking at these lines. The file is composed of individual sources, one per line, and each line of several space-separated fields. The first field tells us what kind of a source the line is describing, such as a source for binary packages (deb) or source code packages (deb-src). The second field is the actual URI of the package source, the third names the distribution whose packages we want (lucid), and the remaining fields tell APT which components to use from the source we're describing—by default, main and restricted.

If you look through the rest of the file, you'll find it's nicely commented to let you easily enable two extra repositories: the very useful universe and the bleeding-edge backports. In general, now that you understand the format of each source line, you have complete control over the repositories you use, and while we strongly recommend against using the backports repository on a server, enabling universe is usually a good idea.

With that in mind, let's get you acquainted with some of the basic command-line package management tools on an Ubuntu system. Ubuntu inherits its package management from Debian, so if you're familiar with Debian, the utilities we'll discuss are old friends.

dpkg

Our first stop is the Debian package manager, dpkg, which sits around the lowest levels of the package management stack. Through a utility called dpkg-deb, dpkg deals with individual Debian package files, referred to as *debs* for their .deb filename extension.

dpkg is extensively documented in the system manual pages, so you can read about the various options it supports by entering man dpkg in the shell. We'll point out the most common dpkg operations: listing and installing packages. Of course, dpkg can also remove packages, but we'll show you how to do that with the higher-level tool called apt-get instead.

Listing Packages　　Running dpkg -l | less in the shell will list all the packages on your system that dpkg is tracking, in a six-column format. The first three columns are one letter wide each, signifying the desired package state, current package status, and error status, respectively. Most of the time, the error status column will be empty.

The top three lines of dpkg output serve as a legend to explain the letters you can find in the first three columns. This lets you use the grep tool to search through the package list, perhaps to look only at removed packages or those that failed configuration.

Installing a Package Manually

There are more than 17,000 packages in the Ubuntu archive for each release. Only a small percentage of those are officially supported, but all the other packages are still held to reasonably rigorous inclusion requirements. Packages in the Ubuntu archive are thus almost universally of high quality and are known to work well on your Ubuntu system.

Because of this, the archive should be the very first place you look when you choose to install new software. On rare instances, however, the software you want to install won't be available in the archive because it's new or because redistribution restrictions prevent it from being included. In those cases, you might have to either build the software from source code, run binaries that the vendor provides, or find third-party Ubuntu or Debian packages to install.

TIP　　**Practice Safe Hex!**
That's a terrible pun. We apologize. But it probably got your attention, so follow closely: Be very, very cautious when dealing with third-party packages. Packages in the Ubuntu archive undergo extensive quality assurance and are practically certain to be free from viruses, worms, Trojan horses, or other computer pests. If you install software only from the archive, you'll never have to worry about viruses again.

With third-party packages, you just don't know what you could be installing. If you install a malicious package, you've given the package creator full control of your system. So ideally, don't install third-party packages at all. And if you must, make absolutely sure you trust the source of the packages!

Impatience is a hallmark virtue of programmers and system administrators alike, so if you were too impatient to read the warning note, do it now. This is serious business. Let's continue: Say you've downloaded a package called myspecial-server.deb. You can install it simply by typing:

```
$ sudo dpkg -i myspecial-server.deb
```

dpkg will unpack the deb, make sure its dependencies are satisfied, and proceed to install the package. Remember what we said about the root account being unusable by default? Installing a package requires administrator privileges, which we obtained by prefixing the command we wanted to execute with sudo and entering our user password at sudo's prompt.

TIP   **A Quick Note on Shell Examples**
In the dpkg example, the dollar sign is the standard UNIX shell symbol, so you don't need to actually type it. We'll use it in the rest of the chapter to indicate things that need to be entered in a shell. On your Ubuntu system, the shell prompt won't be just a dollar sign but will look like this:

user@server:~$

user and *server* will be replaced by your username and the hostname you gave the server during installation, respectively, and the part between the colon and dollar sign will show your working directory. A tilde is UNIX shorthand for your home directory.

apt-get and apt-cache

Now let's jump higher up in the stack. Whereas dpkg deals mostly with package files, apt-get knows how to download packages from the Ubuntu archive or fetch them from your Ubuntu CD. It provides a convenient, succinct interface, so it's no surprise it's the tool that most system administrators use for package management on Ubuntu servers.

While apt-get deals with high-level package operations, it won't tell you which packages are actually in the archive and available for installation. It knows how to get this information behind the scenes from the package cache, which you can manipulate by using a simple tool called apt-cache. Let's see how these two commands come together with an example. Say we're trying to find and then install software that lets us work with extended filesystem attributes.

Searching the Package Cache and Showing Package Information   We begin by telling apt-cache to search for the phrase "extended attributes."

```
$ apt-cache search "extended attributes"
attr - Utilities for manipulating filesystem extended attributes
libattr1 - Extended attribute shared library
libattr1-dev - Extended attribute static libraries and headers
python-pyxattr - module for manipulating filesystem extended
attributes
python2.4-pyxattr - module for manipulating filesystem extended
attributes
rdiff-backup - remote incremental backup
xfsdump - Administrative utilities for the XFS filesystem
xfsprogs - Utilities for managing the XFS filesystem
```

The parameter to apt-cache search can be either a package name or a phrase describing the package, as in our example. The lines following our invocation are the output we received, composed of the package name on the left and a one-line description on the right. It looks like the attr package is what we're after, so let's see some details about it.

```
$ apt-cache show attr
Package: attr
Priority: optional
Section: utils
Installed-Size: 240
Maintainer: Ubuntu Core Developers <ubuntu-deel-
discuss@lists.ubuntu.com>
Original-Maintainer: Nathan Scott <nathans@debian.org>
Architecture: i386
Version: 1:2.4.39-1
Depends: libattr1 (>= 2.4.4-1), libc6 (>= 2.6.1-1)
Conflicts: xfsdump (<< 2.0.0)
Filename: pool/main/a/attr/attr_2.4.39-1_i386.deb
Size: 31098
MD5sum: 84457d6edd44983bba3dcb50495359fd
SHA1: 8ae3562e0a8e8a314c4c6997ca9aced0fb3bea46
SHA256:
f566a9a57135754f0a79c2efd8fcec626cde10d2533c10c1660bf7064a336c82
```

```
Description: Utilities for manipulating filesystem extended
   attributes
 A set of tools for manipulating extended attributes on filesystem
 objects, in particular getfattr(1) and setfattr(1).
 An attr(1) command is also provided which is largely compatible
 with the SGI IRIX tool of the same name.
   .
  Homepage: http://oss.sgi.com/projects/xfs/
Bugs: mailto:ubuntu-users@lists.ubuntu.com
Origin: Ubuntu
```

Don't be daunted by the verbose output. Extracting the useful bits turns out to be pretty simple. We can already see from the description field that this is, in fact, the package we're after. We can also see the exact version of the packaged software, any dependencies and conflicting packages it has, and an e-mail address to which we can send bug reports. And looking at the filename field, the pool/main snippet tells us this is a package in the main repository.

Installing a Package   So far, so good. Let's perform the actual installation:

```
$ sudo apt-get install attr
```

apt-get will track down a source for the package, such as an Ubuntu CD or the Ubuntu archive on the Internet, fetch the deb, verify its integrity, do the same for any dependencies the package has, and, finally, install the package.

Removing a Package   For didactic purposes, we're going to keep assuming that you're very indecisive and that right after you installed the attr package, you realized it wasn't going to work out between the two of you. To the bit bucket with attr!

```
$ sudo apt-get remove attr
```

One confirmation later and attr is blissfully gone from your system, except for any configuration files it may have installed. If you want those gone, too, you'd have to instead run the following:

```
$ sudo apt-get --purge remove attr
```

Performing System Updates   Installing and removing packages is a common system administration task, but not as common as keeping the system up to date. This doesn't mean upgrading to newer and newer versions of the software (well, it does, but not in the conventional sense), because once a given Ubuntu version is released, no new software versions enter the repositories except for the backports repository. On a server, however, you're strongly discouraged from using backports because they receive a very limited amount of quality assurance and testing and because there's usually no reason for a server to be chasing new software features. New features bring new bugs, and as a system administrator, you should value stability and reliability miles over features. Ubuntu's brief, six-month development cycle means that you'll be able to get all the new features in half a year anyway. But by then they will be in the main repositories and will have received substantial testing. Keeping a system up to date thus means making sure it's running the latest security patches, to prevent any vulnerabilities discovered after the release from endangering your system.

Luckily, `apt-get` makes this process amazingly easy. You begin by obtaining an updated list of packages from the Ubuntu archive:

```
$ sudo apt-get update
```

and then you simply run the upgrade:

```
$ sudo apt-get upgrade
```

After this, `apt-get` will tell you either that your system is up to date or what it's planning to upgrade, and it will handle the upgrade for you automatically. How's that for cool?

Running a Distribution Upgrade

When a new Ubuntu release comes out and you want to upgrade your server to it, you'll use a new tool, `do-release-upgrade`. The upgrade tool will switch over your sources.list to the new distribution and will figure out what packages are needed and whether they have any known issues. After it has done this, it will ask you to confirm the update by pressing y or to view the updated packages by pressing d. If you choose to view the updates, merely type y to continue the update, as the tool will not prompt you again.

NOTE   The update process may take a couple of hours and should not be interrupted during that time.

Building Packages from Source   The Ubuntu archive, unlike Debian's, doesn't permit direct binary uploads. When Ubuntu developers want to add a piece of software to the archive, they prepare its source code in a certain way and put it in a build queue. From there it's compiled, built automatically, and—if those steps succeed—pushed into the archive.

Why go through all the trouble? Why not just have the developers build the software on their machines? They could upload binaries to the archive, bypassing the build queue, which can take hours to build software. Here's the catch: Ubuntu officially supports three hardware platforms (Intel x86, AMD64, and ARMHF). Without the build queue, developers would have to build separate binaries of their software for each platform, which entails owning a computer running on each platform (expensive!) or creating complicated cross-compilation toolchains. And even then, sitting through three software builds is an enormous waste of precious developer time.

The build queue approach solves this problem because the automatic build system takes a single source package and builds it for all the necessary platforms. And it turns out that the approach provides you, the system administrator, with a really nifty benefit: It lets you leverage the dependency-solving power and ease of use of `apt-get` and apply it to building packages from source!

Now that you're excited, let's backtrack a bit. Building packages from source is primarily of interest to developers, not system administrators. In fact, as a sysadmin, you should avoid hand-built packages whenever possible and instead benefit from the quality assurance that packages in the Ubuntu archive received. Sometimes, though, you might just have to apply a custom patch to a piece of software before installing it. We'll use the attr package example, as before. What follows is what a session of building `attr` from source and installing the new package might look like—if you want to try it, make sure you install the dpkg-dev, devscripts, and fakeroot packages.

```
$ mkdir attr-build
$ cd attr-build
```

```
$ apt-get source attr
$ sudo apt-get build-dep attr
$ cd attr-2.4.39
```
<apply a patch or edit the source code>
```
$ dch -i
$ dpkg-buildpackage -rfakeroot
$ cd ..
$ sudo dpkg -i *.deb
```

All of the commands we invoked are well documented in the system man pages, and covering them in detail is out of the scope of this chapter. To briefly orient you as to what we did, though, here's a quick description.

1. We made a scratch directory called attr-build and changed into it.

2. `apt-get source attr` fetched the source of the attr package and unpacked it into the current directory.

3. `apt-get build-dep attr` installed all the packages required to build the attr package from source.

4. We changed into the unpacked attr-2.4.25 directory, applied a patch, and edited the package changelog to describe our changes to the source.

5. `dpkg -buildpackage -rfakeroot` built one or more installable debs from our package.

6. We ascended one directory in the filesystem and installed all the debs we just built.

This is a super-compressed cheat sheet for a topic that takes a long time to master. We left a lot of things out, so if you need to patch packages for production use, first go and read the man pages of the tools we mentioned and get a better understanding of what's going on!

aptitude

Around the highest levels of the package management stack hangs aptitude, a neat, colorful textual front end that can be used interchangeably with apt-get. We won't go into detail about aptitude use here; plenty of information is available from the system manual pages and the online `aptitude` help system (if you launch it as `aptitude` from the shell). It's worth mentioning, though, that one of the chief reasons some system administrators prefer `aptitude` over `apt-get` is its better handling of so-called orphan packages. Orphan packages are packages that were installed as a dependency of another package that has since been removed, leaving the orphan installed for no good reason. `apt-get` provides no automatic way to deal with orphans, instead relegating the task to the `deborphan` tool, which you can install from the archive. By contrast, `aptitude` will remove orphan packages automatically.

Tips and Tricks

Congratulations. If you've gotten this far, you're familiar with most aspects of effectively dealing with packages on your Ubuntu server. Before you move on to other topics, though, we want to present a few odds and ends that will probably come in handy to you at one point or another.

Listing Files Owned by a Package   Sometimes it's really useful to see which files on your system belong to a specific package, say, `cron`. `dpkg` to the rescue:

```
$ dpkg -L cron
```

Be careful, though, as `dpkg -L` output might contain directories that aren't exclusively owned by this package but are shared with others.

Finding Which Package Owns a File   The reverse of the previous operation is just as simple:

```
$ dpkg -S /etc/crontab
cron: /etc/crontab
```

The one-line output tells us the name of the owner package on the left.

Finding Which Package Provides a File   Both `dpkg -S` and `dpkg -L` operate on the database of installed packages. Sometimes, you might need to figure out which—potentially uninstalled—package provides a certain file. We might be looking for a package that would install the bzr binary, or /usr/bin/bzr. To do this, first install the package `apt-file` (requires the universe repository), then execute:

```
$ apt-file update
$ apt-file search /usr/bin/bzr
```

Voila! `apt-file` will tell you that the package you want is bzr, with output in the same format as `dpkg -S`.

That's it for our package management tricks—now it's time to talk about security.

Ubuntu Server Security

As a system administrator, one of your chief tasks is dealing with server security. If your server is connected to the Internet, for security purposes it's in a war zone. If it's only an internal server, you still need to deal with (accidentally) malicious users, disgruntled employees, and the guy in accounting who *really* wants to read the boss's secretary's e-mail.

In general, Ubuntu Server is a very secure platform. The Ubuntu Security Team, the team that produces all official security updates, has one of the best turnaround times in the industry. Ubuntu ships with a no open ports policy, meaning that after you install Ubuntu on your machine—be it an Ubuntu desktop or a server installation—no applications will be accepting connections from the Internet by default. Like Ubuntu desktops, Ubuntu Server uses the `sudo` mechanism for system administration, eschewing the root account. And finally, security updates are guaranteed for at least 18 months after each release (five years for some releases, like Dapper), and are free.

In this section, we want to take a look at user account administration, filesystem security, system resource limits, logs, and finally some network security. But Linux security is a difficult and expansive topic; remember that we're giving you a crash course here and leaving out a lot of things—to be a good administrator, you'll want to learn more.

User Account Administration

Many aspects of user administration on Linux systems are consistent across distributions. Debian provides some convenience tools, such as the `useradd` command, to make things easier for you. But since Ubuntu fully inherits Debian's user administration model, we won't go into detail about it here. Instead, let us refer you to www.oreilly.com/catalog/debian/ chapter/book/ch07_01.html for the basics. After reading that page, you'll have full knowledge of the standard model, and we can briefly talk about the Ubuntu difference: `sudo`.

As we mentioned at the end of the installation section (You're Done— Now Watch Out for Root!), Ubuntu doesn't enable the root, or adminis- trator, account by default. There is a great deal of security benefit to this approach and incredibly few downsides, all of which are documented at the man pages for `sudo_root`.

The user that you added during installation is the one who, by default, is placed into the admin group and may use `sudo` to perform system admin- istration tasks. After adding new users to the system, you may add them to the admin group like this:

```
$ sudo adduser username admin
```

Simply use `deluser` in place of `adduser` in the above command to remove a user from the group. (Adding the `--encrypt-home` option to `adduser` will auto- matically set up home directory encryption for the new user.)

One thing to keep in mind is that `sudo` isn't just a workaround for giving people root access. `sudo` can also handle fine-grain permissions, such as saying, "Allow this user to execute only these three commands with super- user privileges."

Documentation about specifying these permissions is available in the sudoers man page, which can be a bit daunting—feel free to skip close to the end of it, until you reach the EXAMPLES section. It should take you maybe 10 or 15 minutes to grok it, and it covers a vast majority of the situ- ations for which you'll want `sudo`. When you're ready to put your new knowledge to use, simply run:

```
$ visudo
```

Be careful here—the sudoers database, which lives in /etc/sudoers, is not meant to just be opened in an editor because an editor won't check the syntax for you! If you mess up the sudoer's database, you might find yourself with no way to become an administrator on the machine.

Filesystem Security

The security model for files is standardized across most UNIX-like operating systems and is called the POSIX model. The model calls for three broad types of access permissions for every file and directory: owner, group, and other. It works in exactly the same way on any Linux distribution, which is why we won't focus on it here. For a refresher, consult the man pages for chmod and chown, or browse around the Internet.

We want to actually look at securing partitions through mount options, an oft-neglected aspect of dealing with system security that's rather powerful when used appropriately. When explaining how to partition your system, we extolled the virtues of giving, at the very least, the /home, /tmp, and /var directories their own partitions, mentioning how it's possible to use special options when mounting these to the filesystem.

Many of the special mount options are filesystem-dependent, but the ones we want to consider are not. Here are the ones that interest us.

nodev   A filesystem mounted with the nodev option will not allow the use or creation of special "device" files. There's usually no good reason to allow most filesystems to allow interpretation of block or character special devices, and allowing them poses potential security risks.

nosuid   If you read up about UNIX file permissions, you know that certain files can be flagged in a way that lets anyone execute them with the permissions of another user or group, often that of the system administrator. This flag is called the setuid (suid) or the setgid bit, respectively, and allowing this behavior outside of the directories that hold the system binaries is often unnecessary and decreases security. If a user is able to, in any way, create or obtain a setuid binary of his or her own choosing, the user has effectively compromised the system.

noexec   If a filesystem is flagged as noexec, users will not be able to run any executables located on it.

noatime   This flag tells the filesystem not to keep a record of when files were last accessed. If used indiscriminately, it lessens security through limiting the amount of information available in the event of a security incident, particularly when computer forensics is to be performed. However, the flag does provide performance benefits for certain use patterns, so it's a good candidate to be used on partitions where security is an acceptable tradeoff for speed.

Deciding which mount options to use on which partition is another fuzzy science, and you'll often develop preferences as you become more accustomed to administering machines. Here's a basic proposal, though, that should be a good starting point:

- /home: `nosuid`, `nodev`
- /tmp: `noatime`, `noexec`, `nodev`, `nosuid`
- /var: `noexec`, `nodev`, `nosuid`

System Resource Limits

By default, Linux will not impose any resource limits on user processes. This means any user is free to fill up all of the working memory on the machine, or spawn processes in an endless loop, rendering the system unusable in seconds. The solution is to set up some of your own resource limits by editing the /etc/security/limits.conf file:

```
$ sudoedit /etc/security/limits.conf
```

The possible settings are all explained in the comment within the file, and there are no silver bullet values to recommend, though we do recommend that you set up at least the `nproc` limit and possibly also the as/data/memlock/rss settings.

TIP   **A Real-Life Resource Limit Example**
Just to give you an idea of what these limits look like on production servers, here is the configuration from the general login server of the Harvard Computer Society at Harvard University:

```
*        -      as       2097152
*        -      data     131072
```

```
*       -       memlock     131072
*       -       rss         1013352
*       hard    nproc       128
```

This limits regular users to 128 processes, with a maximum address space of 2GB, maximum data size and locked-in-memory address space of 128MB, and maximum resident set size of 1GB.

If you need to set up disk quotas for your users, install the quota package, and take a look at its man page.

System Log Files

As a system administrator, the system log files are some of your best friends. If you watch them carefully, you'll often know in advance when something is wrong with the system, and you'll be able to resolve most problems before they escalate.

Unfortunately, your ability to pay close attention to the log files dwindles with every server you're tasked with administering, so administrators often use log-processing software that can be configured to alert them on certain events, or they write their own tools in languages such as Perl and Python.

Logs usually live in /var/log, and after your server runs for a while, you'll notice there are a lot of increasingly older versions of the log files in that directory, many of them compressed with gzip (ending with the .gz filename extension).

Here are some log files of note:

- /var/log/syslog: general system log
- /var/log/auth.log: system authentication logs
- /var/log/mail.log: system mail logs
- /var/log/messages: general log messages
- /var/log/dmesg: kernel ring buffer messages, usually since system bootup

Your Log Toolbox   When it comes to reviewing logs, you should become familiar with a few tools of choice. The `tail` utility prints, by default, the last ten lines of a file, which makes it a neat tool to get an idea of what's been happening last in a given log file:

```
$ tail /var/log/syslog
```

With the `-f` parameter, tail launches into follow mode, which means it'll open the file and keep showing you changes on the screen as they're happening. If you want to impress your friends with your new system administrator prowess, you can now easily recreate the Hollywood hacker movie staple: text furiously blazing across the screen.

Also invaluable are `zgrep`, `zcat`, and `zless`, which operate like their analogues that don't begin with a `z`, but on `gzip`-compressed files. For instance, to get a list of lines in all your compressed logs that contain the word "warthog" regardless of case, you would issue the following command:

```
$ zgrep -i warthog /var/log/*.gz
```

Your toolbox for dealing with logs will grow with experience and based on your preferences, but to get an idea of what's already out there, do an `apt-cache` search for "log files."

A Sprinkling of Network Security

Network security administration is another feature provided largely by the OS, so it's no different on Ubuntu than on any other modern Linux distribution. That means we won't cover it here but will leave you with a pointer.

The `iptables` command is the front end to the very powerful Linux firewall tables. Unfortunately, dealing with `iptables` can be rather difficult, particularly if you're trying to set up complex firewall policies. To whet your appetite, here's `iptables` in action, dropping all packets coming from a notorious time-sink domain:

```
$ sudo iptables -A INPUT -s www.slashdot.org -j DROP
```

Tutorials, how-tos, and articles about iptables are available on the Internet in large numbers, and the system man pages provide detailed information about all the possible options. Spending some time to learn iptables is well worth it because it'll let you set up network security on any Linux machine and will make it pretty easy for you to learn other operating systems' firewall systems if need be.

If you want to just manage a basic firewall on Ubuntu Server, you don't necessarily even need to venture into iptables. Ubuntu provides an excellent front-end called ufw that makes it very easy to add new firewall rules. For more information on ufw, check out the man page for that tool, or if you want a more complete reference, look at the security section of *The Official Ubuntu Server Book*.

Final Words on Security

We've barely even scratched the surface of system security in this subsection, though we've tried to give you good pointers on where to start and where to get the information you need to learn more. But let us give you some sage advice on security in general, since it's a painful truth to learn: There is no such thing as a fully secure system. Securing systems isn't about making it impossible for a breach to occur. It's about making the breach so difficult that it's not worth it to the attacker. This definition is pretty fluid because if your attacker is a bored 14-year-old sitting in a basement somewhere chewing on cold pizza, you can bet that kid will leave your system alone if it's even marginally secure. But if you're keeping around top-secret information, it's a lot more difficult to have the system be secure enough that breaking into it isn't worth it, from a cost/benefit point of view, to the attackers.

Security is also neat because, as a concept, it permeates the entire idea space of computer science. Getting really good at security requires an incredibly deep understanding of the inner workings of computer systems, which has the nonobvious advantage that if you're trying to get a deep understanding of computer systems but don't know where to start, you can start with security and simply follow the trail. Use this to your advantage! Good luck.

TIP   **Getting In Touch**
If you want to tell us why you like Ubuntu Server, or why you hate it, or send us cookies, or just stalk us from a distance, come on in! Go to

https://lists.ubuntu.com/mailman/listinfo/ubuntu-server

to join the ubuntu-server mailing list, visit our page on Launchpad at

https://launchpad.net/people/ubuntu-server,

or jump on IRC. We're on the #ubuntu-server channel on FreeNode. Hope to see you there!

Advanced Topics

A single book chapter isn't the right place to go into great detail on all the features packed into Ubuntu Server. There isn't enough space, and many of the features are quite specialized. But that doesn't stop us from taking you on a whirlwind tour. Our goal here is to give just enough information to let you know what's there and interest you in finding out more about those features that may be relevant to how you use Ubuntu.

Virtualization

If there's been one buzzword filling out the server space for the past couple of years, it's *virtualization*. In August 2007, a virtualization company called VMware raised about a billion U.S. dollars in its initial public offering, and the term virtualization finally went supernova, spilling from the technology realm into the financial mainstream, and soon to CIOs and technology managers everywhere.

Fundamentally, virtualization is a way to turn one computer into many. (Erudite readers will note this is precisely the opposite of the Latin motto on the Seal of the United States, "E Pluribus Unum," which means "out of many, one." Some technologies match that description, too, like Single System Image, or SSI, grids. But if we talked about virtualization in Latin, it would be "Ex Uno Plura.") Why is it useful to turn one computer into many?

Back in the 1960s, servers were huge and extremely expensive, and no one wanted to buy more of them than they absolutely needed. It soon became clear that a single server, capable of running different operating systems at once, would allow the same hardware to be used by different people with different needs, which meant fewer hardware purchases, which meant happier customers with less devastated budgets. IBM was the first to offer this as a selling point, introducing virtualization in its IBM 7044 and IBM 704 models, and later in the hardware of its Model 67 mainframe. Since then, the industry largely moved away from mainframes and toward small and cheap rack servers, which meant the need to virtualize mostly went away: If you needed to run separate operating systems in parallel, you just bought two servers. But eventually Moore's law caught up with us, and even small rack machines became so powerful that organizations found many of them underutilized, while buying more servers (though cheap in itself) meant sizable auxiliary costs for cooling and electricity. This set the stage for virtualization to once again become vogue. Maybe you want to run different Linux distributions on the same machine. Maybe you need a Linux server side by side with Windows. Virtualization delivers.

There are four key types of virtualization. From the lowest level to highest, they are hardware emulation, full virtualization, paravirtualization, and OS virtualization. Hardware emulation means running different operating systems by emulating, for each, all of a computer's hardware in software. The approach is very powerful and painfully slow. Full virtualization instead uses a privileged piece of software called a hypervisor as a broker between operating systems and the underlying hardware, and it offers good performance but requires special processor support on instruction sets like the ubiquitous x86. Paravirtualization also uses a hypervisor but supports only executing operating systems that have been modified in a special way, offering high performance in return. Finally, OS virtualization is more accurately termed "containerization" or "zoning" and refers to operating systems that support multiple user spaces utilizing a single running kernel. Containerization provides near-native performance but isn't really comparable to the other virtualization approaches because its focus isn't running multiple operating systems in parallel but carving one up into isolated pieces.

The most widely used hardware emulators on Linux are QEMU and Bochs, available in Ubuntu as packages qemu and bochs respectively. The big players in full virtualization on Linux are the commercial offerings from VMware, IBM's z/VM, and most recently, a technology called KVM that's become part of the Linux kernel. In paravirtualization, the key contender is Xen; the Linux OS virtualization space is dominated by the

OpenVZ and Linux-VServer projects, though many of the needed inter-faces for OS virtualization have gradually made their way into the Linux kernel proper.

Now that we've laid the groundwork, let's point you in the right direction depending on what you're looking for. If you're a desktop Ubuntu user and want a way to safely run one or more other Linux distributions (including different versions of Ubuntu!) or operating systems (BSD, Windows, Solaris, and so forth) for testing or development, all packaged in a nice interface, the top recommendation is an open source project out of Sun Microsys-tems called VirtualBox. It's available in Ubuntu as the package virtualbox-ose, and its home page is www.virtualbox.org.

If you want to virtualize your server, the preferred solution in Ubuntu is KVM, a fast full virtualizer that turns the running kernel into a hypervisor. Due to peculiarities of the x86 instruction set, however, full virtualizers can work only with a little help from the processor, and KVM is no excep-tion. To test whether your processor has the right support, try:

```
$ egrep '(vmx|svm)' /proc/cpuinfo
```

If that line produces any output, you're golden. Head on over to https://help.ubuntu.com/community/KVM for instructions on installing and con-figuring KVM and its guest operating systems.

TIP   **Point-and-Click Xen**
One Xen-related project to point out is MIT's open source XVM (not to be confused with Sun Microsystems' xVM), which is a set of tools built on top of Debian that allow users to create and bring up Xen guests through a Web browser, complete with serial console redirection, ssh access, and a variety of other goodies. MIT uses the system to offer point-and-click vir-tual machines to any MIT affiliate; the project home page is http://xvm.mit.edu.

Disk Replication

We've discussed the role of RAID in protecting data integrity in the case of disk failures, but we didn't answer the follow-up question: What happens when a whole machine fails? The answer depends entirely on your use case, and giving a general prescription doesn't make sense. If you're Google, for instance, you have automated cluster management tools that notice a machine going down and don't distribute work to it until a technician has been dispatched to fix the machine. But that's because Google's infrastructure makes sure that (except in pathological cases) no machine holds data that isn't replicated elsewhere, so the failure of any one machine is ultimately irrelevant.

If you don't have Google's untold thousands of servers on a deeply redundant infrastructure, you may consider a simpler approach: Replicate an entire hard drive to another computer, propagating changes in real time, just like RAID1 but over the network.

This functionality is called DRBD, or Distributed Replicated Block Device, and it isn't limited to hard drives: It can replicate any block device you like. Ubuntu 9.04 and newer ships with DRBD, and the user space utilities you need are in the drbd8-utils package. For the full documentation, see the DRBD Web site at www.drbd.org.

Cloud Computing

Cloud computing builds on the most interesting aspect of virtualization: you can easily create, pause, and tear down multiple virtual computers, all running on one real bare-metal machine. To the user, those virtual computers behave just like real computers.

With cloud computing, computing power becomes a commodity. You don't need to plan, budget for, and install new computing power months in advance. Instead, ask the cloud for a machine and it's there within seconds. When you're done, throw it away.

It's like the difference between digging a well and turning on a tap. If you have running water from a tap, water remains a precious resource, but it's no longer something you need to invest time in to obtain. If you have cloud computing, computing power may remain limited, but it's much easier to get hold of, share, and repurpose.

If you want cloud computing power, there are a couple of ways to get it: build your own private cloud or buy computing power as and when you need it from one of the big cloud providers, such as Amazon or RackSpace.

Actually, with Ubuntu you can mix and match between using your own private cloud and buying additional resources when you need them.

Ubuntu is at the heart of the cloud computing revolution. Both as the base operating system running cloud compute clusters—the machines that provide the computing power to the cloud—and as the OS that people choose to run in the virtual machines they run in the cloud.

Because it's so new, cloud computing is fast moving, but two dominant approaches to running a cloud have already emerged: Amazon's EC2 and the open source project OpenStack. Ubuntu is at the heart of both. That's great news if you want to experiment, because Ubuntu gives you a range of tools to set up and manage your own cloud.

The two main tools you'll come across are MAAS, otherwise known as Metal As A Service, and Juju. MAAS helps you set up and manage a cluster of servers, and Juju makes it easy to get services running either directly on bare-metal servers or in the cloud.

Using MAAS, you can treat a group of bare-metal servers like a cloud: instead of a bunch of individual servers, you have a computing resource to which you can deploy different services. Using MAAS's Web UI, you can quickly get an overview of how your computing cluster is being used and what's available. Even with just a handful of servers, MAAS is a great way to start treating real machines in a similar way to a cloud.

You can think of Juju as similar to apt-get but for services that run on servers. Juju uses scripts, called charms, that do all the setup necessary to get a particular service running. Let's say you want to run a WordPress server. All you need to do is deploy the correct Juju charm to the server and everything should get set up correctly.

By combining MAAS and Juju, you can relatively easily set up your own private cloud. MAAS helps you manage the real machines, and Juju helps you set up the services you need to run that cloud.

Let's say you want to deploy a specific service to the cloud using Juju. We use Zookeeper in our example. Deploying a service normally begins like this:

```
$ juju bootstrap
$ juju deploy zookeeper
$ juju expose zookeeper
```

At this point, Juju creates a virtual machine instance, installs Zookeeper, and configures it. Use the following to determine the status of the instance:

```
$ juju status
```

When you get the notification that your instance is up and running, you will learn its IP address and can start using it. This process is amazingly quick and easy!

One useful tool that is brand new for 12.04 is the Juju charm store. When Juju started, it was much more difficult to find and deploy services using charms, but with the charm store as a central repository, the process has become much more elegant. Just as APT and related software repositories have made finding and installing software easy, the Juju store is designed to make launching and configuring servers in the cloud easy. There is an interesting difference between how APT and Juju work.

In an APT repository, the software is generally frozen—that is, it will not receive updates for a specific release cycle except perhaps for security updates or minor bug fix updates, and even then the updates are often stored in another repository (e.g., precise-main or precise-security). With Juju, charms can be written by anyone and can be updated within a release cycle for the charm store. It isn't frozen the way APT repositories are. This is important, especially for those who (wisely) choose to run an LTS release of Ubuntu for their servers and who otherwise might need to wait several years before they can install a new version of desirable software or until they upgrade their Ubuntu release version to the next LTS or find a PPA with the software in it.

So, let's say you are working on a development version of Zookeeper and want to quickly create a cloud server instance with the development version deployed to it instead of the stable version. You could simply use the following series of commands instead of the previous set:

```
$ juju bootstrap
$ juju deploy zookeeper
$ juju set zookeeper source=dev
$ juju expose zookeeper
```

By adding only one line, you are deploying the development version! The ability to easily set the source from which to deploy is useful.

Charm authors are given the ability to write these details into their charms. Specifics like versions, sources, and so on, are all in there. If you want to install nodejs, there is no need to search all over for someone's install script in a blog post or a pastebin code snippet. You can use that person's Juju charm. Simple. The charm includes information like which PPA to use and the install script necessary.

Allowing anyone to give you a charm to install software could be dangerous, so some safety and security mechanisms are built in. This is the second reason for the store (after convenience for end users). Charms included in the Juju store go through a community peer review process and an automated build process to test for failures. Anyone can write charms for their own use or to share directly with people, but it takes a little more effort and scrutiny before a charm is included in the store.

There is so much more to be said about Juju, MAAS, and charms that is beyond the scope of this book. If you are interested, see juju.ubuntu.com/ Charms or *The Official Ubuntu Server Book, Third Edition,* also from Prentice-Hall.

Summary

If you've never administered a system before, the transition from being a regular user will be difficult, regardless of which OS you choose to learn to administer. The difficulty stems from the wider shift in thinking that's required. Instead of just making sure your room is clean, now you have to run and protect the whole apartment building. But the difficulty is also educational and rewarding. (We realize they also told you this for your theoretical physics class in college, but we are not lying.) Learning to maintain Ubuntu servers is a great choice for you because you'll benefit from a vibrant and helpful user community, and you'll be working with a top-notch OS every step of the way.

If you're a seasoned administrator who came to see what all the Ubuntu Server fuss is about, stay tuned. The project, though rock solid as far as stability goes, is still in its feature infancy, and the Server Team is working very hard at making it the best server platform out there. We're emphasizing advanced features and we're being very fussy about getting all the little details just right.

In both cases, if you're installing a new server, give Ubuntu Server a try. It's a state-of-the-art system, and we're sure you'll enjoy using it. Get in touch, tell us what to do to make it better, and lend a hand. Help us make Ubuntu rock even harder on big iron and heavy metal!

CHAPTER 9

Ubuntu-Related Projects and Derivatives

- **Recognized Derivatives**
- **Editions**
- **Remixes**
- **Other Distributions**
- **Launchpad**
- **Bazaar**
- **Ubuntu One**
- **Summary**

UBUNTU IS NOT MERELY a complete operating system; it is also the center of a growing ecosystem of distributions. Some, referred to as the partner projects, work closely with and within Ubuntu. Others prefer to work outside the project and are considered full derivatives. Often, these projects are created in order to highlight a specific selection of software or use case, such as the Ubuntu Studio project, which focuses on multimedia creation and editing. Others, like the Lubuntu project, are created by a community of users with specific desires.

Still others are created for reasons connected to the international nature of Linux and open source software. While most Ubuntu development happens in English, there are large developer and user communities in other languages and countries. Thus, a derived distribution might spring up to satisfy that need. There are derived distributions targeted at Christians, Muslims, people with slow computers, and people who prefer to have an Ubuntu system optimized for any of several alternative user interfaces or for use in several different schools and government bureaucracies around the world. Should you use any of these over Ubuntu? We can't answer that question for you. Some of these projects are fully within and, as a result, not mutually exclusive from Ubuntu and others are based on Ubuntu, but distinct projects. One may be more appropriate than another depending on your preferences or circumstances. You can mix, match, and sample these distributions until you find one that works great for you. As we mentioned in Chapter 1, Ubuntu sees these derivatives, also know as flavors, as a sign of a healthy and vibrant community. One of the goals of the project is to make it easier for this type of distribution to appear. We can all expect to see more of them in the future.

Recognized Derivatives

Recognized derivatives, or flavors (Figure 9-1), release on the same schedule, share a common repository of packages, and work in close relation with Ubuntu. There are at the time of publication six officially recognized derivatives—Xubuntu, Ubuntu Studio, Mythbuntu, Kubuntu, Edubuntu, and Lubuntu—which are discussed in more depth later in this chapter. As of the 2011 Ubuntu Developer Summit (UDS-P; Orlando, Florida), Canonical has implemented changes around its derivatives. No longer are there any "supported" derivatives, and all "official" derivatives are referred to as "rec-

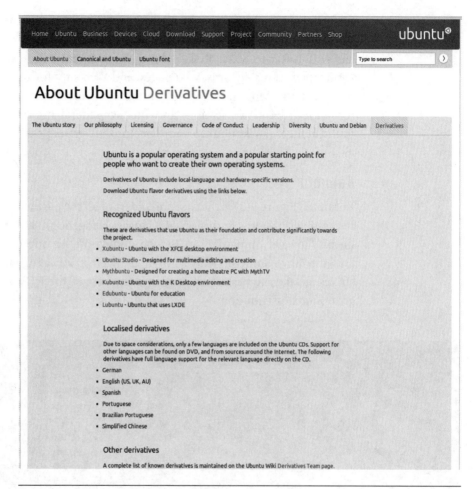

Figure 9-1 Ubuntu.com Derivatives page

ognized" derivatives. Canonical now supplies these recognized derivatives with infrastructure, daily ISO build and publish resources, coordination with the Ubuntu release, and support after the release. However, there are services that Canonical does not offer these recognized derivatives: testing of the derivative images on ISO tracker, automated ISO or upgrade testing, fixing of packages not in Ubuntu desktop or server images, security updates of packages not in main, publishing on http://releases.ubuntu.com, and mastering of the CD or USB images. It is now the responsibility of each of the recognized derivative communities to take ownership of those services.

Like Ubuntu, each of these recognized derivatives has vibrant communities that help develop, maintain, test, support, advocate, and more. Each has IRC (Internet Chat Relay) channels on freenode.net, mailing lists, Launchpad teams, forums, wiki pages, and Web sites for users to actively participate in. More information on these resources is listed under each recognized derivative section, and further general information can be found at https://wiki.ubuntu.com/RecognizedDerivatives.

Kubuntu

Kubuntu (Figure 9-2) is the first and oldest of all the partner projects. First released alongside Ubuntu 5.04 (Hoary Hedgehog), Kubuntu, which means "toward humanity" in Bemba, builds on the strengths of the K Desktop Environment (KDE) rather than GNOME as Ubuntu does. It strives to take the best of Ubuntu and the best of the KDE to produce a great Linux distribution.

Figure 9-2 Kubuntu 12.04 desktop

Like Ubuntu, Kubuntu makes the following commitments: Kubuntu will provide the very best translations and accessibility infrastructure that the free software community has to offer; Kubuntu will always be free of charge, and there is no extra cost for an "enterprise" version; and Kubuntu will always provide the latest and best software from the KDE community.

Kubuntu is a complete desktop but one built around KDE and Qt. Kubuntu opts for a more traditional blue and makes only a few other visual changes. The project is led by the Kubuntu Council (an elected group of developers) and an army of volunteers. The Council includes:

- Christian Mangold

- David Wonderly

- Harald Sitter

- Jonathan Riddell

- Jonathan Thomas

- Scott Kitterman

TIP   **Kubuntu Resources**
IRC: #kubuntu
Mailing list: http://lists.ubuntu.com/mailman/listinfo/kubuntu-users
Launchpad Team: https://launchpad.net/~kubuntu-members
Forum: www.ubuntuforums.org
Wiki page: https://wiki.kubuntu.org/Kubuntu

TIP   **Kubuntu**
Kubuntu can be found at www.kubuntu.org.

Edubuntu

Edubuntu (Figure 9-3) is a version of Ubuntu for use in schools and other educational environments and uses the thin client technology of the Linux Terminal Server Project (LTSP) as well as a number of programs aimed at the educational market, such as GCompris and the KDE Education suite.

Figure 9-3 Edubuntu 12.04 desktop

It is led by a team council that coordinates and participates heavily in its development; the members are listed here:

- Scott Balneaves
- Jonathan Carter
- Jordan Erickson
- Alkis Georgopoulos
- Stéphane Graber
- Marc Gariépy

One of Edubuntu's unique features is the inclusion of the LTSP in an easy-to-use, out-of-the-box installer. LTSP uses a different method of deploying clients over a network than is used in traditional computer deployments. Instead of full-powered computers, LTSP uses thin clients, less capable, cheaper computers that connect to a larger server and have it do all the processing work. LTSP is covered in greater detail in *The Official Ubuntu Server Book, Second Edition*, also available from Prentice Hall.

For most of those reading this book, Ubuntu is an alternative operating system for an extraordinarily exciting generation of users. No team or project within Ubuntu has done more to target, support, and grow this group of users than the Edubuntu project.

The community-driven Edubuntu project aims to create an add-on for Ubuntu specially tailored for use in primary and secondary education. Edubuntu exists as a platform consisting of tools for teachers and administrators. The real thrust, of course, and the real purpose, is to put free and open source software into the hands of children. In doing so, Edubuntu provides children with a flexible and powerful technological environment for learning and experimenting. Based on free software, it offers educational technologies that are hackable and that can ultimately be used by students and teachers on *their own terms*. Distributed freely, its gratis nature serves an important need for schools where technology programs are always understaffed and underfunded. Fluent in Ubuntu and in free software, the children who, right now, are growing up using Edubuntu are offering the Ubuntu community a glimpse of where it might go and the generation of Ubunteros who may take us there.

While the Ubuntu, Kubuntu, and Xubuntu (another recognized derivative covered later in this chapter) desktops highlight the products of the GNOME, KDE, and Xfce communities respectively, the Edubuntu project aims to provide the best of everything in Ubuntu—properly tailored for use in schools and as easy to use as possible. One thing that made Edubuntu popular was its amazing ability to integrate thin clients, allowing the use of one powerful machine (the server) to provide many very low-powered, often diskless machines (the clients), with their entire OS. This model, while uninteresting for most home or business users using workstations and laptops, is a major feature in classroom settings where it can mitigate configuration and maintenance headaches and reduce the cost of classroom deployments substantially.

In 2008, it was decided that the developers of Edubuntu should focus more on bringing the best educational applications to the desktop rather than trying to maintain an entire distribution of their own. As a result, Edubuntu is no longer a distribution like Ubuntu, Kubuntu, or Xubuntu, but rather an "add-on" for users. What this means is that you can easily install Edubuntu using the Ubuntu Software Center located in your Unity launcher found on your desktop. Once the Ubuntu software Center opens, type *Educational Desktop for Ubuntu* or *Educational Desktop for Kubuntu* in the search window.

> **TIP**   **Edubuntu Resources**
> IRC: #edubuntu
> Mailing list: https://lists.ubuntu.com/mailman/listinfo/edubuntu-users
> Launchpad Team: https://launchpad.net/~edubuntu-members
> Forum: www.ubuntuforums.org
> Wiki page: http://wiki.ubuntu.com/Edubuntu

> **TIP**   **Edubuntu**
> Edubuntu, along with more detailed installation instructions and options, can be found at www.edubuntu.org.

Lubuntu

Lubuntu (Figure 9-4) gained its official recognized derivative status during the 11.10 release cycle and strives to provide an even lighter and faster desktop by using the Lightweight X11 Desktop Environment (LXDE), by default, in place of GNOME, KDE, or Xfce. While LXDE can be built on many current Linux distributions, it is the native environment of Lubuntu alone.

Lubuntu is targeted at "normal" PC and laptop users running on low-spec hardware and who may not know how to use command-line tools. In most cases, they just don't have enough resources for all the bells and whistles of the "full-featured" mainstream distributions.

> **TIP**   **Lubuntu Resources**
> IRC: #lubuntu
> Mailing list: https://lists.ubuntu.com/mailman/listinfo/lubuntu-usersv
> Launchpad Team: https://launchpad.net/~lubuntu-desktop
> Forum: http://ubuntuforums.org/tags.php?tag=lubuntu
> Wiki page: https://wiki.ubuntu.com/Lubuntu

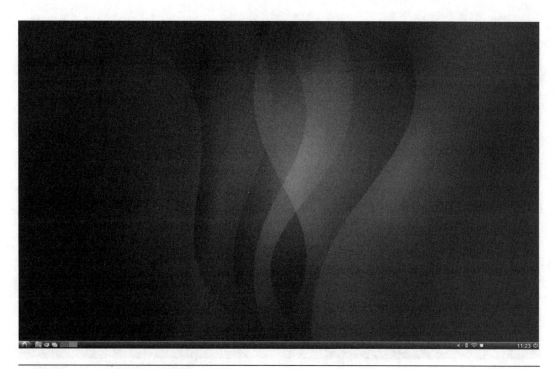

Figure 9-4 Lubuntu 12.04 desktop

TIP   **Lubuntu**
Lubuntu can be found at http://lubuntu.net.

Xubuntu

Xubuntu (Figure 9-5) is a version of Ubuntu built on top of the Xfce window management system. In Xubuntu, Xfce and its associated applications play a role analogous to KDE in the context of Kubuntu. Xfce is small and lightweight compared to the much fancier GNOME and KDE. It uses less memory and fewer CPU cycles than either of the alternatives in a normal configuration. While this means that Xubuntu is often seen as having fewer features or being less user-friendly than Ubuntu or Kubuntu, it also means that it runs faster, is more responsive, and tends to run very quickly on older or less powerful computers, where the weight of either GNOME or KDE may make the system prohibitively slow. As a result, Xubuntu has been used frequently by computer recyclers, by the

Figure 9-5 Xubuntu 12.04 desktop

owners of old computers, and by those who just want to squeeze out better performance from their hardware using a more efficient interface.

Like Kubuntu, Xubuntu is community driven and began outside the project in the universe repository of Ubuntu. In releases 5.04 and 5.10, Xfce 4 was supported by a special Xfce Team in Ubuntu. Due to the great work done on Xfce, Xubuntu was brought into the fold and became Ubuntu's third partner project and a part of the main Ubuntu repository, for release 6.10, where it has remained since.

TIP   **Xubuntu resources can be found at:**
IRC: #xubuntu
Mailing list: https://lists.ubuntu.com/mailman/listinfo/xubuntu-users
Launchpad Team: https://launchpad.net/xubuntu-desktop
Forum: www.ubuntuforums.org
Wiki page: http://wiki.ubuntu.com/Xubuntu

TIP   **Xubuntu**
Xubuntu, can be found at www.xubuntu.org

Ubuntu Studio

Ubuntu Studio (Figure 9-6) is a derivative of Ubuntu that is designed and optimized for multimedia production. The system includes a wide variety of applications useful to those engaging in audio and video recording, mixing, editing, synthesis, and production as well as graphics production and manipulation. It contains a modified kernel that allows the system to reduce latency for audio in ways that dramatically improve performance in professional audio recording and manipulation, but the kernel may be inappropriate in other environments. Its first release was based on Ubuntu 7.04.

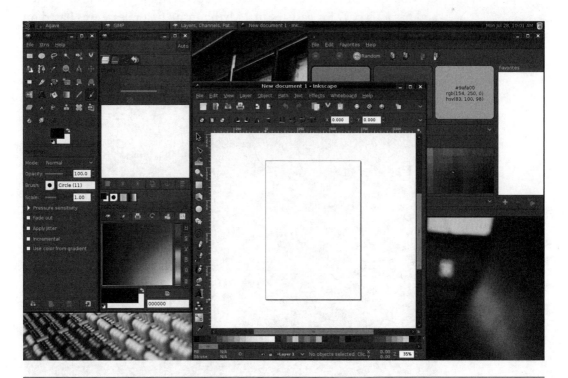

Figure 9-6 Ubuntu Studio 12.04 desktop

TIP   **Kubuntu Ubuntu Studio Resources**
IRC: #ubuntustudio
Mailing list: https://lists.ubuntu.com/mailman/listinfo/ubuntu-studio-users
Launchpad Team: https://launchpad.net/~ubuntustudio
Forum: www.ubuntuforums.org
Wiki page: https://wiki.ubuntu.com/UbuntuStudio

TIP   **Ubuntu Studio**
Ubuntu Studio can be found at www.ubuntustudio.org.

Mythbuntu

MythTV is one of the most popular pieces of home theater software, but it has a bit of a reputation as a beast to set up. Mythbuntu (Figure 9-7) is designed to make that setup easy. Like Xubuntu, Mythbuntu uses Xfce as a desktop environment, has a custom-made Mythbuntu Control Center, and has a LiveCD for easy testing. Mythbuntu's first release was based on Ubuntu 7.10.

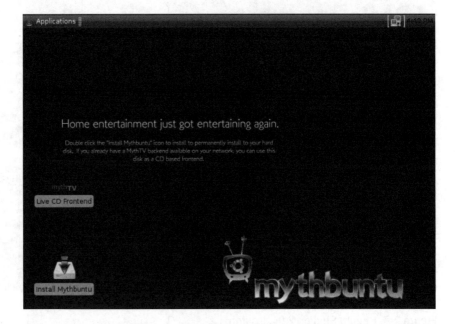

Figure 9-7 Mythbuntu 12.04 desktop

TIP   **Mythbuntu Resources**
IRC: #mythbuntu
Mailing list: www.gossamer-threads.com/lists/mythtv/users/
Launchpad Team: https://launchpad.net/mythbuntu
Forum: http://ubuntuforums.org/forumdisplay.php?f=301
Wiki page: www.mythbuntu.org/wiki

TIP   **Mythbuntu**
Mythbuntu can be found at www.mythbuntu.org.

Editions

Official Ubuntu editions include the Ubuntu desktop, server and cloud and are fully supported by Canonical.

Ubuntu Server Edition

Ubuntu Server Edition was created with the aim of making Ubuntu easy to install and use on servers. The Server Edition was officially launched with Ubuntu 5.04 and initially focused on making certain that the highest quality server applications were available for easy installation and configuration, including MySQL, Apache, and others.

The most recent work has involved improvements to the cloud computing capabilities of Ubuntu Server.

Ubuntu Cloud

Ubuntu Cloud (Figure 9-8) aims at providing you with all the tools and services needed to build your own cloud infrastructure with Ubuntu. Whether at an enterprise or individual level, Ubuntu Cloud allows you to manage cloud workloads on your own servers and send identical workloads to the public cloud when you need extra capacity.

Ubuntu Cloud is more than just infrastructure. Systems administrators, dev-ops engineers, and users can use Juju—DevOps Distilled™—charms to deploy, orchestrate, and scale services in the public, private, or hybrid cloud.

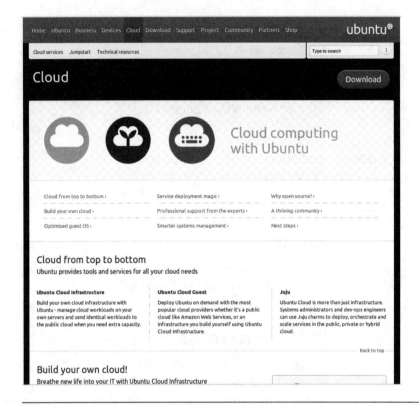

Figure 9-8 Ubuntu Cloud

To learn more about Ubuntu Server Edition, we recommend *The Official Ubuntu Server Book, Third Edition,* also available from Prentice Hall.

TIP   Ubuntu Server Edition
Ubuntu Server Edition can be found at www.ubuntu.com/business/server/overview with further infomation at www.ubuntu.com/cloud, http://cloud.ubuntu.com, and https://juju.ubuntu.com.

Remixes
Ubuntu Desktop Business Remix

The Ubuntu Desktop Business Remix (Figure 9-9), which launched during the 12.04 release cycle to be a starting point for large-scale corporate

Figure 9-9 Ubuntu Cloud infrastructure

desktop deployments, was inspired by a review of common changes made by IT departments deploying Ubuntu on that scale. As a result of that review, a common set of standards was formed and became the basis for this remix.

The remix retains all the goodness of Ubuntu and is compatible with all Ubuntu-certified hardware, apps, and tools. What is different is the addition of business-focused tools from the standard Ubuntu and partner archives and removal of the home-user-oriented apps. The remix contains no modified or enhanced package, and it gets its security updates from the same place as standard Ubuntu. The remix is meant to be a convenient starting point that includes many of the common changes made by IT administrators who deploy Ubuntu in a corporate setting.

The first release of this remix contains the Adobe Flash plug-in, VMware View, and the OpenJDK 6 Java runtime environment. The social networking and file-sharing applications, games, and development/sysadmin tools have been removed.

At the time of publication, this remix is for 32-bit x86 machines, English-only, and installation images are available now for free download with registration at www.ubuntu.com/business/desktop/remix.

TIP   **Ubuntu Desktop Business Remix**
Ubuntu Desktop Business Remix can be found at www.ubuntu.com/business/desktop/remix.

Other Distributions

Some distributions generally work outside of the Ubuntu community and usually have their own package repositories. They may not release at the same time as Ubuntu. In the past, several of these derived distributions have been built directly upon other distributions, such as Debian, which is also the base for Ubuntu. The changes that Ubuntu developers make in the process of creating the distribution have been seen as positive and useful as a foundation for others with custom needs or desires. The list of derivative distributions has grown rapidly, and as distributions come and go, the list is constantly in flux. While in the first edition of this book, our list was nearly comprehensive, the size of the derivative distribution community has grown so much that compiling a complete list for this book is no longer possible. Instead, we provide a bit of the flavor of the diversity of derived distributions with some examples of the oldest and most visible derived distributions to give you an idea of the scope of the community.

Guadalinex

Guadalinex is the GNU/Linux distribution developed and promoted by the regional government of Andalusia, the most populated autonomous community in Spain with almost 8 million inhabitants. It is currently one of the largest free software implementations worldwide, with more than 200,000 desktops—and increasing. The project is a consequence of the unanimous support of the Andalusian Parliament on the Information Society and Innovation policies approved in 2002 and 2003, urging all the regional institutions to promote and use free software and open licenses. This makes the Guadalinex initiative unique in the world.

Guadalinex was initially released in 2003, and the first two versions were based on Debian. In 2005 the Guadalinex project decided to develop the third version deriving from Ubuntu. Guadalinex version 3 was released in January 2006 based on Ubuntu 5.10 (Breezy Badger), making it the first major Ubuntu derivative. The project is part of a government plan to implement free software as the default option in the public schools. At the beginning of 2006, this project involved 500 schools and approximately 200,000 desktops equipped with Guadalinex and free software only. These numbers increase every year as new courses start every September and new computers are purchased (about 40,000 in 2006). This initiative alone puts Guadalinex in the top position as the biggest free software implementation worldwide. Additionally, the software is used in public Internet access centers, senior centers, libraries, and women's associations, as well as citizens' homes. Guadalinex is merely one example of many Ubuntu derivatives created by or in cooperation with governments for use in schools and bureaucracies. It is now only one among many massive deployments of Ubuntu in these settings.

TIP   **Guadalinex**
Guadalinex can be found at www.guadalinex.org.

Linux Mint

Because Ubuntu is dedicated to using free software by default as much as possible, it does not come with proprietary media codecs installed. That was the reason Linux Mint was originally created. Over time, it has developed a community that focuses on creating an easy-to-use-and-install Linux desktop that is nice to look at with a focus on making things as simple and enjoyable as possible, especially for newcomers. The distribution is completely compatible with and uses the Ubuntu software repositories. The main differences are in the look and feel as well as choices for software installed by default. Linux Mint also produces a Debian-based version.

TIP   **Linux Mint**
Linux Mint can be found at linuxmint.com.

TIP   **More Derivatives**
A list of official and recognized derivatives is kept at www.ubuntu.com/products/whatisubuntu/
derivatives, and even more are listed at wiki.ubuntu.com/DerivativeTeam/Derivatives.

Launchpad

As we mentioned in Chapter 1, most of Canonical's technical employees
do not work on Ubuntu. Rather, they work on infrastructure. The majority of this infrastructure is a large collection of services that work together
to provide the framework through which Ubuntu is built. This superstructure of related applications is collectively referred to as Launchpad. While
it has several non–Web-based systems, it is almost wholly accessible over
the Web.

While Launchpad (Figure 9-10) is primarily used to develop Ubuntu, the
infrastructure was designed to be useful for any free software project and is
becoming more popular. It aims to provide these projects with the code
tracking, bug tracking, and translation tracking software necessary to
more easily and more powerfully collaborate with others and to develop
free and open source software. Each of these functions (code, bug, and
translation tracking) is highly integrated, making it much more ambitious, and potentially much more powerful, than traditional Web-based
solutions with similar goals. Early on, the Launchpad Web page described
the project as follows:

> A collection of services for projects in the Open Source universe. You can
> register your project, and then collaborate with the Open Source commu-
> nity on translations, bug tracking, and code.

That description continues to be valid even as the project has expanded
with support and specification modules. In addition to code, bug, and
translation tracking, Launchpad provides the ability to deal with code, not
just on a per-package or per-project level but on the distribution level as
well. If a bug has been reported against a piece of software in Ubuntu, it is

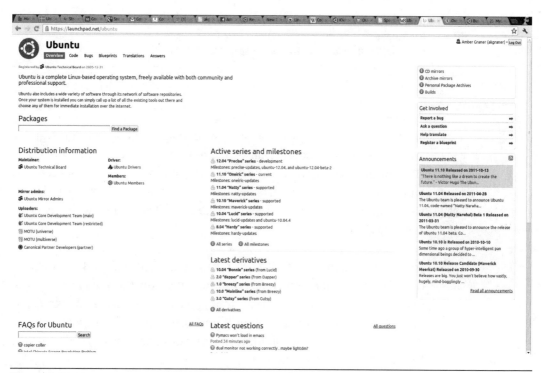

Figure 9-10 Ubuntu project in Launchpad

visible to both the upstream and downstream projects. The project can track how its software evolves over time and see, at a glance, whether bugs apply or not. Developers can track translations in a similar way.

The best way to understand Launchpad is to see it in action. This section walks through the individual pieces of Launchpad in more depth. Much of the Ubuntu infrastructure is highly integrated into Launchpad. If you have created an account for contributing to the wiki or ordering CDs at https://shipit.ubuntu.com, you already have a Launchpad account.

Once a source of controversy in the free and open source software world was the fact that the source code to Launchpad was not distributed. This changed on July 21, 2009, when Launchpad and all of its components, including code hosting and Soyuz, were officially made open source using the GNU Affero General Public License, version 3 (AGPLv3).

TIP   **Launchpad**
Launchpad can be found at www.launchpad.net.

Soyuz

Soyuz is the distribution and archive management software integrated into Launchpad. It handles all of the automatic building of software in Ubuntu on each of the architectures and the integration of successfully built software into the archive. Soyuz means "union" in Russian and is the name of the spacecraft that Mark Shuttleworth traveled in during his voyage to space.

Soyuz works almost entirely behind the scenes. It was first activated in early February 2006, but had no initial effect on the way software was uploaded or downloaded in Ubuntu. What Soyuz does is integrate the process by which software is built and inserted into different parts of the Ubuntu archive. The building of software cannot be tracked using the Launchpad Web infrastructure.

TIP   **Recent Builds**
The status of recent builds in Ubuntu can be found at https://launchpad.net/distros/ubuntu/+builds.

Launchpad Translations

Translations, commonly called Rosetta, is a Web-based translation system integrated into Launchpad (Figure 9-11). It was the first piece of Launchpad to be publicly released. It is codenamed Rosetta after the Rosetta Stone, the famous piece of dark gray granite with the same text in three scripts that led to the deciphering of Egyptian hieroglyphics.

Rosetta is a Web-based version of a "PO" file editor. In other words, it provides a simple mechanism by which translators can view a list of untranslated phrases or strings and then translate each of them into their language. At the moment, the system works only with translations *from* English. Rosetta's non–Web-based predecessors include Kbabel and Gtranslate,

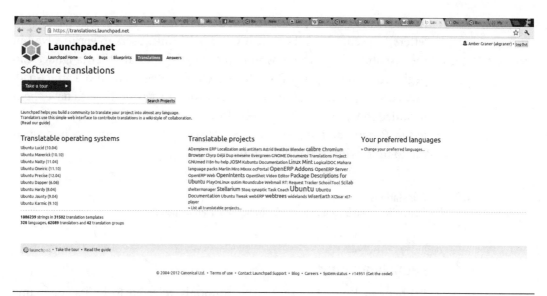

Figure 9-11 Ubuntu translations in Launchpad

both of which can be downloaded and installed on Ubuntu. By putting this functionality on the Web and integrating it into the archive management scripts, Rosetta lowers the barrier of entry for translation and increases the chance that a translation will make it into the distribution.

Rosetta includes each of the translatable strings contained in every application in Ubuntu. When new software is uploaded into Ubuntu, Rosetta will check to see if any strings have changed or been added. Changes to a string that has previously been translated will result in the translation being marked as fuzzy until a translator can check the translation and the new string, make any necessary changes, and then mark the translation as no longer fuzzy. By tracking new strings, Rosetta can easily prompt translators with new strings to translate as they appear as well as provide statistics on the percentage of strings within a particular application or within all of Ubuntu that have been translated into a particular language.

As users translate strings, they build up positive "karma" within the system—an innovation that has now been deployed to many other parts of Launchpad. Users can also work together in localization teams (called l10n teams because the word *localization* has ten letters between its first and last letters). Rosetta provides a great way for Ubuntu users to get involved in the distribution. Anybody who knows English and another language can begin contributing. Because the system is integrated into Launchpad, users do not need to submit their translations a second time to have them included in Ubuntu—the project already has them. After they are submitted in Rosetta and approved, new translations are automatically pushed out to users who use Ubuntu in those languages.

TIP   **Translations**
Translations can be found at https://translations.launchpad.net.

Launchpad Bugs

Launchpad Bugs (Figure 9-12), commonly referred to by its codename Malone, is a Web-based bug system like the Mozilla project Bugzilla, which might be familiar to some users. It provides a location where users can file

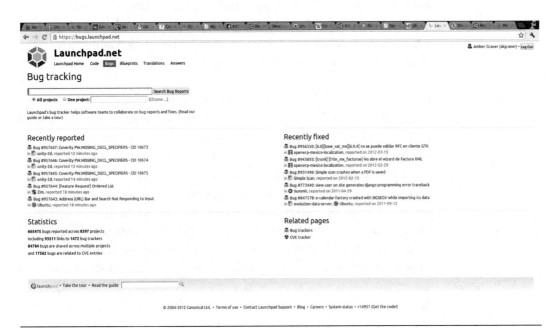

Figure 9-12 Ubuntu Bugs in Launchpad

bugs they find in their Ubuntu software by using easily accessible pieces of software such as Bug Buddy or by reporting over the Web. Malone's name is a reference to the gangster movie musical *Bugsy Malone*.

Malone's first role is to provide a location where users can submit bugs. Malone is not just a way to collect complaints, though. Rather, its job is to track and record a bug through its full life cycle, from report to close. Bugs can be assigned to a particular developer or reassigned. If the bug is, in fact, the result of another application, the bug can be reassigned to another package. Bugs can be rated according to severity, or tagged and categorized in any number of useful manners. Information, files, and patches that fix a bug can be uploaded into Malone. When the bug has been resolved, it can be closed. The Malone bug report provides a single venue in which to collect information from the bug submitter, the bug fixer, the upstream maintainer if necessary, and any other involved party.

All of this, of course, is exactly what you would expect from any usable modern bug tracker. Where Malone aims to distinguish itself from its competitors is through its integration in Launchpad. First and foremost, this means that users of Malone can track the status of a bug as it relates to a particular patch or a particular piece of code. Because Ubuntu supports *every* release for 18 months and some releases, such as Ubuntu 10.04 LTS, for much longer, it's important that Ubuntu be able to track which bugs show up in which releases. As derivative works of Ubuntu are created in Launchpad, Malone also allows these derivatives to use Malone to see whether bugs submitted against Ubuntu or other distributions apply to their code and, if so, to quickly grab a fix.

As with Rosetta, Launchpad karma can be built up by fixing, reporting, and interacting with bugs over time. Bug triage that involves closing irreproducible bugs and merging duplicate bugs is one way that users can build up their karma. Of course, simply running developer versions and submitting new bugs is another great way to build good karma.

TIP   **Bugs**
Bugs can be found at https://bugs.launchpad.net.

The Launchpad Blueprint Tracker

The Launchpad Blueprint Tracker (Figure 9-13), or Blueprints, is Ubuntu's custom specification and feature-tracking system. Blueprints provides a way that users can create specification pages, linked into the existing Ubuntu wiki, for features they would like to see in Ubuntu. Other interested parties can use Blueprints to subscribe to specifications or proposals they are interested in to collaborate on the development of the specification and to track progress. Over time, users working in the wiki and in Blueprints help new ideas through a process that starts with "brain-dump"—a very rough collection of ideas and brainstorming—and ends with an implemented feature. In Ubuntu, this process involves (1) review by the community and trusted members and (2) approval by decision makers and the Ubuntu Technical Board or by appropriate team leaders and councils. Blueprint provides technology to support this process and ensure that nothing important is dropped on the floor.

In particular, Blueprints helps leaders and decision makers on Ubuntu prioritize features and specifications and ensure that work is progressing on necessary features toward on-time completion for releases. As a result, Blueprint is used as both the primary specification tracker and the major release management tool for Ubuntu.

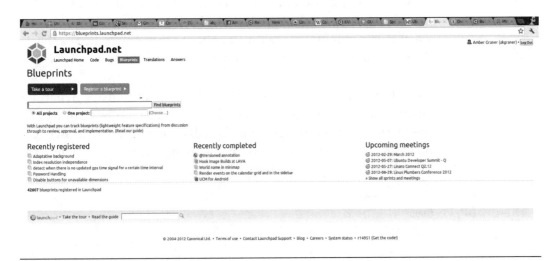

Figure 9-13 Launchpad Blueprint tracker

While Blueprints is extremely useful for technical specifications, it is also used heavily for developing and tracking community-related proposals as well as for brainstorming stages into implementation. Blueprints also has features designed around sprints and conferences to help organize sessions and coordinate groups to bring forward specifications. As a final bit of trivia, it's interesting to note that Blueprints was also written largely by Ubuntu founder and financier Mark Shuttleworth himself!

TIP   **Blueprints**
Blueprints can be found at https://blueprints.launchpad.net.

Launchpad Answers

Launchpad Answers (Figure 9-14) is a technical support tracker built within Launchpad for use by Ubuntu and other free software projects hosted in the system. It allows community members to file support requests and other community members to help resolve those requests. Unlike most other systems, questions can be asked and answered in a variety of languages. Launchpad Answers tries to complement other forms of

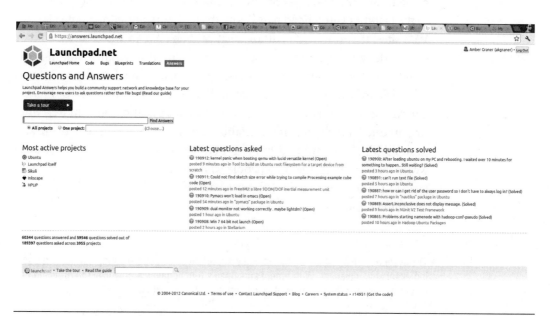

Figure 9-14 Launchpad Answers

community support in Ubuntu by providing a familiar ticketing system that also catalogs answered questions, allowing users to easily find answers to questions that others have asked before. Users can file support requests and communicate with volunteer community support contacts to provide more information, to discuss issues, and to note that their issues are resolved. In addition to storing the answers in a way that makes them searchable, Launchpad Answers helps contextualize support requests by integrating them with other Launchpad features to show the connections and context of relevant bugs, translations, people, teams, and the variety of versions in the variety of releases tracked by Launchpad. Of course, karma can be built by interacting with Launchpad Answers and, in particular, by answering questions.

TIP   **Answers**
Answers can be found at https://answers.launchpad.net.

Other Functionality

In addition to the visible flagship products within Launchpad just discussed, Launchpad has several other important uses. We've already alluded to the fact that Launchpad handles all the authentication for all the Ubuntu Web sites. If you want to edit or create a Web page in the Ubuntu wiki or even order a CD, you must first create an account in Launchpad. In addition to holding a username and password, a Launchpad account can contain rich information about each individual, including a GNU Privacy Guard encryption key, wiki pages, contact information, and more. More important, Launchpad also contains representations of every team and group within Ubuntu and handles permission within the entire Ubuntu world. For example, the only people who are allowed to upload core packages to Ubuntu are people who are part of the Ubuntu Core Developers Team in Launchpad.

NOTE   The system is also playing an increasingly important role in coordinating sprints and tracking events in a calendar. With time, Launchpad's functionality is only likely to grow, and its help in supporting the new type of development will grow with it.

Bazaar

Bazaar (Figure 9-15) is a distributed revision control system. What does that really mean? First, a revision control system is a program that tracks how the source code of a program changes. It tracks what each specific change was, such as the addition of a new piece of code, as well as who made the change. It also allows a developer to roll back to a previous version or create a branch, or a separate and parallel code version, to try a new idea without forcing the change on the main code.

The second key piece about Bazaar is that it is distributed. Traditional revision control systems have a single place where the code is stored. Only certain people can access this place and change the code there. A distributed revision control system is different in that there is no single place for code storage. Each branch a developer is working on is equal, and they all take code from each other. This system is much like a number of equal merchants at a bazaar, hence the name.

Bazaar started out as a fork of the Arch distributed revision control system. (A fork means that the developers disagree on where to take the

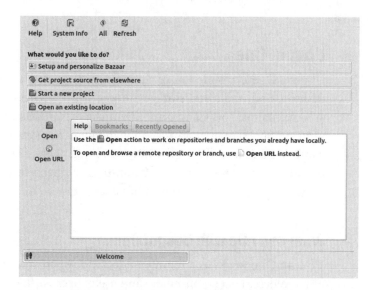

Figure 9-15 Bazaar Explorer (can be installed from the Ubuntu Software Center)

program, and they break into different groups to work toward each group's different goals.) However, Bazaar 2 was completely rewritten, as it was found that the then-current code did not work in the long term.

TIP   **Bazaar**
Bazaar can be found at http://bazaar.canonical.com.

Launchpad Ground Control

Launchpad Ground Control is a new project that aims to make the use of the collaborative features of Launchpad and Bazaar easier for everyday users. To accomplish this, a new package may be installed by users on their computer that integrates Launchpad with their desktop, enabling the use of Launchpad and Bazaar without using the command line. It does so in a way that is completely compatible with all the command-line methods, so it is possible to switch between the methods without harming the project at hand.

TIP   **Ground Control**
Ground Control can be found at https://launchpad.net/groundcontrol.

Ubuntu One

Ubuntu One is cloud storage that integrates perfectly into your Ubuntu desktop. Both the cloud storage and the desktop client were created and are maintained by Canonical. Canonical also runs the Ubuntu One service. Users sign up for an account and may then sync files between their computer and a server on the Internet. From there, files may be accessed by other computers with an Ubuntu One client installed, via a Web browser or using a paid mobile phone service.

What Can I Do with Ubuntu One?

Ubuntu One works as a remote folder into which you can place files and other folders. That is convenient and useful because these may then be easily accessed from other systems. However, other cloud storage services have this functionality, so it is not what makes Ubuntu One unique.

In addition to files, you can set Ubuntu One to synchronize your contacts, notes made with Tomboy, and your Firefox bookmarks. Not only that, but your Ubuntu One account can be used via Banshee Music Player and other Linux media players like Rhythmbox to purchase and legally download music from well-known artists and groups. When you purchase music, it is automatically placed in your Ubuntu One account, so it may then be accessed from any location. Ubuntu One Mobile allows you to stream this music to your Android or iOS4 phone.

How Much Does Ubuntu One Cost?

Profits from paid Ubuntu One options go back to Canonical, which supports Ubuntu development and pays many of the developers who make Ubuntu.

How Do I Begin?

To begin, click the Ubuntu One icon in the Launcher. This opens the Ubuntu One Control Panel, as shown in Figure 9-16. This is the starting point for most of what is discussed in this chapter.

If you do not have an account and want to sign up, click Join Now to sign up for an account. Account options include:

- **Ubuntu One Basic (Free).** This provides 2GB of storage to sync files, contacts, bookmarks, and notes between an unlimited number of computers and the cloud; Web access; and the ability to use the Ubuntu One Music Store. This account is free.

- **Ubuntu One additional storage.** Additional storage may be purchased in 20GB chunks.

Figure 9-16 Launching Ubuntu One from the Ubuntu Unity Launcher

- **Ubuntu One Mobile.** This option gives the ability to stream all stored music from your Ubuntu One cloud to your Android phone or iPhone and to sync your contacts with an Android phone, iPhone, Blackberry, and others.

Additional storage and Ubuntu One Mobile are modular; neither requires the presence or absence of anything other than a basic account.

TIP   You can learn more about how to sign up for and use Ubuntu One at https://one.ubuntu.com.

The remainder of this chapter assumes you have created an Ubuntu One account and signed in to your account via the Ubuntu One Control Center. Once you sign in, the Ubuntu One Control Center will reveal new options, as in Figure 9-17.

The top of the Ubuntu One Control Center displays a bar that shows your current use compared to your total available space and tells you if File Sync is disconnected, in progress, or up-to-date.

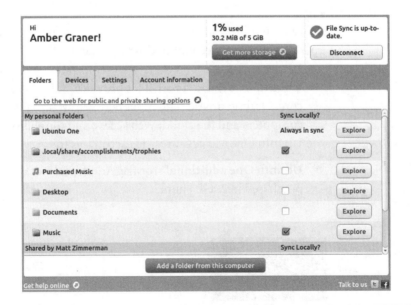

Figure 9-17 Ubuntu One Welcome Screen. When you are logged in, Ubuntu One Control Panel helps you manage your account and Ubuntu One use.

Below the storage meter are four tabs that reveal different options. Click Account to see and edit your account details. Click Cloud Folders to select folders from your personal cloud that you want synchronized to the device you are using. Click Devices to manage devices that are connected to your Ubuntu One cloud and their settings. Click Services to manage synchronization for specific data types and services like files, contacts, and bookmarks. Additional software packages may be needed to provide some of these services. If so, Ubuntu One will inform you, and installation of necessary packages requires only the click of a button and entering your user account password (not your Ubuntu One account, but your user account, because permission to install software must be established and authorized with a password).

TIP Most of what is discussed in this chapter may also be accessed and managed via the Web interface. Log in at https://one.ubuntu.com.

Syncing Files

Click the File Manager icon from the Launcher. An Ubuntu One folder has been created for you in your /home directory. Place any file or folder that you want to store in your Ubuntu One cloud storage into this folder, and it will automatically be synchronized between your device, the cloud, and from there any other devices you have connected to your Ubuntu One account.

From any other location in File Manager, you can right-click on a file or folder to reveal a pop-up menu. Hover over Ubuntu One in this menu to reveal a submenu that allows you to share, synchronize, publish, and more using Ubuntu One. If you want to stop synchronizing a shared file, right-click and select Stop Synchronizing on Ubuntu One.

You can also upload, access, and manage your files from the Web interface.

Syncing Contacts

Enable the Contacts service from the Services tab in the Ubuntu One Control Panel.

Click Applications in the Launcher and find Evolution Mail and Calendar. Once open, click the Contacts button at the lower left. Click to select your Personal Address Book from the list on the left. Open the Actions menu at the top and select Copy All Contacts To... from the list of options. Select Ubuntu One and click OK. From this moment, all your contacts in Evolution will be synchronized with your Ubuntu One cloud as well as to any other devices connected to the same account.

To make the Ubuntu One synced address book the default address book in Evolution, again click the Contacts button at the lower left of Evolution Mail and Calendar. Click to select the Ubuntu One address book from the list on the left. Open the Actions menu at the top and select Address Book Properties. In the window that pops up, mark the checkbox next to Mark as Default Address Book and click OK.

You can also create, view, edit, and delete contacts from the Web interface.

Syncing Bookmarks

Enable the Bookmarks service from the Services tab in the Ubuntu One Control Panel.

Click Firefox Web Browser from the Launcher to browse the Web. All bookmarks in Firefox will be synchronized with your Ubuntu One cloud storage and from there to any other Ubuntu device running Firefox and attached to your account.

Special Features of Ubuntu One Mobile

Ubuntu One already allows you to synchronize all your music, including files purchased from the Ubuntu One Music Store and others that you upload, to the cloud and to all other devices running Ubuntu and attached to your account. For a monthly fee, you can stream your music to your Android mobile phone or iPhone.

Ubuntu One Mobile also lets you sync your contacts from your Ubuntu One account to your mobile device. This option is supported by Android, iPhone, Blackberry, Nokia, and others.

More features are promised. For the latest news, see https://one.ubuntu.com/mobile.

Summary

In addition to building a great OS that many people use, the Ubuntu project has developed an OS that those building other operating systems use as a basis to build from. This has come in the form of both internal partner projects and external derivative distributions. Together, these span languages, continents, and markets. Also, Ubuntu is tightly linked to Canonical's other projects: Launchpad and Bazaar. Bazaar provides a compelling version control system, and Launchpad provides a one-stop show for bugs, translations, and much more.

CHAPTER 10

The Ubuntu Community

- Venues
- Teams, Processes, and Community Governance
- Getting Involved
- Submitting Apps to the Ubuntu Software Center
- Summary

COMMUNITY IS A WORD OFTEN used in discussions of Ubuntu. Early articles about Ubuntu bore subtitles asking, "Would you like some community with that?" The earliest press releases and communiqués from the project emphasized a "community-driven approach" to operating system development and distribution. In fact the highest-level governance board in Ubuntu is called the Community Council and Canonical, Ltd. employs a full-time community team, which is lead by Jono Bacon, one of the authors of early editions of this book. It is to that end that we have made a very conscious decision to spend an entire chapter of this book describing the Ubuntu community. In fact, every edition has been dedicated to the Ubuntu community!

Still, while the Ubuntu community is important, it is not always easy to succinctly describe it. Ubuntu is, in large part, developed and funded by Canonical. The community, almost by definition, extends far beyond Canonical. The Ubuntu project has members and self-declared activists (Ubunteros), but the Ubuntu community is more than even those with such explicitly declared relationships. The project contains a wide variety of different venues for participation. But while the community is active in each of these areas, its scope is even wider.

The Ubuntu community is the collection of individuals who build, promote, distribute, support, document, translate, and advocate Ubuntu—in myriad ways and in myriad venues. Most people in the Ubuntu community have never met, talked with, or heard of each other. Members of the community are linked by their contributions, both technical and nontechnical, and by Ubuntu itself. These contributions have built Ubuntu as a distribution, as a social movement, as a set of support infrastructures, and as a project. In short, they have built Ubuntu *as a community*. While any active software development project has a number of people making contributions, not every project has a community.

Community is also a term that represents a promise by the Ubuntu project to remain inclusive. The focus on community means that volunteers are not only welcome but also essential. It means that Ubuntu is a "place" where individuals can come together to create something greater than the sum of its parts. The word *community* gives a nod to the fact that while much development work is paid for by Canonical, and while some people contribute more hours, more effort, more code, more translations, more documentation, or more advocacy work to Ubuntu than others, no individual or subgroup can take credit for everything that Ubuntu has become. In Ubuntu, no contribution is expendable. Having a community also reflects Ubuntu's goal to provide a low barrier for entry for these contributions. Anyone who cares about Ubuntu can contribute to the project and can, in whatever ways are most appropriate, become a participant in the Ubuntu community.

This chapter provides a bird's-eye view of the venues and processes in which the Ubuntu community is active. First, it takes a tour through the venues through which the Ubuntu community both consumes and communicates information. It continues by looking at the way the community is organized and the processes by which that organization works. Finally, it walks you through the ways *you* can participate in the Ubuntu community and contribute to its success.

Venues

As we described in Chapter 1, transparent and public communication was an early goal of the Ubuntu project. Technical and community decisions are made publicly and are accessible to all interested parties. When this is impossible (e.g., when there is a face-to-face meeting and it's simply not possible for *everyone* interested to attend), the community attempts to publish summaries and minutes and to provide avenues for feedback. Ubuntu contains no "member only," "developer only," or "decision maker only" back channels except to preserve individual privacy or security—and the Ubuntu community refuses to create them. All work in Ubuntu occurs in places where *everyone* can view the work, and anyone who agrees to engage constructively and respectfully can participate.

Of course, this activity is public only to those who know where to find it. This section tries to document the venues for communication in Ubuntu as completely as possible. It describes the places where discussions of development, support, and advocacy take place. While nobody can engage in communication in *all* of the venues described, knowledge of what exists allows participants to be more informed when they need to choose the right place to ask a question or to make a suggestion.

Mailing Lists

The single most important venue for communication in Ubuntu is the Ubuntu mailing lists. These lists provide the space where all important announcements are made and where development discussions take place. There are, at the time of this writing, more than 300 public e-mail lists. This number is constantly growing. However, great care is taken by the Ubuntu Community Council to ensure that this list stays current as the community continues to enjoy its growth.

An up-to-date, full page of mailing lists for Ubuntu can be found at https:// lists.ubuntu.com, where users can see a list of available mailing lists, view archived discussions, and subscribe to lists through a Web interface.

Lists are one of the oldest forms of communication by e-mail. A mailing list provides a single e-mail address that, when mailed to, will then relay the received message to a large number of people. In Ubuntu, lists are topical, and individuals can subscribe to a mailing list if they want to receive information on the list's topic. All mailing lists at Ubuntu are hosted at lists.ubuntu.com. If you would like to send a message to a list, simply e-mail *<mailing list name>*@lists.ubuntu.com, replacing *<mailing list name>* with the name of the list you are trying to mail.

With a few exceptions (e.g., the e-mail lists for the Technical Board or Community Council), *anybody* can subscribe to any Ubuntu list. In most cases, the capability to send e-mail to lists is restricted to list members (membership in lists is, of course, open to anyone). This means that all e-mail sent to a list from someone who is not a member of that list is put into a queue to be reviewed by a human moderator before it is broadcast to list members. This is done as an antispam measure. Users can subscribe to lists and then configure the system to never send e-mail. For several e-mail lists, *all* messages are moderated. This is largely to ensure that lists remain "low volume" or "announcement only."

Ubuntu's mailing lists are run by the popular Mailman software, which may be familiar to some users. Mailman makes it simple to subscribe to lists, to unsubscribe, and to configure any number of options about mail delivery. One popular option is to receive a daily digest of messages rather than a separate e-mail each time a new message is sent. This is all available through a Web interface at https://lists.ubuntu.com. Users can also subscribe to lists by sending an e-mail with "subscribe" in the subject line to *<mailing list name>*-REQUEST@lists.ubuntu.com.

While each list plays an important role in the Ubuntu community, the following central lists warrant a little more detail. You might find it a good idea to subscribe to them.

ubuntu-announce   This fully moderated list relays all important announcements for the Ubuntu project and usually contains less than one e-mail per week. It is the place where new releases are announced and where other important information can be found first. If you use Ubuntu, you may want to consider subscribing to this list. If you subscribe to only one list, this should be it.

ubuntu-devel-announce   This fully moderated list contains announcements related to the development of Ubuntu. It is low volume and contains one to three e-mails per week. If you work with code in Ubuntu, use a development release, or contribute on any technical level, you should be on this list. This is the list that everyone involved in development for Ubuntu is expected to read.

ubuntu-devel-discuss   This list is the primary open list for general-purpose discussion of Ubuntu development. If you are looking to contribute to Ubuntu in any technical way, you should subscribe to this list and begin to follow the discussion. The list has a relatively high volume of e-mails.

ubuntu-devel   This list is a moderated list for discussion of Ubuntu. While subscribing remains free, posting to the list is restricted to those who are Ubuntu developers or to chosen other developers. Others may post, but all posts are checked by a moderation team.

Internet Relay Chat

While mailing lists provide the primary venue for asynchronous communication (i.e., not at the same time), there is still an important need for synchronous, or real-time, collaboration. Internet Relay Chat (IRC) fills this niche. While it was designed primarily for group (i.e., many-to-many) communication in channels, it is also equipped with private messaging capabilities that facilitate one-to-one communication—all instantaneously. It is very similar to instant messaging or chat room communication. While time zones and a round globe make it difficult for the global Ubuntu community to meet at the same time, many users and developers take advantage of IRC's capability to let anyone chat about an issue in real time or to ask a question and have it answered immediately.

Like mailing lists, IRC channels provide a venue for a variety of different types of communication in a variety of different subcommunities in Ubuntu. There are many different channels, including channels in a variety of languages.

All official Ubuntu IRC channels are located on the FreeNode IRC network, which also hosts a range of other free and open source software projects. Users can connect to IRC using several pieces of software in Ubuntu, including Pidgin, XChat-gnome (Figure 10-1), IRSSI, and a FreeNode webchat client is available for users who aren't using a local application on their machine for IRC but would like to join the channels from time to time (Figure 10-2). Mailing lists such as the loco-contacts@lists.ubuntu.com. Will assist users in finding the right help and support, #ubuntu is designed for help and support. When joining any channel, users should carefully read the topic as many frequently asked questions are answered there, and moderators of the channel can be annoyed by users who ask questions the moderators have already taken the time to answer in the channel's topic.

Currently the #ubuntu channel is usually the biggest channel on the FreeNode network, with over 1,000 simultaneous users at most times—and it's continuing to grow—especially around releases. Another important channel is #ubuntu-devel, which is reserved for discussion of Ubuntu development. Similarly, Kubuntu users hang out in #kubuntu and developers in #kubuntu-devel. Edubuntu and Xubuntu have similarly named user and support channels. To keep #ubuntu focused on support, all general chatter has been moved to #ubuntu-offtopic, and there are similar channels for Kubuntu, Edubuntu, and Xubuntu. Support for development releases has moved to #ubuntu+1. Maintaining channels with specific purposes has allowed the support community to stay focused and help as

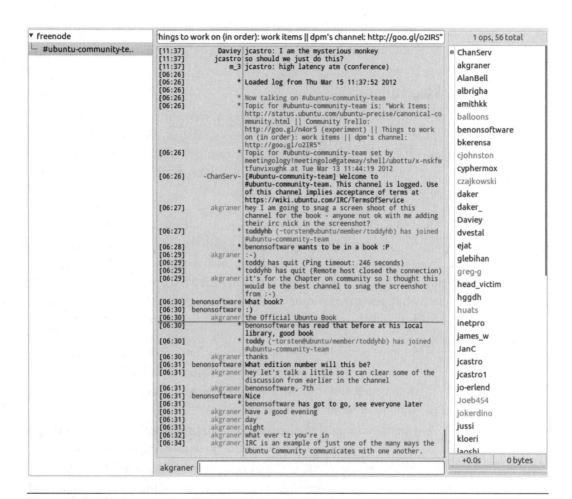

Figure 10-1 XChat-gnome is an IRC client that allows Ubuntu users to connect to the Ubuntu IRC channels.

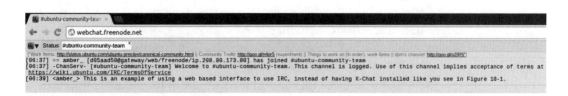

Figure 10-2 FreeNode webchat client sign-in screen and view of the #ubuntu-community-team IRC channel on freenode.net

many people as possible. A full list of channels can be found at https://help.ubuntu.com/community/InternetRelayChat.

Web Forums

The official Ubuntu forums are the most frequently used venues for communication in Ubuntu. For a number of reasons, many users prefer communication through a Web-based forum or bulletin board over mailing lists. The Ubuntu forums were created to satisfy this group and have done so with amazing success.

The forums are accessible online at ubuntuforums.org and have shown an impressive amount of usage. Statistics as of the time of writing show activity of more than 10 million messages on more than 1.5 million topics. The forums also boast more than 1 million registered users with around 10,000 online at any given moment. The forums continue to grow explosively. The topics discussed in the forums run the gamut in categories like these:

- Support discussions, including spaces for questions about specific hardware (e.g., Dell computers with Ubuntu preinstalled, or networking and multimedia cards) and specific use cases (e.g., desktop or server users)
- Ubuntu community discussions, including spaces for discussions by people working on art for Ubuntu, those working in science and education, and those developing new documentation and tutorials
- Forum-specific community discussion spaces, including several social spaces and places for administrative and community governance discussions

Each category includes subforums, each containing many threads. Many of these forums provide important spaces dedicated to important community discussions, including:

- A forum to highlight community announcements and news
- A discussion area for support for a variety of third-party projects built on top of Ubuntu that are useful primarily to Ubuntu users or that otherwise serve the Ubuntu community
- Forums for discussion and planning for local community teams (discussed later in this chapter) from across the world

By covering such ground, the Ubuntu forums provide an impressive support resource. They offer an excellent venue for both asking questions and answering questions, both receiving support and making important contributions to the Ubuntu community. If you are interested in any of these, the forums are a good place to begin.

The only caveat regarding the forums worth mentioning is that they are not frequently used by those developing Ubuntu—although there are exceptions to that rule. If users want to send messages directly to the Ubuntu *developers*, the forums may not provide the most effective tool. If users want to get involved in technical contributions to the project, they will, in all likelihood, have to augment their forums' patronage with the use of mailing lists or Launchpad.

The forums were founded by and are moderated and maintained entirely by volunteers, and are governed by the Forums Council (discussed later in this chapter), which currently contains no Canonical employees.

Wikis

Since nearly day one, a large chunk of Ubuntu documentation and support has taken place in the official Ubuntu wiki. In case you don't already know, a *wiki*—pronounced "wik-ee"—is a Web site where any viewer can add, remove, or edit content. The first wiki was created by Ward Cunningham in 1995, and wikis have shown themselves to be an extremely effective tool for collaborative writing in recent years. The term is shortened from *wiki wiki*—Hawaiian for "quick." Many wikis have been created. Most famous among these wikis is the online encyclopedia Wikipedia, which now contains more than 2.3 million articles in the English version alone.

There are several Ubuntu wikis, but two are central to the community. The first is the community support and documentation wiki at https://help.ubuntu.com/community (Figure 10-3). It is edited and directed by the Ubuntu Documentation Team and focuses on issues of community-produced technical documentation for Ubuntu. The second wiki is at https://wiki.ubuntu.com and is meant to be used for everything else. The documentation wiki can be thought of as a project to build an expansive manual through community contributions and editing. The general-purpose wiki is used for specification writing and traffic, conference

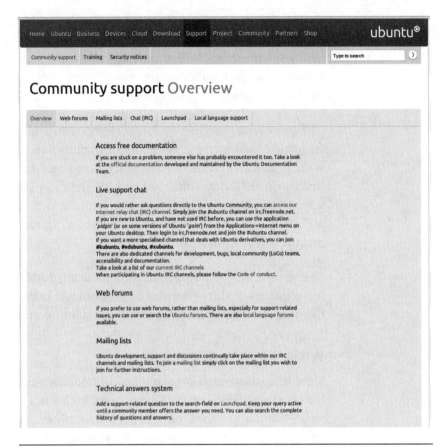

Figure 10-3 Front page of the Ubuntu community support and documentation wiki

organization, meet-ups, pages for teams and individuals involved in Ubuntu, and absolutely anything else that is in written form and relevant to the Ubuntu community. Both wikis can be edited, added to, or reorganized by anyone in the community who creates an account, and edits are unrestricted. Since registration is required, each change can be traced to a particular user.

Unlike other documentation that ships with Ubuntu, anyone can fix an error, inaccuracy, or out-of-date fact in the wiki. As a result, there is no good way to determine whether information in the wiki is correct. It cannot be subjected to the same type of quality assurance workflow that a document such as this book might be. However, it is also *much* more likely to be up-to-date in the quickly changing world of Ubuntu development, where there is a new release every six months. The wiki provides a venue for this level of up-to-date information with a low barrier to entry and, as a result, acts as an invaluable resource for the community.

The two major wikis each run the Moin Moin wiki software, and the use and operation of the wikis is identical. To use the wikis, you can either search or browse them. Searching is the most common way to get information from the wiki, and users can easily search either titles or the full text of the wiki. To achieve the best results, it is usually best to search titles and then the text to ensure that you look for more relevant information first.

For people who prefer to browse, the general-purpose wiki is divided into a number of categories that include the following:

- Resources
- Community
- Events
- Releases

The documentation is browsable in sections that try to serve users at different stages of familiarity with Ubuntu or with particular types of problems. The major divisions in the community documentation wiki include these:

- General help and information for new users
- Help for those switching from Mac OS X, Windows, or another Linux distribution who want a quick guide using analogies they are familiar with
- A large variety of information for people to read after they have installed Ubuntu and have questions about applications or types of use
- Information on maintaining and troubleshooting Ubuntu installs
- Help on connecting and configuring hardware

Most of these categories are relatively self-explanatory. Additionally, the general wiki provides a prominent link to information and support resources in languages other than English. The comprehensive list at www. ubuntu.com/support/community/locallanguage provides both links to pages within the wiki that include documentation and information in languages other than English and links to more than a dozen other wikis that are in another language entirely. Users looking for wiki pages in a language other than English are advised to visit this page.

The Fridge

The Fridge (https://fridge.ubuntu.com) is the quirky community portal for Ubuntu. In many Western cultures, refrigerators provide a central sort of "bulletin board" in a family's home. Because refrigerators are magnetic, children and parents can use magnets to hang pieces of paper that they want to share with the community of people who come in contact with that fridge. For children, this often includes good grades, news reports, or other information that someone is proud of or wants to share. The Fridge tries to create such a shared resource within the Ubuntu community. The Fridge home page is shown in Figure 10-4.

The Fridge is perhaps best described as the community portal for Ubuntu. It is part news site, part grassroots marketing and advocacy site. It hosts developer interviews, news, a picture gallery, a calendar with a list of upcoming events, polls, a list of Ubuntu-in-the-press citations, and much more. The core content on the site is arranged as a Web log. Users frequently set The Fridge as their home page or subscribe to the site via its RSS feed. The Fridge is unique in the community in that it appeals to a wide variety of Ubuntu participants—developers, advocates, translators, users—and provides a venue where each group can share information with others. There is a story every two to three days on The Fridge, although this may increase to up to several stories a day with time. Users can comment and discuss each story in the comments section on the Fridge.

Anyone can contribute content to The Fridge. If you would like to contribute, you can do so by sending your suggestions for features, articles, or even a piece of original work (such as an article, photo, or event review) to editor.ubuntu.news@ubuntu.com or by following any of the suggested ways on the https://wiki.ubuntu.com/Fridge/Submit.

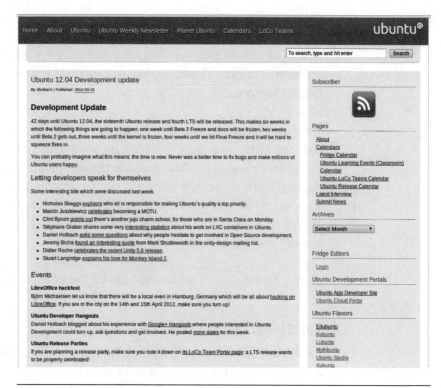

Figure 10-4 The Fridge home page

Ask Ubuntu.com

Ask Ubuntu at http://askubuntu.com is a free and community-driven question and answer site designed to make it easy for users to get answers to Ubuntu-related questions. It's also a place for users to share their knowledge about the Ubuntu Platform.

The site concentrates on answers that are voted on by the community and peer reviewed by other members of the site, which can keep the information up-to-date and topical.

The Ask Ubuntu Web site features the ability for users to ask and answer questions, and, through membership and active participation, to vote questions and answers up or down and edit questions and answers in a wiki fashion. Users of Stack Overflow can earn reputation points and "badges"; for example, a person is awarded 10 reputation points for receiving an "up" vote on an answer given to a question, and can receive badges for their valued contributions. All user generated content is licensed under a Creative Commons license.

From here users will have access to answer or ask questions as well as search and view all the questions that have already been asked. Users do not have to register or login in to have access to the site. For those users who wish to register, there are several ways this can be accomplished. If you have an account on Google, Yahoo!, myOpenID, Facebook, your Ubuntu account, AOL, or OpenID, you can associate that account to your AskUbuntu account and sign in using any of those accounts.

More information on AskUbuntu can be found at http://askubuntu.com.

Social Media

Social media sites such as Facebook, Twitter, Google+, and identi.ca are also used to disseminate information to the community as well.

Facebook: facebook.com/ubuntulinux
Twitter: http://twitter.com/ubuntudev
identi.ca: http://identi.ca/ubuntudev
Google+: https://plus.google.com/u/1/100887841569748798697/posts

Developer Summits, Sprints, and Rallies

While the vast majority of the work of the Ubuntu community takes place online, Ubuntu contributors do, from time to time, meet face to face. Since Ubuntu was first released, there have been several public developer summits, sprints and rallies organized and funded by Canonical. Highlights include:

■ The Mataró Sessions in Mataró, Catalonia, Spain, in December 2004—the first Ubuntu development summit

■ The two named Ubuntu conferences in 2005: Ubuntu Down Under in Sydney, Australia, in April and the Ubuntu Below Zero in Montreal, Canada, in November

- Ubuntu Developer Summit Mountain View at Google Headquarters in Mountain View, California, in November 2006
- Ubuntu Developer Summit-O in Budapest, Hungary—in May 2011
- Ubuntu Developer Summit-P in Orlando, Florida for the second time—in November 2011, the most recent developer summit held at the time of writing

With Canonical, Ubuntu tries to organize the developer summits so that they occur once per release, usually toward the very beginning of a release cycle, so that the specifications and goals for the forthcoming release can be discussed, thrashed out, and decided upon. These meetings move around the globe geographically so that, over a several-year period, a large percentage of the Ubuntu community will be able to attend at least one summit and meet with other developers.

While the format changes slightly each time, these meetings have been between one and two weeks in length. Frequently, a given attendee stays for only one week. At Ubuntu Below Zero, for example, the second week was devoted almost entirely to discussing, implementing, and developing infrastructure related to Launchpad (see Chapter 9). The format of these summits has changed as the attendees have experimented with different methods for structuring the events and maximizing the efficiency of these short periods. One common theme, though, is a process of writing specifications. Through remote participation the developer summits are now available for people who can't attend in person. Remote participation enables off-site attendees to interact via the Internet in designated IRC channels and public EtherPad instances, and many of the sessions are now videotaped as well.

At developer summits, attendees describe features that they would like to see in the next Ubuntu release. At an arranged time or in a series of meetings, a small set of interested community contributors and developers works to draft a written specification. This process of drafting involves brainstorming and ends up with a formal, approved spec that describes a problem or need and provides a detailed description of how it will be fixed or implemented. While these specifications are often technical in nature, they are also used to describe goals that may pertain to localization, documentation, or community building. For example, both The Fridge and the planning of each summit began as a specification. With time, these specifications are categorized in terms of priority for the upcoming release. Later, individuals will claim or be assigned some set of these specs. Paid developers at Canonical, frequently take responsibility for the highest-priority technical specs. Each specification is written up and improved as a blueprint on Launchpad so that Ubuntu developers and contributors who cannot attend the summit are still able to participate.

These summits also address issues within the community. For example, at the last UDS—UDS-P in November 2011—Ubuntu community manager, Jono Bacon, took the opportunity to schedule a two-day leadership summit in conjunction with the UDS event to address the scaling needs of the community. Many of the Ubuntu leaders attended to discuss how they could help grow not only their own leadership abilities but those of the Ubuntu community as well.

These conferences have, so far, occurred in hotels with conference centers and have been attended by up to several hundred people. The exception was the 2006 conference, which was graciously hosted by Google. The meetings have been wholly organized and funded by Canonical, which ensures that its employees attend and also distributes funds for other active volunteers to travel. This funding tends to be divided up based on the contributions of volunteers over the last release cycle and their geographic proximity to the summit location. This is done to minimize travel expenditures and to ensure that users around the world get a chance to attend a conference when it comes near them.

In addition to the biannual summits, Canonical, organizes a number of sprints/rallies each year. These sprints/rallies tend to be one to three-week intense collocated work sessions that involve a team or subteam tasked with a well-defined goal. They provide a time when team members can write code, write documentation, make plans, or do whatever else is necessary to fulfill that goal. The sprints tend to be smaller, less than 100 people, while the rallies can often be over 100 people; yet both attempt to squeeze large amounts of work into a short period of time and have earned a reputation for being exhausting, fulfilling, amazingly productive, fun experiences. These sprints/rallies are work sessions and are usually limited to a group of Canonical, employees; however, on occasion, they may also include volunteer attendees.

User Conferences

Developer summits and sprints are effective but are primarily of interest to technically minded people or individuals who are already very actively involved in the Ubuntu community. Their goal is to accomplish work through high-bandwidth face-to-face interaction among existing teams. User conferences try to provide an alternative space for users who are not yet actively involved in the community. These conferences attempt to bring people up to speed on Ubuntu and to provide a space for community building, support, and networking.

While many local community teams have regular meetings and their own Ubuntu events, there have been several larger-scale Ubuntu user conferences to date, and several more are currently being planned. These conferences fall into two major classes. The first class is a set of laid-back, lightly organized, day-long "unconferences" called Ubucons (short for Ubuntu Conferences). Ubucons have been held many times, the first two at Google headquarters, in Mountain View and in New York City, and others are designed to coincide with the much larger Linux World conferences that many other Ubuntu users attend. The unconference format means that much of the schedule is left up in the air until the morning of the meeting and that many of the attendees are encouraged to come prepared with their own demonstrations, talks, and workshops and with a list of things they would like to learn. Attended by a group of about a hundred users and a handful of developers, Ubucons have provided a simple way for users to connect with each other. Additionally, Ubucons have, to date, also provided space for "installfests" where users can bring computers and have Ubuntu installed on their machines by other Ubuntu users, developers, and aficionados.

Any active group of Ubuntu users can plan a Ubucon, and Ubucons have taken place in a variety of locations around the world. For example, Ubucon's now take place in conjunction with such events as the Southern

California Linux Expo, Ohio Linux Fest, Southeast Linux Fest, and others. This piggybacking onto the larger events worked so well that in 2010, several others permitted an Ubucon to be organized as a smaller part of their larger event and the practice continues into 2012. Ubucons are becoming more popular because Ubuntu users are already attending the larger events, LoCo teams can afford to organize the Ubucons because the venue costs are quite low and can usually be covered by only one sponsor, they are free events, and popular Ubuntu speakers often are already attending the larger event and are willing and happy to add some participation in the Ubucon to their schedule.

While conferences and summits act as a site for major technical advances in brainstorming and development, they are also fun and enjoyable experiences. They provide a venue for users to put faces to names, IRC nicks, and e-mail addresses, and they provide for enjoyable, humorous, and productive interaction. In addition to work, there are frequent card-playing, eating, drinking, and athletic activities. Many Ubuntu users from the local area who've attended because they were curious have gone on to become some of the community's most important contributors. Attending a conference is like taking a drink from an Ubuntu fire hose. It is frequently overwhelming but can ultimately be a useful, productive, and rewarding experience as well.

Planet Ubuntu

For a window into the people who make Ubuntu what it is, the blog aggregator Planet Ubuntu (http://planet.ubuntu.com) is a great place to start (Figure 10-5). A blog aggregator is basically a blog of blogs that retrieves the latest posts from Ubuntu members who have chosen to add their blogs to the system and then publishes a single blog in reverse chronological order. Although much of the content in Planet Ubuntu is about Ubuntu, as a window into the Ubuntu membership, Planet Ubuntu also includes information from the personal lives of community members. In this way, Planet Ubuntu provides a good way for participants to put their stamp on the Ubuntu community and for others to see what the Ubuntu community is doing.

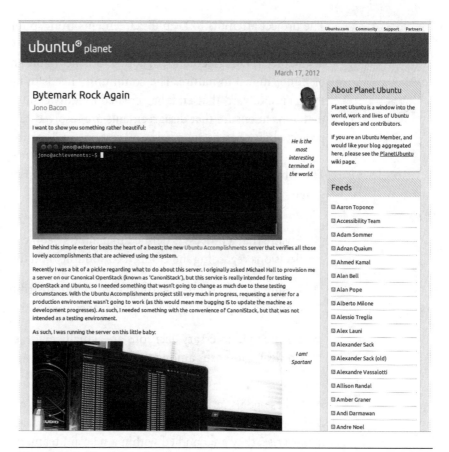

Figure 10-5 Planet Ubuntu

Teams, Processes, and Community Governance

Ubuntu operates under the famous hacker mantra of "rough consensus and running code." The project attempts to forge consensus, to make good technical decisions, and to move forward. It attempts to minimize politicization wherever possible and to distribute power to those who are best at getting good work done. Mark Shuttleworth explains, "This is not a democracy, it's a meritocracy. We try to operate more on consensus than on votes, seeking agreement from the people who will have to do the work."

The project attempts to keep disagreements from spiraling out of control by enforcing mutual respect at all times with its Code of Conduct described in Chapter 1. Disagreements, of course, are inevitable and can be technical or nontechnical in nature. The community needs to be able to deal with these and, toward that end, has created a lightweight governance system that aims to ensure that disagreements are resolved carefully and that the project always has a strong, fair, and responsive direction.

The Ubuntu Web site describes the goals of its community governance system as threefold.

1. Ensure that a process is defined that allows people to contribute to decisions regarding the Ubuntu community and distribution.

2. Ensure that decisions regarding the Ubuntu distribution and community are made in a fair and transparent fashion.

3. Ensure that necessary decisions are actually made, even when there is no clear consensus among the community.

With these goals in mind, Ubuntu's system is based on the delegation of decision-making power to small and medium-sized teams. When disagreements arise, they are handled within a relevant team. In the cases of some larger teams, team councils handle a variety of dispute resolutions in a very structured fashion. When teams cannot resolve their own disagreements or when there are disagreements between teams, issues are forwarded to the council or board which governs that area of the community and at times can and may be escalated to either the Community Council or the Technical Board—depending on whether the issue is technical in nature. As the financier and the project's progenitor, Shuttleworth sits on both boards and occupies a special position as the self-appointed benevolent dictator for life (SABDFL). Users can participate in the Ubuntu governance structure by serving on teams, and as Ubuntu members and maintainers, they have a voice in approving members of both the Community Council and the Technical Board.

Teams

Most work in Ubuntu is delegated to a set of teams, each responsible for a particular area of work in Ubuntu. A sample of important teams (which is by no means complete) might include the forums, marketing, art, documentation, kernel, server, laptop, and translation teams. Anyone with an interest in a particular aspect of the Ubuntu project can join a team's discussion and contribute to its decisions.

When participants feel that a particular area is under-served, they can go ahead and build a new team by beginning work and writing up a proposal for consideration by the Community Council, which approves the creation of all new teams. Rather than catalyzing work with the creation of a team, the Community Council likes to recognize existing work with official team status. Teams should always involve the participation of several individuals. There are no one-man or one-woman teams in Ubuntu.

Several teams are so large and important that they have built their own more advanced governance structures in the forms of team councils. These councils are appointed by the community council from active members and leaders within the team and act as delegates of the Community Council for that team and its domain in the project. These team councils have regular meetings, resolve conflicts, report to the Community Council, and in some cases even grant membership on behalf of the Community Council. Current large teams with councils include the Forums, Edubuntu, Kubuntu, and MOTU teams. More on these later in this chapter.

The Ubuntu Community Team at Canonical

As mentioned at the beginning of this chapter, Canonical understands and appreciates what an important part the Ubuntu community plays in the success and growth of each Ubuntu release. The Ubuntu community team at Canonical is a five-person team lead by Jono Bacon, the Ubuntu community manager, and includes Michael Hall, external project developer relations; Daniel Holbach, Ubuntu community development liaison; David Planella, Ubuntu translations coordinator; Jorge Castro, Cloud community liaison; and Nickolas Skaggs, Ubuntu QA community coordinator. As you can see, each team member focuses on various areas of the community.

The community team members specialize in their respective areas of the Ubuntu project. They each work with their area of the community to help educate, encourage and ignite greater participation. This also helps establish trust relationships with Canonical, upstream software projects, ustream videocasts, and the wider community, which helps maintain a healthy and inclusive community that is empowered to develop, design, and influence the direction and growth of the Ubuntu project.

The Ubuntu community team has implemented the following new opportunities to engage the Ubuntu community:

For the Ubuntu App Developer Community
Ubuntu App Developer Web site: http://developer.ubuntu.com

Ubuntu App Developer Blog: http://developer.ubuntu.com/community/app-developer-blog/

Facebook: https://www.facebook.com/ubuntuappdev

Twitter: www.twitter.com/ubuntuappdev

indenti.ca: www.identi.ca/ubuntuappdv

Google +: https://plus.google.com/u/1/111697084657487423167/posts

For the Ubuntu Developer Community
Ubuntu Packaging Guide: http://developer.ubuntu.com/packaging/html/

Facebook: www.facebook.com/ubuntudev

Twitter: www.twitter.com/ubuntudev

ident.ca: www.identi.ca/ubuntudev

Google +: https://plus.google.com/u/1/107265043789873157543/about

For the Cloud Community
Ubuntu Cloud Portal: http://cloud.ubuntu.com

Getting Involved: http://cloud.ubuntu.com/community/interact/

Juju: https://juju.ubuntu.com/

Facebook: https://www.facebook.com/ubuntucloud

Twitter: www.twitter.com/ubuntucloud

identi.ca: www.identi.ca/ubuntucloud

Google+: https://plus.google.com/u/1/109091305842368633411/posts

Foss Boss blog: http://foss-boss.blogspot.com

Local Community Teams

Local community teams, affectionately referred to as LoCos in the community, are an extremely important type of team. Each LoCo is responsible for promoting, supporting, and representing Ubuntu in a particular locale. These locales are usually geographical and frequently countrywide, although in some situations they may overlap geographically. Ubuntu tries to encourage LoCos to work together whenever possible.

LoCos are like Linux User Groups (LUGs) and may often work closely with or be associated with a LUG. LoCos are often involved in localization or translations of Ubuntu into local languages and in advocacy in local schools, public administrations, and communities. The best LoCos meet regularly for social events, talks, and discussion. Often, they meet for installfests, where team members help new users install Ubuntu onto their computers. Representatives of LoCos are asked to assist with localization matters, to speak on behalf of the Ubuntu project at local conferences and trade shows, and to organize a booth or presence at such events.

Canonical, Ltd., provides each team with a mailing list and a domain name (usually in the form of ubuntu-<*CC*>.org, where *CC* is the country's two-letter country code). Canonical also is willing to host LoCo Web pages, wikis, forums, blogs, download areas, and additional mailing lists. LoCos are open to participation by anyone.

Want to find a Local Community team near you? All you have to do is go to the Ubuntu Local Community Team Directory site at http://loco. ubuntu.com/ begin by selecting your region of the world on the map or by clicking the team tab at the top of the page and either action will bring up a list of current LoCo teams.

MOTUs

Another very special team that deserves an in-depth description in this book is the MOTUs. The MOTUs are the maintainers of Ubuntu's Universe software package repository, and the acronym stands, jokingly, for Masters of the Universe. MOTUs call themselves "the brave souls who try to keep the Universe section of Ubuntu in shape." They are community members who spend their time adding, maintaining, and supporting as much as possible the software found in Universe.

MOTUs are package maintainers. They maintain, as a group, the vast majority of packages in the Ubuntu archive. Several of the packages that have been well maintained by the MOTUs have, with time, migrated into the main component and become an official part of the Ubuntu distribution. Because Ubuntu does not make support or quality promises regarding the packages in universe, the MOTU team provides a way for maintainers to sharpen their teeth and (since it's sometimes unavoidable) make mistakes before jumping into the higher-responsibility packages in main.

The roles and responsibilities of the MOTUs are many. Some important ones are that MOTUs

- understand packaging concepts and have substantial experience uploading packages through a sponsor.
- apply this knowledge by uploading new packages and updating existing packages in the universe component.
- may also contribute to the main component in cooperation with a core developer.
- answer questions of other developers in order to expand their understanding of packaging work.
- provide guidance for prospective Ubuntu developers regarding technical issues.

MOTU contributors are the people who are interested in contributing to Ubuntu and are learning how to package and work in the Ubuntu development community. They primarily work by using MOTUs as sponsors for their work. There are no requirements or exams to pass to become a

MOTU contributor, just a willingness to learn and a commitment to the Ubuntu Code of Conduct. Many of these contributors do graduate to full-fledged MOTUs, and many MOTUs eventually are granted full-core developer status. This three-step system is the process by which almost all new maintainers learn to maintain packages in Ubuntu.

The Community Council

The Community Council and the Technical Board are the highest-level governance structures within Ubuntu. The Community Council, as it pertains to all Ubuntu members and activities, is arguably the most powerful team within the Ubuntu project. The Community Council is charged with supervising the social structures, venues, and processes of the project.

The Community Council's day-to-day work involves five major areas in Ubuntu. The first, and the most straightforward, is the maintenance of the Ubuntu Code of Conduct. The Community Council is the only body that can approve revisions to the code. Because the Community Council does not ask each member to "reagree" to the code when it is changed, each of these revisions must be fully within the spirit of the previous drafts. At the time of this writing, the Ubuntu Community Council is drafting version 2.0 of the Code of Conduct in order to combine the Code of Conduct and the Leadership Code of Conduct to highlight and emphasize the importance leaders play in the Ubuntu community.

The second charge of the Community Council is the arbitration of disputes that cannot be handled within a particular team or that arise between teams. These are generally disputes about the Code of Conduct that may require clarification of a part of the Code of Conduct or a description of whether any of the code was in fact violated by a particular action or behavior. However, the Community Council's purview is not limited to Code of Conduct violations, and the Community Council is available to handle disputes in any nontechnical situation. In most situations, the Community Council does not take action against individuals but, rather, helps group members come to agreement or consensus among themselves. If this fails, the Community Council can ask a maintainer or other member of the community to apologize and refrain from particular behavior or to leave the community. The Council promises that nobody will be asked to leave without a substantial review and an opportunity to defend him- or herself.

A third area of council work is the creation and dissolution of teams and the appointment of team leaders. New teams are proposed to the Community Council in the manner described earlier in the section on teams, and the Community Council either approves the request or asks the proposer to wait. Defunct or inactive teams can similarly be dissolved by the Community Council. In cases where team leadership is requested, the Community Council can appoint leaders of teams or shift leadership to different team members. In most situations, the appointment of team leaders is an internal team matter but, when requested, the Community Council is available to intervene.

Fourth, the Community Council is ultimately responsible for approving and welcoming new members to the project, described in more depth in the upcoming subsection on membership.

Finally, the Community Council is responsible for all community-related structures and processes. New types of teams, requirements for membership, and core philosophical documents should first be approved by the Community Council. Community members who wish to suggest new structures or processes can submit their proposal to the Community Council for discussion and approval.

The Community Council meets every week on the first and third Thursday of each month in IRC and the second and fourth Thursday of each month for an informal "face-to-face" using Google+Hangouts. Any community participant can submit an item or proposal for discussion by the Community Council. Meetings are open to the community, but the Council seeks only consensus or votes from Council members—although it consults representatives from the team that submitted the proposal and other community members. If an open meeting becomes too noisy, the Council reserves the right to move to a private channel for the duration of the meeting. To date, this has never happened. In all situations, full transcripts of meetings are published immediately following a Community Council meeting. The Community Council at the time of this writing consists of Mark Shuttleworth, Daniel Holbach, Elizabeth Krumbach, Milo Casagrande, Scott Richie, Laura Czajkowski, Martin Albisetti, and Charles Profitt. At the time of this writing, the Ubuntu Community Council now contains four Canonical employees: Shuttleworth, Albisetti, Czajkowski, and Holbach. Appointments to the board are made by Shuttleworth and subject to confirmation by a vote among all members. Appointments are for a period of two years.

The Technical Board

The Ubuntu Technical Board is responsible for the Ubuntu project's technical direction. By handling all technical matters, the Technical Board complements the Community Council as Ubuntu's highest rung of project governance. In particular, the Technical Board is responsible for three major areas of Ubuntu policy: package policy, release feature goals, and package selection. Also, the Technical Board is available to arbitrate any technical disagreements or issues within or between teams in a manner similar to the one described earlier in relation to the Community Council.

The Technical Board's first responsibility is Ubuntu's package policy. The Technical Board maintains the policy document, which describes the processes and standards to which all Ubuntu packages are held. Since the policy is constantly evolving, each Ubuntu release is associated with a specific version of the Ubuntu package policy as determined by the Technical Board. Any suggestions or proposals about policy are suggested to and considered by the Technical Board.

Also, the Technical Board is responsible for maintaining Ubuntu's feature goals for each release. During each release cycle, there is a date defined as Feature Freeze, after which no new features are added. The Technical Board sets these dates and decides when and if the rules can be bent for a particular feature or piece of software.

Finally, the Technical Board is responsible for maintaining the *list* of pieces of software (i.e., packages) in Ubuntu. In this capacity, the Technical Board determines which software is installed in the default desktop installation and which packages qualify for full support as part of the main component of Ubuntu. Users and developers can propose a particular piece of software for inclusion in main, the base install, or a desktop install. In all cases, the ultimate decision will be made by the Technical Board.

Like the Community Council, the Technical Board meets at least every two weeks on IRC. Also like the Community Council, any user can submit an item or proposal for discussion by the Technical Board prior to the scheduled meeting. Meetings are open to all interested parties, although decision making and voting is restricted to Technical Board members. Full transcripts and rules about noise, as they pertain to the Community Council, also apply to the Technical Board. The Technical Board at the time of this writing comprises Matt Zimmerman as board chair, Soren Hanson, Stéphane Graber, Colin Watson, Kees Cook, Martin Pitt, and Mark Shuttleworth. Nominations for the Technical Board are considered at the beginning of each release cycle. Like the Community Council, appointments are made by Shuttleworth but are subject to confirmation by a vote among the maintainers instead of all members. Appointments are made for a period of one year.

Other Councils and Boards

Ubuntu Forum Council   The Ubuntu Forums are led by a small group of people called the Forum Council. The council is currently made up of seven community members, listed here by their usernames on the forums:

- Artificial Intelligence
- bodhi.zazen
- cariboo907
- coffeecat
- Iowan
- overdrank
- s.fox

> Wiki page: https://wiki.ubuntu.com/ForumCouncil
> Mailing list: ubuntu-forums-council@lists.ubuntu.com

Ubuntu IRC Council   The IRC Council is the group that is ultimately responsible for governing the IRC channels and interfacing between IRC and the rest of the Ubuntu community and governance systems. Members include Juha Siltala, Ben Rubin, Alan Bell, and Matt Wheeler.

> Wiki page: https://wiki.ubuntu.com/IrcTeam/IrcCouncil
> Mailing list: irc-council@lists.ubuntu.com

Ubuntu LoCo Council   The LoCo Council governs the LoCo community, makes decisions on resource allocations, deals with conflict resolution and makes decisions about where the project should move forward. Members include Sergio Meneses, Greg Grossmeier, Christophe Sauthier, Paolo Sammicheli, Chris Crisafulli, and Laura Czajkowski.

> Wiki page: http://loco.ubuntu.com/loco-council/
> Mailing list:loco-council@lists.ubuntu.com

Edubuntu Council   The Edubuntu Council oversees Edubuntu, providing technical guidance, community governance, and ensuring the health of the project. Members include: Alkis Georgopoulos, Jonathan Carter, Marc Gariépy, Scott Balneaves, and Stéphane Graber.

> Wiki page: https://wiki.kubuntu.org/Edubuntu/Council
> Mailing list: edubuntu-users@lists.ubuntu.com

Kubuntu Council   The Kubuntu Council oversees Kubuntu, providing technical guidance, community governance, and ensuring the health of the project. Members include Christian Mangold, Jonathan Riddell, Jonathan Thomas, Harald Sitter, and Scott Kitterman.

> Launchpad Team: https://launchpad.net/~kubuntu-council
> Mailing list: jr@kubuntu.org

Ubuntu Developer Membership Board   The Ubuntu Developer Membership Board is the group responsible for considering and approving applications to become members of the Ubuntu Core Developer team. Members include Benjamin Drung, Cody A. W. Somerville, Iain Lane, Barry

Warsaw, Micah Gersten, Stephan Rivera, and Stéphane Graber, with the Ubuntu Technical Board as its administrator.

> Wiki page: https://wiki.ubuntu.com/DeveloperMembershipBoard
> Mailing list: developer-membership-board@lists.ubuntu.com

Ubuntu Membership Approval Boards   The Ubuntu Membership Approval Boards are made up of the following three boards which are responsible for considering application for Ubuntu Membership based on each geographical region associated with each membership board.

1. **Ubuntu Membership Board—Americas Region.** Members include Belinda Lopez, Elizabeth Krumbach, Greg Grossmeier, Martin Albisetti, Mathieu Trudel-Lapierre, Nathan Handler, n0rman, and Penelope Stowe.

   > Wiki page: https://wiki.ubuntu.com/Membership/RegionalBoards/Americas
   > Mailing list: ubuntu-membership-board-americas@lists.ubuntu.com

2. **Ubuntu Membership Board—Asia and Oceania Region.** Members include Eleanor Chen, Emmet Hikory, Jared Norris, Khairul Aizat Kamarudzzaman, Matthew Lye, Melissa Draper, Muhammad Takdir, oneleaf, Robert Collins, ZhengPeng Hou, and amachu.

   > Wiki page: https://wiki.ubuntu.com/Membership/RegionalBoards/AsiaOceania
   > Mailing list: ubuntu-membership-board-asia-oceania@lists.ubuntu.com

3. **Ubuntu Membership Board—Europe, Middle East, and Africa Region.** Members include Laura Czajkowski, David Rubin, Iulian Udrea, Jonathan Carter, Oliver Grawert, and Stéphane Graber.

   > Wiki page: https://wiki.ubuntu.com/Membership/RegionalBoards/EMEA
   > Mailing list: ubuntu-membership-board-emea@lists.ubuntu.com

The SABDFL

Mark Shuttleworth jokingly refers to himself as Ubuntu's SABDFL—self-appointed benevolent dictator for life. He plays an admittedly undemocratic role as the sponsor of the Ubuntu project and the sole owner of

Canonical. Shuttleworth has the ability, with regard to Canonical, Ltd. employees, to ask people to work on specific projects, feature goals, and bugs. He does exactly this.

Shuttleworth also maintains a tie-breaking vote on the Technical Board and Community Council but has never used this power and has publicly said that he will not use it lightly. In situations where the boards are split and there is no one "right" answer, the SABDFL will provide a decision instead of more debate. The SABDFL exists to provide clear leadership on difficult issues and to set the pace and direction for the project. In exchange for this power, he has the responsibility to listen to the community and to understand that the use of his SABDFL authority can weaken the project.

Ubunteros and Ubuntu Members

Membership in the Ubuntu project is one official way that the project recognizes sustained and significant contributions. The first level of membership in Ubuntu is as an Ubuntero. Ubunteros are Ubuntu activists and can be any person in the Ubuntu community who has explicitly committed to observing the Ubuntu Code of Conduct. Ubunteros are self-nominated and self-confirmed. Using Launchpad, participants can generate a GPG encryption key and "sign" the Code of Conduct as a way of pledging to uphold it within the Ubuntu community. By doing so, that participant automatically gains status as an Ubuntero.

The next, more significant, step is official membership. Official membership is available to any Ubuntero who has demonstrated a significant and sustained set of contributions to the Ubuntu community. These contributions can be of any kind—technical or nontechnical—but need to be of a form that can be represented to one of the Ubuntu membership boards, under the authority of the Community Council. The membership board before which a candidate appears will consider each application individually. A non-exhaustive list of some of the types of contributions that qualify appears in the following section on getting involved. The membership boards try to be flexible in the variety of different types of contributions that will be accepted in consideration of membership.

Ubuntu members are responsible for confirming, by voting, all nominations to the Ubuntu Community Council. They also may be asked by the Community Council to vote on resolutions put to the general membership. In exchange, members gain the right to an @ubuntu.com e-mail address and the right to carry Ubuntu business cards. Membership lasts for two years and is renewable. Members who fail to renew their membership will be marked as inactive but, with renewed activity and a simple procedure that involves approval of the Community Council, can be easily reactivated.

The process to become a member is relatively straightforward and is documented in depth on the Ubuntu Web site. Most important, it requires that users document their contributions on a wiki page that includes links to code, mailing list messages, specific forms of documentation that clearly demonstrate their involvement, and/or other relevant material. Membership applications also need to include testimonials on work and involvement in Ubuntu from current Ubuntu members.

Getting Involved

Users can participate in the Ubuntu community on a variety of levels and in a multitude of ways. The following subsections, adapted largely from a page with links to relevant resources online on the Ubuntu Web site (www.ubuntu.com/community/participate), provides a good list of ways in which people can get a running start in the Ubuntu community.

Ubuntu Online Events

The Ubuntu community organizes several online IRC events each cycle with the goal of teaching what is new with each release, helping to encourage more users to become developers, helping current developers become more proficient developers, encouraging LoCo teams and members, encouraging users to become contributors and more.

The following are the various events and the list continues to grow with each release:

Ubuntu Open Week: https://wiki.ubuntu.com/UbuntuOpenWeek

Ubuntu App Developer Week: https://wiki.ubuntu.com/UbuntuAppDeveloperWeek

Ubuntu Developer Week: https://wiki.ubuntu.com/UbuntuAppDeveloperWeek

Ubuntu User Days: http://wiki.ubuntu.com/UserDays

Ubuntu Cloud Days: https://wiki.ubuntu.com/UbuntuCloudDays

Advocacy

The easiest way for someone to contribute to the Ubuntu community is simply by telling others about Ubuntu. Advocacy frequently occurs in a variety of ways. One good method involves joining or starting a LoCo team. LoCos, described earlier in this chapter, provide a method through which you can get involved in Ubuntu activities. If users do not have a LoCo and do not have the critical mass of users to start one, they might help build support by giving a talk about Ubuntu to a local Linux User Group or other technical group. Ubuntu members and LoCo teams can order CDs at no cost and can distribute them. Through these and other means, advocacy provides a great way to spread the word about Ubuntu and offers a low-barrier opportunity to make contributions to the community. Many community members share resources such as fliers, posters, cd covers, banners etc., on the Spread Ubuntu website (http://spreadubuntu.neomenlo.org/en/). Spread Ubuntu is an official ubuntu resource which is community driven and dedicated to helping provide various tools and resources to users, teams, and community members to aid in advocacy efforts.

Support

One of the most meaningful ways that users can contribute to Ubuntu is by helping others use the software. Users can do this by joining the support-oriented mailing lists, IRC channels, or forums, as described in detail earlier in this chapter. By responding to requests for help in each of these venues, users can help other users get up and running on Ubuntu. Even if users are themselves beginners, the knowledge they gain in solving even simple problems enables them to help users who run into the same issues, and community member Fabián Rodríguez sums this up nicely with, "Every user is someone's guru."

Ideas and Feedback

Another way to contribute to Ubuntu is by helping steer the direction of the project by describing a vision or providing ideas. This can be done by participating in discussion and brainstorming sessions at conferences and on the Ubuntu wiki. By monitoring specifications as they are written and creating feedback, especially at early stages, users can make meaningful contributions. However, users contributing ideas should remember that talk is cheap. Users are wise to work with others to help turn their visions into reality.

Documentation

When a user is stumped by a problem, chances are good that other users will also be frustrated by it. If users are not in a position to write code to change the situation, they may be able to help others by writing up their experiences and documenting the solution. Ubuntu has a vibrant documentation team and community, and writing documentation is a great low-barrier way to make meaningful contributions to the Ubuntu community.

Users aiming to contribute to Ubuntu's documentation would be advised to take notes as they puzzle through problems and to document solutions when they find them. Before writing, users should also check to see whether documentation for a particular problem already exists. When it does, users would be wise to choose to improve or augment existing documentation rather than write a new document. Similarly, users can also make meaningful contributions by reading through existing documentation and fixing factual, technical, stylistic, spelling, and grammar errors. Users who spend a large amount of time working on documentation may, with time, also want to join the Ubuntu Documentation Team, which can help organize and coordinate this work in terms of Ubuntu documentation goals.

Artwork

For those users who feel that their strengths are primarily artistic, there are many ways to improve the style and feel of the Ubuntu desktop through wholly artistic contributions. For example, Ubuntu is always in need of new ideas for wallpapers, icons, and graphical themes. Inkscape, similar in many respects to Adobe Illustrator, is a great piece of free software in

Ubuntu that proves useful for this type of work. As with documentation, there is an Ubuntu Art Team that helps coordinate artistic work within the Ubuntu community.

Translation and Localization

The discussion of LoCos should have already made it clear that translation is a great way that anyone with a firm understanding of English and another language can contribute to the Ubuntu community. Translation through Rosetta (described in Chapter 9) allows users to translate as little as a single string or as much as an entire application. Through its easy interface and Web-based nature, it provides a low-barrier road to contribution. Serious translators should join a local community team and the ubuntu-translators mailing list so that they can stay in touch with other Ubuntu translators.

Quality Assurance and Bugs

Quality assurance (QA) is something for which many companies hire special engineers. In Ubuntu, the Development Team relies on the Canonical QA team and the community to test software before it is released to let developers know about problems so that the bugs can be squashed before the vast majority of users ever see it. To test software, users merely need to upgrade to the latest development version of Ubuntu and to upgrade regularly. When users helping out with QA find bugs, they should report them in the Ubuntu bug-tracking system, Malone. They can also help by "triaging" bugs, closing or merging duplicates, or verifying bugs and adding information to a bug's description. If you intend to become involved in QA, you should subscribe to the ubuntu-devel-announce mailing list, consider monitoring ubuntu-devel and following the Ubuntu QA Community Coordinator (described earlier in this chapter on the Ubuntu community team at Canonical), and join the #ubuntu-testing IRC channel on irc.freenode.net.

Programming and Packaging

The final way that users can contribute to the Ubuntu community is through the production of code. Because Ubuntu is free and open source software, users can get access to every piece of software that Ubuntu supports. This allows users to package additional software for inclusion in Ubuntu, to fix bugs, and to add features. Developers, like people testing software, should subscribe to the ubuntu-devel-announce mailing list and should consider monitoring ubuntu-devel, too. The best way to begin making contributions is then through the MOTU team as a MOTU hopeful, as described earlier. Users can also look through a list of specifications to find a project that they find personally interesting. In some situations, there are even bounties available—small amounts of money offered to those who fulfill a small feature goal that has remained unfilled for some period of time.

Submitting Apps to the Ubuntu Software Center

The App Review Board (ARB) is a new volunteer group that is ultimately responsible for governing the application review process of open source gratis apps and how it interfaces with the rest of the Ubuntu community and governance systems.

The ARB has a number of rights and responsibilities and is ultimately responsible for approving quality applications for availability to Ubuntu users. The ARB evaluates applications, resolving disputes in applications following the existing dispute resolution system, and sends reports or representatives to Community Council members to weigh in on issues of membership and to update the council on the ARB business.

Summary

Ubuntu is a vibrant and diverse community that is active around the world and in many languages. Its activities happen primarily online in a variety of virtual venues, including mailing lists, IRC, Web forums, wikis, social media, ustream videocasts, developer and cloud portals, as well as two special Web-based community portals known as The Fridge and Planet Ubuntu. Ubuntu complements this virtual activity with real-life meetings and conferences. The Ubuntu community is broken down into a variety of teams and processes. At the top of this government structure is the Ubuntu Community Council, the Technical Board, and SABDFL Mark Shuttleworth. Through a variety of ways, this community is designed to facilitate contributions easily. Ultimately, these contributions are recognized through a process culminating in official project membership and enfranchisement.

Index

***... (asterisks), password security, 63
. (dot), in configuration folder names, 112
; (semicolon), sequential command execution, 196
- (dash), in command line options, 186
&& (ampersands), conditional command execution, 196
* (asterisk), wildcard, 195
@ (at sign), in command-line username, 184
? (question mark), wildcard, 195
| (vertical bar), pipe symbol, 118, 186–187
$ (dollar sign), UNIX shell symbol, 184, 218
~ (tilde), home directory indicator, 184, 190

A
Access for disabled users, 20
Accessibility plug-ins, 177
addgroup command, 194
Adding. *See also* Creating.
  groups, 194
  packages, 90–91
  programs, 90–91
  search engines to Firefox, 76
  text to files, 193
adduser command, 71, 193
Administrator privileges, 104
Adobe Flash, Firefox support, 77–78
Adobe Illustrator equivalent. *See* Inkscape.
Adobe InDesign equivalent. *See* Scribus.
Adobe Photoshop equivalent. *See* GIMP (GNU Image Manipulation Program).
Advocacy, community opportunities, 307
Albisetti, Martin, 301, 304
Allocating drive space, 43–48
Alternate install CDs, 34. *See also* Installing Ubuntu from alternate install CD.
Amachu, 304
AMD64 support, 35
Ampersands (&&), conditional command execution, 196
Anagrams, 156
Answers program, 29
Appearance tool, 169–170

313

PRENTICE HALL

REGISTER

THIS PRODUCT

informit.com/register

Register the Addison-Wesley, Exam Cram, Prentice Hall, Que, and Sams products you own to unlock great benefits.

To begin the registration process, simply go to **informit.com/register** to sign in or create an account. You will then be prompted to enter the 10- or 13-digit ISBN that appears on the back cover of your product.

Registering your products can unlock the following benefits:

- Access to supplemental content, including bonus chapters, source code, or project files.
- A coupon to be used on your next purchase.

Registration benefits vary by product. Benefits will be listed on your Account page under Registered Products.

About InformIT — THE TRUSTED TECHNOLOGY LEARNING SOURCE

INFORMIT IS HOME TO THE LEADING TECHNOLOGY PUBLISHING IMPRINTS Addison-Wesley Professional, Cisco Press, Exam Cram, IBM Press, Prentice Hall Professional, Que, and Sams. Here you will gain access to quality and trusted content and resources from the authors, creators, innovators, and leaders of technology. Whether you're looking for a book on a new technology, a helpful article, timely newsletters, or access to the Safari Books Online digital library, InformIT has a solution for you.

informIT.com

THE TRUSTED TECHNOLOGY LEARNING SOURCE

Addison-Wesley | Cisco Press | Exam Cram
IBM Press | Que | Prentice Hall | Sams

SAFARI BOOKS ONLINE

DVD-ROM Warranty

Prentice Hall warrants the enclosed DVD to be free of defects in materials and faulty workmanship under normal use for a period of ninety days after purchase (when purchased new). If a defect is discovered in the DVD during this warranty period, a replacement DVD can be obtained at no charge by sending the defective DVD, postage prepaid, with proof of purchase to:

Disc Exchange
Prentice Hall
Pearson Technology Group
75 Arlington Street, Suite 300
Boston, MA 02116
Email: disc.exchange@pearson.com

Prentice Hall makes no warranty or representation, either expressed or implied, with respect to this software, its quality, performance, merchantability, or fitness for a particular purpose. In no event will Prentice Hall, its distributors, or dealers be liable for direct, indirect, special, incidental, or consequential damages arising out of the use or inability to use the software. The exclusion of implied warranties is not permitted in some states. Therefore, the above exclusion may not apply to you. This warranty provides you with specific legal rights. There may be other rights that you may have that vary from state to state.

More information and updates are available at:
informit.com/ph

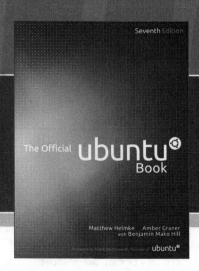

Your purchase of *The Official Ubuntu Book, Seventh Edition* includes access to a free online edition for 45 days through the **Safari Books Online** subscription service. Nearly every Prentice Hall book is available online through **Safari Books Online**, along with thousands of books and videos from publishers such as Addison-Wesley Professional, Cisco Press, Exam Cram, IBM Press, O'Reilly Media, Que, Sams, and VMware Press.

Safari Books Online is a digital library providing searchable, on-demand access to thousands of technology, digital media, and professional development books and videos from leading publishers. With one monthly or yearly subscription price, you get unlimited access to learning tools and information on topics including mobile app and software development, tips and tricks on using your favorite gadgets, networking, project management, graphic design, and much more.

STEP 1:

STEP 2:

form.

34.99